The Art of
Defense in
Chess

The Art of Defense in Chess

by

Andrew Soltis

DAVID McKAY COMPANY, INC.

NEW YORK

794.1
So ✓

Library of Congress Cataloging in Publication Data

Soltis, Andrew.
    The art of defense in chess.

    1.   Chess—Openings.   I.   Title.
GV1450.S64   794.1'22   74-25728
ISBN 0-679-13043-8

MANUFACTURED IN THE UNITED STATES OF AMERICA

Brolt 6/76 9.95

Contents

INTRODUCTION:

What is Defense?

"Chess first of all is art."—*Mikhail Tal*
"Chess is a struggle."—*Emanuel Lasker*

A relatively obscure game from a relatively obscure event:

Khlyavin-Zhdanov, Latvian Championship 1961—*1. P–K4 P–QB3 2. N–QB3 P–Q4 3. N–B3 P–KN3 4. P–Q4 B–N2 5. P–KR3 P–QR3?! 6. B–KB4 N–B3?! 7. P–K5 N–N1 8. Q–Q2 P–QN4 9. B–K2 P–R3 10. 0–0–0 P–K3*

It doesn't take long to conclude that White has a very strong game. He has developed nearly all of his pieces while Black's only developed piece, his KB, bites on granite. Black's queenside is full of holes on black squares and he has just locked in his

QB. A quick mating attack is assured, you might conclude. And you would be right:

> 11. P–KN4 N–Q2 12. B–N3 B–B1! 13. QR–B1 N–N3 14. N–Q1 P–QR4 15. N–K1 P–N5 16. N–Q3 N–B5 17. Q–K1 Q–N3 18. P–N3 QxP! 19. PxN Q–R8ch 20. K–Q2 PxP 21. N–B4 QxRP 22. K–K3 B–QN2 23. Q–Q2 P–N4 24. N–R5 P–B6 25. Q–Q3 R–Q1 26. Q–K4 B–B4ch 27. K–B3 R–Q5 28. Q–K3 Q–Q4ch and mates.

Yes, Black delivered the mate. And in less than 20 moves from the diagram. Actually with a good understanding of defensive play the game's result is not at all surprising. But that understanding is the most difficult chess knowledge to acquire.

Consider for a minute the instructional books you've read. One group tells you how to gain the initiative in the opening. Another group explains how to convert that initiative into a solid advantage during the middlegame. The endgame books go the final step and describe how that tangible advantage is transformed into a decisive margin that forces mate or resignation.

The trouble with this is twofold: (1) For every player who has the initiative, the attack or a material advantage there is another player—his opponent—who is fighting to minimize this and turn the tables, and (2) Most chess games are not won; they are lost. That is, with precise play even a very bad game can be saved. It takes several mistakes to lose.

Very little in the English language chess literature will give the improving player much of an idea of how he can minimize his opponent's advantage and avoid losing. Most players don't know why they lost a particular game. We blame an oversight, a surprise move, a misconception, when the real culprit is a series of errors—some mistakes of attitude, some mistakes of strategy and some of tactics. But most chess books are written only to help the prospective winner understand why he won.

The aim of this book is to outline the principles and tactics of defense and explore their application in typical game situations. Defense can be defined as *the protection of weakness,* which can mean the warding off of the desperation attack of a positionally beaten opponent. It can mean protecting chronic weaknesses so long and so tenaciously that a "hopeless" position is held. It can mean diverting attention from your weaknesses by seizing counterplay in a balanced position.

Defense is unpopular because it is fun to attack. Yet improving your defensive skill will improve your whole game much more than learning a new opening or a few tricks in rook-and-pawn endings. There will always be some positions which you will have to defend. You can't attack all the time. The great masters of attack—Alekhine, Tal, Spielmann and Marshall—could also defend well, and that is why they were among the greatest players of all time. Yet the great defensive masters—Steinitz, Lasker, Capablanca, Botvinnik and Petrosian—were world champions for 80 of the last 110 years.

First, let's dispose of some myths.

(1) *Defense Is Dull.* Defense, like the game as a whole, is 90 percent tactics. In fact, it could be argued that the absence of general principles for defensive play puts a greater emphasis on tactics for the defender than for the attacker.

In this position, from Ryumin-Verlinsky, Moscow 1933, White is desperately fighting off a two-pawn deficit. He is the defender despite the apparent activity of his pieces. The Black

QP ties up one heavy piece, however. But White fights back with 76. *R–KB1!! P–Q8(Q)* 77. *Q–K6ch!*

If Black takes the queen—becoming two queens ahead—he is mated by rook checks on KB8 and KR8. 77. . . . *K–R2* is forced, but then 78. *N–B8ch* (not 78. QxQ QxPch and . . . QxN) forces 78. . . . *QxN* 79. *Q–N6ch! K–N1* 80. *Q–K6ch* and draws by perpetual check.

Or take the Perlis-Marshall game from Karlsbad 1911. It began:

1. P–K4 P–K4 2. N–KB3 N–QB3 3. B–N5 P–QR3 4. B–R4 N–B3 5. Q–K2 B–B4 6. P–Q3 P–Q3 7. P–B3 0–0 8. 0–0 B–KN5 9. B–K3 P–QN4 10. B–N3 Q–Q2 11. QN–Q2 K–R1 12. P–KR3 B–R4 13. K–R2 QR–Q1 14. B–N5 N–K2 15. BxN? PxB 16. P–N4? BxNP! 17. PxB QxP 18. R–KN1 Q–R4ch 19. K–N2 N–N3! 20. K–B1 N–B5

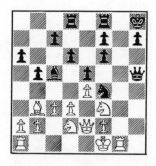

White's position appears resignable since 21. Q–Q1 NxP or 21. . . . Q–R6ch crumbles and his king's protection. Perlis's defense was inspired: *21. P–Q4!! PxP 22. PxP NxQ 23. KxN BxP 24. R–R1.*

The idea is to drive the Black queen away from the kingside so that White can play RxRPch! followed by a perpetual check with White's other rook. For example, had Black taken the queen immediately at move 21, then 22. KxN PxP would allow 23. R–R1 Q–N5 24. QR–KN1 Q–Q2 (24. . . . Q–B5 25. R–R4) 25. RxPch!! and Black's king cannot escape checks from KN1 and KR1. If the king goes to KN5 it will be mated by R–KR4.

Play continued with *24. . . . Q–QB4 25. QR–QB1* and Black was forced to sacrifice his queen back to preserve winning chances. (Notice that 25. NxB QxN 26. RxPch would *not* draw because of *26. . . . KxR 27. R–R1ch K–N3 28. R–N1ch K–R4 29. R–R1ch K–N5 30. R–N1ch K–B5,* as Vidmar pointed out in the tournament book.) White managed to draw with *25. . . . BxNP 26. RxQ PxR 27. B–Q5 P–B5 28. N–B1 R–Q3? 29. N–K3 B–K4 30. N–B5 R–N3 31. N–R6· K–N2 32. N–B5ch K–R1 33. N–R6* and a repetition of moves.

(2) *Defense Is Monolithic.* The charge that defensive play is mechanical, unimaginative and with little room for variety is also unfounded. There are several kinds of action we call defensive. For illustration, see what happens in a typical opening when an attacking idea is introduced: *1. P–K4 P–QB4 2. N–KB3 P–Q3 3. P–Q4 PxP 4. NxP N–KB3 5. N–QB3 P–K3 6. P–KN4.*

White initiates a kingside pawn storm with his last move. His intention is P–N5 followed by P–KB4 and/or P–KR4. This will drive off one defensive piece, Black's KN, and enable White to open lines around the Black king with P–KB5 and P–N6. Black has a broad choice:

(a) He can *strike back in the center* with 6. . . . P–Q4 or 6. . . . P–K4. This is a traditional response. It is hoped that with an open center the kingside advance will be exposed as a weakness rather than a strength. But here the action is premature—6. . . .

P–Q4 7. PxP NxQP 8. B–N5ch B–Q2 9. NxN PxN 10. Q–K2ch Q–K2 11. B–K3 discombobulates Black's pieces and leaves him with a weak QP, while 6. . . . P–K4 7. B–N5ch followed by N–B5 must give White a powerful positional hold of the center and kingside.

(b) He can *exchange off potential attacking pieces.* Another wise policy in many situations—but here 6. . . . N–B3 7. P–N5 NxN? 8. QxN N–Q2 9. B–K3 (stopping further trades by . . . Q–N3) leaves White in a dominating control of the center.

(c) He can *restrain* White's advance. The move 6. . . . P–KR3 is quite reasonable, although it must be realized that White can still play 7. P–N5 and thereby open up kingside lines. Potentially White could profit from the half-open KN-file but he could also lose his KRP. Black's KN is allowed to remain at its post.

(d) He can ignore the threat and just *develop.* That is, he can play 6. . . . N–B3 and after 7. P–N5 N–Q2 bring his KN to activity on QB4 or K4. Black can be better developed within a few moves so that he can seize the attack by fighting back on the kingside with . . . P–KR3 or running to the queenside for counterplay.

(e) Finally, he can seek immediate *counterplay* on the opposite wing. With 6. . . . P–QR3 Black prepares . . . P–QN4–5, . . . B–N2 and . . . R–B1. Should White stop to take queenside precautions his kingside attack may run out of steam.

Each of these responses has something going for it. In different positions a policy of exchanging may be better than one of counterplay. But the important point is that Black does have a choice. That was a typical example of the defender facing an attacking plan. Now consider the alternatives when faced with an immediate and dangerous threat, e.g., *1. P–K4 P–K3 2. P–Q4 P–Q4 3. N–QB3 B–N5 4. P–K5 P–QB4 5. P–QR3 BxNch 6. PxB Q–B2 7. Q–N4.*

This is another double-edged opening of considerable analytical importance. But we're more concerned with Black's method of handling the threat of 8. QxNP, which would win not only a pawn but the KR as well. The choice includes:

(a) *Immediate protection*—Black can handle the threat in two simple ways, 7. . . . P–KN3 or 7. . . . K–B1. There is something objectionable in both. The pawn move makes big holes in the kingside at KB3 and KR3. The king move forfeits castling. Wilhelm Steinitz's introduction of the theory of economical defense helped stamp out such moves. Is there a cheaper way of meeting the threat? In other words, is there some defense that makes fewer concessions?

(b) *Defense with tempo*—With 7. . . . P–B4 Black discovers protection along his second rank by his queen. But he also attacks the White queen with his KBP and White must lose a tempo to defend against the threat.

(c) *Counterthreat*—With 7. . . . N–K2 Black sacrifices a pawn but hopes to keep the initiative through his own threats after 8. QxNP R–N1 9. QxP PxP. White then is faced with 10. . . . QxBPch and 10. . . . QxKPch.

(d) *Defense and counterattack in the center*—7. . . . P–B3! is now considered the best response because it defends KN2 while striking at White's center. Although not as forcing as 7. . . . P–B4, this move creates more problems for White. With his queen off on the kingside he is not well prepared for a fight in the center.

Again a broad choice, which is repeated almost every time one player makes a threat.

(3) *Defense Is Unrewarding.* The charge is that the best you can hope for from successful defense is a draw and therefore you are putting in a lot of work at the board for a minimum return.

The answer is, first, that you don't *choose* to defend. Some positions demand it. Aside from a few countergambits, you can't compete for the initiative in the early stages of most openings when you play the Black pieces. Secondly, defense pays off repeatedly *because it is difficult to master.* Emanuel Lasker observed that the defender, who is alert because he is defending and is worried about getting mated, often upsets the lazy attacker whose moves may seem easy to find. Thirdly, there are frequent instances of a defender winning despite having a very bad position. The attacker presses too hard in a position that doesn't justify it and overextends his forces.

Here is another case of the Q–KN4 threat by White:

Portisch-Taimanov, Budapest-Leningrad match 1959— 1. P–QB4 P–K3 2. N–QB3 B–N5 3. P–K4 P–QB4 4. Q–N4?! K–B1! 5. N–B3 N–KB3 6. Q–R4 P–Q3 7. B–K2 N–B3 8. 0–0 P–KR3 9. P–KR3?

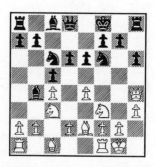

White's attack is premature and his failure to provide an avenue of retreat for his queen leaves him with inadequate

control of the center. Black has given up castling, but his reward
will be a vigorous counterattack in the next few moves:

9. . . . *R–R2!! 10. N–K1 N–Q5 11. B–Q1 P–KN4! 12. Q–KN3
P–K4 13. P–KR4? N–K3 14. N–B2 BxN 15. NPxB N–B5 16.
P–Q4 R–N2 17. Q–R2 NxKP 18. B–B3 NxQBP 19. PxKP PxKP
20. B–N2 P–N5 21. B–Q5 QN–K7ch 22. K–R1 P–N6! 23. PxP
NxPch 24. K–N1 N(B)–K7ch 25. K–B2 Q–B3ch and White
Resigned.*

After 4 Q–N4 Black wasn't in a position to do anything but
defend his weakness at KN2 for the next move. But once the
weakness was covered, Black could think about counterattack.
And his counterattack was grounded in better foundation than
White's premature attack. For a similar instance:

Charousek-Maroczy, Nagy-Tetney 1897—*1. P–K4 P–K3 2.
P–Q4 P–Q4 3. N–QB3 N–KB3 4. B–KN5 B–K2 5. BxN BxB
6. P–K5 B–K2 7. Q–N4 0–0 8. B–Q3 P–QB4 9. Q–R3 P–KN3
10. PxP N–B3! 11. P–B4 BxP 12. N–B3*

White's kingside play forced Black's . . . P–KN3, an unpleasant
but hardly critical concession. However, Black has actually obtained a lead in development and the advantage of the two
bishops as a result of White's kingside intentions. Black ex-
ploits this by opening up the position on the side of the board
where he is theoretically inferior:

12. . . . P–B3! 13. Q–R6 R–B2 14. PxP QxP 15. P–KN3 B–R6!
16. N–Q1 B–B1 17. Q–R4 N–Q5 18. NxN QxN 19. Q–N5 B–Q2
20. P–KR4? B–K2 21. Q–R6 P–K4! 22. P–R5 P–KN4! 23. B–N6
R–N2! 24. P–B3 Q–N3 25. PxNP Q–Q1! 26. B–B2 B–QB1! and
White Resigned. An amusing finish. A Q is lost.

Since defense can mean so many different things—counter-play, parrying of threats, restraint, countersacrifice, stonewalling
—it is not unusual for a defensive virtuoso to win regularly by
accepting the unpopular side of double-edged positions. With
the Black pieces, how else can you regularly play to win?

Viktor Korchnoi, the world's leading master of counterplay,
explains his own very successful style this way:

"Emanuel Lasker once remarked that when there is an equal
position on the board the game rarely has much content and
usually results in a draw. The chessplayer who does not like
draws—and I belong to that group of players—is bound to dis-
turb the equilibrium in some way. [The choice] is to sacrifice
something and by that to take over the initiative, or to allow
one's opponent to attack. . . .

"I do not like to attack first or to sacrifice my pieces and
pawns. I prefer to give my opponent the opportunity to begin
an attack, to weaken his pawns and sacrifice something to me,
and then when the moment comes, I return to him what was
sacrificed."

Korchnoi has extended his style to what can be called provocateur chess. He is eager to be placed on the defense if he
feels that his position can survive attack well. In 1969 he began
a tournament game with:

1. P–Q4 N–KB3. 2. P–QB4 P–B4 3. P–Q5 P–K4 4. N–QB3
P–Q3 5. P–K4 B–K2 6. P–KN3 0–0 7. B–N2 QN–Q2 8. Q–K2
P–QR3 9. P–QR4 P–QN3 10. K–Q1!?

Aside from mistakenly picking up his king and being forced to move it under the "touch-move" rule, the only explanation of 10. K–Q1 is that it entices Black into a hasty counterattack with . . . P–KB4. That is exactly what Korchnoi's young Czech opponent did:

10. . . . N–K1 11. P–B4 P–B4? 12. KPxP KPxP 13. BxP N–K4 14. P–KN4! P–QN4 15. BxN PxB 16. RPxP N–Q3 17. N–B3 B–N2 18. K–B2 PxP 19. PxP P–K5 (Desperation) 20. N–Q2 RxR 21. RxR P–K6 22. QxP B–N4 23. QxP BxN 24. KxB Q–N4ch 25. K–B2 Q–B5 26. R–K1 N–B5 27. R–K2 QxNP 28. P–Q6! BxB 29. P–Q7! N–Q3 30. QxN QxPch 31. K–N3 Q–B2ch 32. K–N4! Resigns.

The final argument in support of defense is this: The only thing close in personal satisfaction to a brilliant sacrificial attack sustained against a strong opponent is a finely conceived, multi-faceted defensive win over such an opponent.

Our illustrative game for this chapter is:

1958 SOVIET CHAMPIONSHIP SEMIFINALS

ZAITSEV   SHAMKOVICH

1. P–K4 P–QB4 2. N–KB3 P–K3 3. P–Q4 PxP 4. NxP P–QR3 5. N–QB3 Q–B2 6. B–Q3 N–QB3 7. B–K3 N–B3 8. O–O NxN 9. BxN B–B4 10. BxB QxB 11. Q–K2 P–Q3 12. P–QR4?! B–Q2 13. K–R1 P–K4! 14. P–B4 R–QB1 15. QR–K1 O–O 16. P–B5 B–B3 17. R–B3!

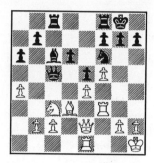

Black's eighth and ninth moves are *simplifying* ideas which ease his defensive chores. In connection with . . . P–K4 they allow Black to play a middlegame in which his bishop is superior to White's. Meanwhile White has a burgeoning attack involving R–N3 and Q–Q2 followed by RxPch or Q–N5 or Q–R6. Why should such an attack be dangerous to Black? Because he has exchanged off the most effective defender of KN2 on the tenth move. That same trade also gave him strong control of black squares in the center and on the queenside.

17. . . .   Q–N5!

Black has excellent chances and he should preserve his queen. On 17. . . . KR–K1 18. Q–K3! or 17. . . . P–QN4 18. PxP PxP 19. BxP BxB 20. QxB Black also has a good game but his winning chances are fewer. First, Black *strikes back at an enemy weakpoint.*

18. Q–Q2   P–R3!

The maxim that the defender should "never move his kingside pawns" needs an addition—"without good reason." Steinitz's principle of economy requires Black to find the least disruptive method of answering the threat to his KN2. ("Like a first-rate boxer, who in the nick of time and with an almost imperceptible movement evades the blow," as Lasker put it.)

Here, Black prepares to meet 19. R–N3 with 19. . . . K–R2 followed by 20. . . . QxNP or 20. . . . P–Q4. The direct 18. . . .

QxNP walks into 19. R–N3 N–K1 20. P–B6 or 19. . . . P–N3
20. N–Q1, a more "expensive" defense.

19. R–R3!   P–Q4!

A *break in the center* is necessary to Blacks' survival now.
On the natural 19. . . . QxNP White has 20. RxP!!, e.g., 20. . . .
PxR 21. QxP (threatening at least a draw with queen checks)
N–R2 22. P–B6. Black can avert the sacrifice on his KR3 with
19. . . . K–R2, but then 20. P–N4! P–Q4 21. P–N5 is stronger since
21. . . . NxP 22. NxN wins a piece.

But after 19. . . . P–Q4 White hasn't time for 20. RxP because
Black can safely ignore it: 20. . . . PxP! 21. RxN PxB 22. Q–N5
Q–KB5, and Black must win the ending. The Black queen on
QN5 is perfectly placed to watch the queenside, the center and
the fifth rank.

20. PxP   NxP

White is still deterred from 21. RxRP by the *line blocking*
21. . . . N–B5, which threatens KN2 as it cuts communication
between White's queen and rook. On 21. RxKP Black's task is
eased by 21. . . . QxNP, the move he's been threatening for
four moves but can only play now. After he takes off the QNP
he will be threatening White's N, creating threats on the last
rank and working on pins.

21. R–K4!   QxNP
22. N–Q1   Q–R8!

This *restraining* move holds White's QN and Q in place while it indirectly defends KN2. The interplay of defensive ideas is not unusual in a complex game. The queen move is necessary because despite all of Black's fine play up to here he could have squandered it all by playing 22. . . . Q–N3 which overlooks 23. QxP!! PxQ 24. R–N4ch K–R2 25. P–B6ch and mates.

23. R–N4!   P–K5!

Another fine move which serves multiple purposes—(1) meeting the threat of 24. RxPch!, (2) maintaining last rank threats, e.g., 24. RxRP is met by 24. . . . N–K6!, and (3) causing line interference on the K5 square. After 24. RxPch QxR 25. R–N3, Black wins with 23. . . . PxB 26. QxRP QxR 27. PxQ KR–K1.

24. BxKP   . . .

White must capture with some piece on K4, and if he uses the rook he removes a key attacking piece and gives Black time for 24. . . . N–B6!.

24. . . .   KR–K1!

Black *seizes open lines* while giving his king a flight square. That this is vital for victory is indicated by a variation pointed out by Soviet analyst Fridstein: 25. R(3)–N3! and now 25. . . . K–B1! 26. RxP RxB 27. R–N8ch K–K2 28. RxR Q–B8!! overloading the White queen because of the threat of mate on the first rank.

25. P–B3   . . .

This tricky move closes the access of Black's queen to the kingside and again threatens 26. RxPch. How is it to be defended?

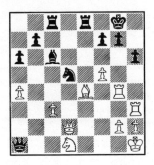

25. . . .   **N–B5!**

Another line-blocking shot which decides the game. Black threatens both . . . NxR and . . . QR–Q1. But White cannot capture the knight with his queen, and on 26. RxN Black responds 26. . . . BxB followed by . . . QR–Q1. Finally on 26. BxB QR–Q1 or 26. RxPch KxR 27. Q–Q4ch P–B3, White is hopeless. White has one last try.

26. P–B6!   . . .

And it is dangerous because White can mate on 26. . . . NxR 27. RxPch K–B1 28. Q–Q6ch, or 26. . . . QR–Q1 27. B–R7ch! K–R1 28. PxPch KxB 29. RxPch! KxR 30. QxNch, or finally 26. . . . P–N3 27. RxN BxB 28. RxP QR–Q1 29. R–R8ch! KxR 30. R–R4ch K–N1 31. R–R8ch KxR 32. Q–R6ch. Such beautiful lines are usually pointed out only when the attacker wins. But . . .

26. . . .   **P–KN4!**

This solves all problems because of the shift of defensive pieces: e.g., 27. RxRP BxB 28. RxPch B–N3!.

The rest of the game is easy:

27. B–R7ch KxB 28. RxP R–KN1 29. Q–B2ch R–N3 30. RxR PxR 31. R–K3 R–Q1 32. R–K1 NxP 33. R–K7ch K–R1 34. Resigns. A very satisfying victory.

The Art of
Defense in
Chess

CHAPTER ONE:

The Spirit of Defense

One reason that defense is the least well understood aspect of chess is the absence of general principles to guide the student. There are simply stated golden rules for every other role a player may assume during a game ("Passed pawns must be pushed in the ending," "Avoid loss of time in the opening," "The attacker needs open lines," and so on), but the great defenders have left us remarkably little to chew on.

Steinitz and Lasker, despite their attention to the elastic nature of defensive positions, were primarily concerned as teachers with the exploitation of weakness. And Lasker, who more than anyone else tried to find the loopholes in the general principles of attack, left little in the way of a theoretical legacy. But he did leave a spirit and philosophy of defense.

Before we look at the tactical devices and strategic themes of defense, it's important to take stock of the mental attitudes that must take the place of general principles. Good defense is a matter of attitude as much as anything else. Some players are defeated the minute they lose the initiative; they are discouraged when they can no longer attack. Others excel at defense because they accept the task of defense as a challenge—as much of an adventure as pulling off a sacrificial mating attack. But usually, as David Bronstein suggests, "The pawn sacrificer is uplifted while the person forced to accept a sacrifice is invariably upset."

How should you act as a defender? You should adopt an

1

attitude somewhere between the "cheerful pessimism" and the "creative skepticism" that Fred Reinfeld ascribed to Lasker. You may have an inferior game, but it takes a great deal to lose. The onus is as much on the attacker as on you. No matter how poor your prospects appear (barring a forced mate or loss of material), you won't lose unless you make further mistakes.

EXPLOITABLE AND UNEXPLOITABLE
WEAKNESS

Look back at that bizarre Latvian game in the Introduction. Who really stands better?:

The tendency to pronounce White confidently in the lead is based on his advantage in development and the weakness of Black's queenside and center. However, development is a value that varies in significance with the openness of a position. In the Morphy era of 1. P–K4 P–K4 games development took on great importance because every position was crosscut by open lines. But in the diagram we have a closed position with no open files and several stifled diagonals.

Both players, in fact, must redevelop their pieces on new squares because their original development doesn't jell with the middlegame pawn structure. Black, who is about to redevelop his KB by moving it from a blockaded line at KN2 to an excellent vista at KB1, stands quite well in terms of development!

More important is the nature of the weaknesses on both sides of the board. Black has "holes" on his weakened black squares such as Q3, QB4, KB3 and QN3. They are weak because they've lost all or part of their pawn protection. Remember that we defined defense in the Introduction as the protection of weaknesses. With the closed nature of the position and the misplacement of the White minor pieces, *these weaknesses are unexploitable.*

True, if he could just get the White QB to Q6, or open the K-file or somehow bring a N to QB5, White would have a terrific game. But as it is, many moves must be made before White will be able to exploit the obvious weaknesses.

Now look at the game from Black's chair. White has made no pawn weaknesses on the queenside where his king is housed, and none of his central or kingside squares is beyond pawn protection. His pieces appear well placed. But actually White's queenside is easily attackable by way of . . . N–Q2–N3–B5 and the recapture with the QNP if the knight is taken on B5. In the meanwhile White has to take several preparatory steps to make his minor pieces work. He needs P–KB4 and P–KN4 in preparation for P–KB5 before he can release the pent-up, potential energy of his pieces.

Now, does this seem fair to White who ostensibly hasn't made a single mistake while Black has been losing time and retreating his pieces behind weaknesses? But White *has* made a mistake, a bad one: 10. 0–0–0??. If he had castled kingside and begun to exploit the queenside with P–QR4, the shoe would be on the other foot. This simple difference—plus the series of mindless attacking moves that followed—is what cost White the game.

This principle of exploitation vs. unexploitable weakness is the most important single lesson to be learned in defense. Fre-

quently the defender is called upon to restrain or impede the
attacker's advance by making moves which appear to be weakening. It's a matter of judgment in deciding whether it's worth
it. Take this example, a 1959 game between Svetozar Gligoric
and Vassily Smyslov:

> 1. P–Q4 N–KB3 2. P–QB4 P–KN3 3. N–QB3 P–Q4 4. PxP
> NxP 5. P–K4 NxN 6. PxN B–N2 7. B–QB4 P–QB4 8. N–K2 O–O
> 9. O–O N–B3 10. B–K3 Q–B2 11. R–B1 R–Q1 12. P–KR3 P–N3
> 13. P–B4

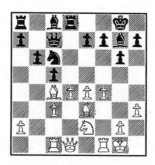

White threatens P–B5, followed by opening up a dangerous
initiative on the KB-file and liberating his QB. Black can prevent
this with a pawn blockade, but these advances would aerate
his king position. Yet if Black's kingside is made porous, White
will not be able to exploit it immediately. This is why 13. . . .
P–K3! 14. Q–K1 B–N2 15. Q–B2 N–R4 16. B–Q3 P–B4! is so
strong: stopping the obvious danger and slowing the opponent's
initiative is more important than conceding holes which *might*
be infiltrated later.

In the 1959 game White followed the familiar attacking
principle of closing the center so that he could advance on the
wing, a very poor strategy at this point: 17. P–K5?? P–B5! 18.
B–B2 N–B3! 19. P–N4 N–K2 20. K–R2 Q–B3 21. N–N3 P–QN4,
and Black held the initiative on both sides of the board.

The lesson of exploitable weaknesses is a common one in modern opening systems. Black accepts a backward QP in the Najdorf Variation of the Sicilian (1. P–K4 P–QB4 2. N–KB3 P–Q3 3. P–Q4 PxP 4. NxP N–KB3 5. N–QB3 P–QR3 6. B–K2 P–K4) or an isolated QP in the Tarrasch Defense to the Queens Gambit (1. P–Q4 P–Q4 2. P–QB4 P–K3 3. N–QB3 P–QB4 4. BPxP KPxP 5. N–B3 N–QB3 6. P–KN3 and later QPxBP) without trepidation because experience has shown that there is a great deal of Black counterplay to overcome before White can realistically think of exploiting the pawn weakness.

Weakness, therefore, is not static but is related to traditional values of force and time. Given time enough, almost any position is repairable. Also, if an attacker is continuously pressed with diversions, he won't have time to penetrate the most helpless weaknesses.

Consider the following position:

It's easy to spot holes in the Black kingside at KR6 and KB6. Naturally these can be exploited if there is a White QB on the board. On the other hand, White's kingside has its share of white-square weakness. If Black has only a black-squared bishop left during a complex middlegame, White is relatively safe. And in a rook ending both king positions are relatively safe. Similarly, a wide-open position with weaknesses is best exploited with rooks on the board, and a closed game is best exploited with knights.

DYNAMIC PLAY VS. SAFETY

One of the many trade-offs in a game of chess is this: If your pieces are all well placed for the protection of your weaknesses, they are probably incapable of exploiting your opponent's. Given time, your opponent can shift his power to the weakest link in your chain of defense.

This is why counterplay is the No. 1 priority of defense—even at the expense of other values such as king safety, pawn structure, material and development. This is more fully examined in Chapter 4, but here we want to show the desirability of counterplay. With rigid obeisance to the need for safety, the most you can hope for in a game is a draw. Protecting yourself doesn't win games.

Tigran Petrosian is Black in the above position, a game from the 1962 Olympiad vs. Andreas Duckstein of Austria. The Caro-Kann Defense has given Petrosian chances for an attack on the KR-file after . . . B–K2, . . . R–R3 and . . . QR–R1. But White can handily meet that danger with QR–Q1 and RxR or KR–K1 and B–K5. Trading off pieces is the oldest defensive idea in the game.

Petrosian evaluated the dangers and played *18. . . . P–R4!!* Yes, Black is inviting the destruction of his pawn protection near the K. But he has judged that Black will obtain sufficient dynamic play to keep White busy. King safety won't come into question for several moves, Petrosian reasoned. That is, Black's king safety. On 19. PxP BxP 20. QR–N1, for example, Black would mate with 20. . . . RxP! 21. KxR R–R1ch 22. K–N1 NxN.

White sought exchanges, but after *19. QR–Q1 RxR 20. RxR R–R5! 21. PxP BxP 22. P–R6?! P–N3 23. R–K1 K–R2*, Black won in phenomenal style—by advancing his king to the sixth rank with queens still on the board. The destruction of White's queen-side pawns eventually cost him the game.

Another surprising example of dynamism taking precedence over safety is Guimard-Unzicker, Buenos Aires 1960:

1. P–Q4 N–KB3 2. P–QB4 P–K3 3. N–QB3 B–N5 4. B–N5 P–KR3 5. B–R4 P–B4 6. P–Q5 P–QN4 7. P–K4 P–N4!? 8. B–N3 NxKP 9. B–K5

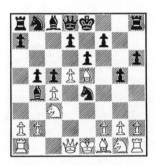

And here Black plays *9. . . . 0–0!*. Surely Black cannot castle into an attack such as this, you might say. It's easy to see that White has a queen, two good bishops and a pawn-break (P–KR4) available for mate.

Yet the castling move does several important things for Black. It removes his K from the K-file and prepares to mine the center with . . . KPxP and . . . R–K1. It also rescues his KR without the clumsy . . . R–KN1 or weakening . . . P–B3. The critical question is: Can Black obtain the chief benefits of castling before White seizes a decisive initiative?

One method of attack is 10. Q–R5!, but 10. . . . P–Q3! is

adequate, e.g., 11. QxRP PxB! 12. B–Q3 KPxP 13. PxP B–B4 or 11. B–Q3 NxN 12. QxP N–K5ch! 13. K–K2 PxB 14. BxN P–B4. White must seek sanctuary in perpetual check before Black's material takes effect.

In the game, White played *10. B–Q3*, and Black could have transposed into the above line with 10. . . . NxN. However, he chose the riskier *10. . . . PxQP!?* in order to answer 11. PxQP with 11. . . . R–K1. White played *11. KBxN PxB 12. Q–Q5 N–B3 13. B–Q6* and was crushed after *13. . . . BxNch 14. PxB Q–B3!*. Black won 11 moves later.

COURAGE AND UGLY MOVES

Since we're on the subject of the proper mental attitudes, one of the most important is the willingness to make moves which look ugly—if not suicidal. The temptation is to play it safe by making the quietest, least volatile move in view. But double-edged "ugly" moves are often the best—sometimes the only good ones—in a position. The tactical demands of the position—those which exempt it from the general rules of safety—may dictate rapid retreat of well-developed pieces, or a forced march by your king, or the general advance of your protective shell of pawns. The significant lesson here is that a defender must be willing to take up the challenge.

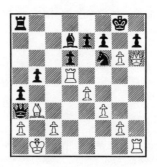

This position comes from a 1970 Yugoslav game and developed out of a highly theoretical variation of the Sicilian Dragon: *1. P–K4 P–QB4 2. N–KB3 P–Q3 3. P–Q4 PxP 4. NxP N–KB3 5. N–QB3 P–KN3 6. B–K3 B–N2 7. P–B3 N–B3 8. Q–Q2 0–0 9. B–QB4 Q–R4 10. B–N3 B–Q2 11. 0–0–0 N–K4 12. K–N1 KR–B1 13. P–KR4 P–QN4 14. B–R6 BxB 15. QxB RxN 16. PxR QxBP 17. N–K2 Q–B4 18. N–B4 P–QR4 19. P–R5 P–R5 20. NxP NxN 21. R–Q5 Q–R6 22. PxN.*

At first glance, it appears that Black can calmly ignore the kingside crises with 22. . . . PxB. Then if White plays 23. PxRPch, Black can hide with 23. . . . K–R1.

But on closer inspection, Black saw the beautiful forced mate —23. PxRPch K–R1 24. Q–N7ch!! KxQ 25. P–R8(Q)ch! RxQ 26. R–N5ch and 27. RxR. Black's position is critical. He has no *zwischenzug* (intermediate forcing move) to upset the threat. He cannot trade pieces in time. And if he captures the pawn on his KN3, he is either mated in one move or subjected to a deadly discovered check.

At this point the defender can reason *à la* Sherlock Holmes. If all the possible ("reasonable") defenses don't work, he must try the impossible. Black coldbloodedly plays *22. . . . BPxP!!*.

There isn't any choice. The alternatives are: hoping that White (a grandmaster, by the way) would overlook the queen sacrifice possibility or resigning. But it turns out that Black is incredibly safe since there is no better discovered check than *23. R–N5ch*. The game continued *23. . . . PxB 24. RxPch K–B2!* (*24. . . . PxR??* 25. QxPch K–B1 26. R–R8ch mates) *25. Q–N7ch! K–K3 26. RxNch PxR 27. Q–N4ch K–K4! 28. Q–N3ch K–K3 29. Q–N4ch,* and a draw was agreed. White had losing chances in the complications (*25. RxNch? PxR 26. QxRPch K–B1!* allows Black to escape).

It takes another kind of willpower to retreat. Often in defending a bad game it is essential to maintain certain outposts for several moves in order to delay the opponent's advance. But the voluntary retreat has its merits, not the least of which is that it is usually the most unexpected move in a given position. The logic of retreat is this: Your opponent has committed his pieces to a certain pawn structure. By rearranging your forces, you expose his pieces to charges of misplacement. Moving backward can be very profitable—Contedini-Euwe, Leipzig 1960: 1. P–K4 P–K4 2. N–KB3 N–QB3 3. B–B4 B–B4 4. P–B3 B–N3 (a retreat to anticipate P–Q4) 5. P–Q4 Q–K2 6. 0–0 P–Q3 7. P–KR3 N–B3 8. R–K1 0–0 9. P–QR4 P–QR3 10. N–R3

White threatens to play B–KN5 and bring his knight powerfully to Q5 via QB2 and K3. This would break Black's efforts to maintain a strong point at K4. At this juncture the former world champion begins a common but surprising series of redeveloping moves which forestalls White's threats and prepares Black's kingside counterattack:

10. . . . K–R1! 11. N–B2 N–KN1 (to support the KP with . . . P–B3) 12. N–K3 B–R2 (to anticipate N–Q5) 13. N–Q5 Q–Q1 14. B–K3 P–B3 15. P–QN4 QN–K2! 16. PxP? NxN 17. BxN BxB 18. RxB BPxP

Black already stands better due to his ready-made counterplay on the KB-file (. . . Q–B3, . . . N-K2–N3–B5). A few more errors by White decided the game: *19. B–N3 Q–B3 20. P–B4 N–K2 21. P–B5 PxP 22. PxP N–N3 23. Q–Q5? BxP! 24. PxB N–R5! 25. NxN QxPch 26. K–R1 QxR 27. N–B5? QxRPch 28. K–N1 R–B3 and White Resigned.*

A similar example is Tarrasch-Alekhine, Baden-Baden 1925: 1. P–K4 P–K4 2. N–KB3 N–QB3 3. B–B4 B–B4 4. P–B3 B–N3 5. P–Q4 Q–K2 6. 0–0 N–B3 7. R–K1 P–Q3 8. P–QR4 P–QR3 9. P–R3 0–0 10. B–KN5 P–R3 11. B–K3 Q–Q1! 12. B–Q3 R–K1 13. QN–Q2 B–R2! 14. Q–B2 PxP (strong because 15 PxP allows counterplay via 15. . . . N–QN5) 15. NxP N–K4 16. B–B1 P–Q4! 17. QR–Q1 P–B4 18. N(4)–N3 Q–B2 19. B–KB4 N–B6ch 20. NxN QxB 21. PxP? B–B4! and Black won quickly—22. B–Q3 BxP 23. PxB QxN 24. RxRch RxR 25. B–B1 R–K4 26. P–B4 R–N4ch 27. K–R2 N–N5ch 28. PxN RxNP 29. Resigns.

Or, for yet another example—Schiffers-Steinitz, match 1896:

1. P–K4 P–K4 2. N–KB3 N–QB3 3. B–N5 B–B4 4. 0–0 Q–B3 5. P–B3 KN–K2 6. P–Q4 PxP 7. B–N5 Q–N3 8. QBxN BxB 9. PxP 0–0 10. N–B3 P–Q3 11. N–Q5

Black's defensive appearance is misleading because in every retreat there is the seed of counterattack and advance. The game continued *11. . . . B–Q1 12. Q–Q3 N–N1!*, threatening . . . P–QB3. The QP would then be weak but not readily attackable.

After a redeployment of force (*13. B–B4 P–QB3 14. N–B4 Q–R3 15. N–K2 N–Q2 16. N–N3 N–N3 17. B–N3 B–B2 18. QR–B1 B–Q2*), White erred in trying to force matters with *19. P–Q5—* rather than the correct redeploying 19. N–Q2. Steinitz quickly took over the momentum with *19. . . . P–QB4 20. N–Q4? P–N3 21. P–B4? QR–B1!* and won shortly after *22. QN–K2 P–B5 23. BxP NxN 24. RxN B–N4!.*

Even less palatable than retreat is the movement of the king in some fashion other than castling. In the golden age of Romanticism, Morphy and his imitators always castled quickly to bring their rooks into play and safeguard the king. But the king is not always well placed in a corner, as Steinitz later showed, and the rooks are not necessary in many middlegames. King moves can be powerful—if the defender overcomes his bias against them. To wit—Keres-Richter, Munich 1944:

1. P–QB4 P–K4 2. N–QB3 N–KB3 3. N–B3 N–B3 4. P–Q4 PxP 5. NxP B–N5 6. B–N5 P–KR3 7. B–R4 P–KN4?! 8. B–N3 P–Q3 9. R–B1 NxN 10. QxN B–KB4 11. P–KR4

White wants to force new kingside holes (. . . P–N5) to be exploited later. Black has to meet the 12. PxP threat, and he does it with the shocking *11. . . . K–Q2!!*, which establishes communication between his Q and KR. It also threatens 12. . . . N–K5 followed by . . . NxB or . . . B–B4.

Besides making the courageous decision to move his king so early, Richter also had to calculate that 12. B–K5 could be met by 12. . . . B–B4 13. BxN BxQ 14. BxQ QRxB, with a fine ending. Keres saw this, and he also rejected 12. P–B3 and 13. B–B2, the conservative, consolidating continuation.

He chose *12. R–Q1*, with a threat of 13. P–B5. However, *12. . . . N–K5 13. Q–K5* as played was met by *13. . . . BxNch 14. PxB NxB 15. PxN B–N3*, giving Black a much safer position than his spatially superior opponent. Black won a long ending.

Sometimes in desperation the best practical chance may be the confusion of a king advance. The opponent, who might win through a variety of simpler ways, looks for the pretty mating finish that just might be there. The defender is using the desire of every player to play beautiful games as a psychological weapon. Even if the mate exists, the attacker still has to find it.

This is Littlewood-Barden from Hastings 1961–62, and things are pretty dismal for White. He has sacrificed a piece for a very speculative attack, but Black's countersacrifice of the Exchange gives him a murderous initiative. On 25. K–K2 Black wins simply by taking the rook on K1. Therefore, White played the provocative 25. *K–Q3!?*.

Black took up the challenge with 25. . . . *N–N5ch 26. K–B4 B–N2!*, threatening checks on QN4 and QB6. If White captures the knight with his king, he is mated by queen checks on B6 and R4. There followed 27. *N–Q4 N–Q4! 28. RxPch! BxR 29. NxB N–K6ch 30. K–B5.*

Black's play has been superb, and now he just has to eliminate the dangers of Q–N6ch and P–Q7ch. From White's point of view his position is so hopeless that his king-walk is as good as anything else. The "proper" end of the game would have been 30. . . . *Q–K4ch* and 31. . . . *QxN*, after which White would be two pieces behind and about to be mated.

But, in time pressure, Black still sought the beauty-mate. He played 30. . . . *Q–B6ch?? 31. K–N6 NxR*, overlooking the response 32. *NxBch K–Q2 33. N–K8ch!*. White won back his rook after 33. . . . *K–K3 34. Q–K7ch K–Q4 35. N–B7ch K–Q5 36. Q–N7ch K–K5 37. QxR*, and Black postponed resignation with a few checks. Black's defeat can only be blamed on the confusion created by White's king march.

If this example isn't surprising enough, who would believe that White could win from this position:

This is Karpov-A. Zaitsev, USSR 1970, which began *1. P–K4 P–QB3 2. P–Q4 P–Q4 3. N–QB3 PxP 4. NxP N–Q2 5. N–KB3 KN–B3 6. NxNch NxN 7. N–K5 B–B4 8. P–QB3 P–K3 9. P–KN4 B–N3 10. P–KR4 B–Q3! 11. Q–K2 P–QB4 12. P–R5? B–K5 13. P–B3 PxP 14. Q–N5ch N–Q2 15. NxP B–N6ch 16. K–K2 P–Q6ch 17. K–K3! Q–B3 18. KxB.*

After *18. . . . QxN* material was equal, but White's king was in the center of the board. What counts, however, is control of territory. Black cannot contest the king's presence on K4 easily, and thus the White king position may be an unexploitable weakness. After *19. R–R3 P–QR3 20. Q–N5 P–R3? 21. Q–K3! P–K4 22. KxP B–B5 23. Q–N1 0–0–0 24. K–B2 BxB 25. RxB! QxRP 26. R–R2* White survived, and even won the game.

One further unappetizing but frequently rewarding theme of defense is the advance of one's protective shield of pawns. Every good instinct of the defender suggests that these protecting blocks shouldn't be budged. Yet defense is the art of finding exceptions to the rules of attack. Naturally, the advance of protecting pawns is something you have to calculate well because one misstep means the difference between crushing the attacking force or choosing suicide.

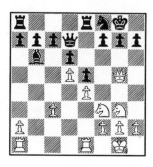

The position above is from an early game of Mikhail Tal's which began 1. P–K4 P–K4 2. N–KB3 N–QB3 3. B–B4 B–B4 4. P–QN4 BxNP 5. P–B3 B–R4 6. P–Q4 P–Q3 7. B–KN5 KN–K2 8. P–Q5 N–QN1 9. BxN KxB! 10. Q–B1 N–Q2 11. 0–0 R–K1 12. N–R4 K–B1 13. N–B5 N–B4 14. N–N3 N–Q2 15. N–Q2 B–N3 16. N–B3 K–N1 17. R–K1 N–B1 18. B–N5 B–Q2 19. BxB QxB 20. Q–N5.

By bringing his king to safety—often called "castling by hand" —Tal has survived the first crisis with his extra pawn intact. Now he faces a new danger from the intrusion of the White queen and knights, e.g., N–R5 and N–R4–B5.

Black's defense begins with 20. . . . P–B3!, which either gains time through the advance of the Black knight or drives White's queen out of the dangerous zone. White remained in the vicinity with 21. Q–R5 N–N3 22. N–B5 N–B5 23. Q–R4, and Black's 23. . . . K–R1 prepared a surprise which White should have anticipated with 24. P–N3 N–Q6 (24. . . . P–N4 25. Q–R6) 25. R–K2. But White saw only the . . . N–Q6 threat and he played 24. QR–Q1.

Now Black played 24. . . . P–KR4!?, a bolt from the blue which should best be ignored. White realized that 25. P–N3?? P–N4 26. NxNP PxN 27. QxNP N–R6ch costs the game. So he played 25. P–N4? which was answered by 25. . . . P–N4! 26. Q–N3 Q–R2, and if 27. P–KR4 Black could open up the deadly file with 27. . . . PxNP 28. QxP R–KN1.

White tried 27. PxP, and after 27. . . . P–N5! 28. N(3)–R4

NxRP 29. Q–Q3 N–B5 30. Q–N3 N–R6ch 31. K–B1 BxP! 32. QxNP BxR! 33. N–N6ch K–N1 34. N(5)–K7ch K–B2, Black was high and dry.

A case in miniature of this effect is Timman-Gligoric, Amsterdam 1971: 1. P–K4 P–K4 2. N–KB3 N–QB3 3. B–N5 P–QR3 4. BxN QPxB 5. 0–0 P–B3 6. P–Q4 PxP 7. NxP B–Q3 8. Q–R5ch P–N3 9. Q–R4?. This is inferior to the retreat of the queen to B3. Black here played 9. . . . P–KR4! threatening to trap the White queen with 10. . . . P–KN4. White took strong measures: 10. P–K5! PxP 11. B–N5 B–K2 12. KN–B3 BxB 13. NxB B–KB4 14. QN–B3 N–R3, which were just enough to hold the balance. In the actual game Black was soon on top after 15. Q–N3 N–B2 16. QN–K4 NxN 17. NxN Q–B3 18. P–KB4? P–K5 19. QR–Q1 QxP!. He won in 31 moves.

TAKING TIME FOR THE IMPORTANT THINGS

The temptation for the defender is to castle, bring out pieces quickly and launch counterthreats. This isn't so easy, however, for several reasons. The rapid mobilization of force and placement of the king may just encourage the other side to pinpoint his attack at the right spot. That's exactly what Khlyavin did in the Latvian game cited in the Introduction. Also, the simple development of pieces and castling isn't so simply accomplished in modern sophisticated openings which are separated by light years from the Giuoco Piano or King's Gambit. (Wilhelm Steinitz did take 32 moves to castle in a game versus Zukertort in their 1886 match.)

The experienced defender knows that under certain circumstances, such as a closed center, he can take his time with developing moves. He can reorder his priorities by making improvements and repair jobs before coordinating his pieces. A good example of the 1934 Soviet Championship:

Savitsky-Veresov—1. P–K4 P–QB3 2. N–QB3 P–Q4 3. N–B3 N–B3?! 4. P–K5 N–K5 5. N–K2 B–N5 6. KN–N1! N–B4 7. P–KB3 B–Q2 8. P–Q4 KN–R3 9. P–B3 P–K3 10. P–QN4?!

Black has been thrown into retreat, and White is ready to redevelop his pieces with a view to a strong kingside attack involving P–KB4, N–B3, N–N3 and B–Q3. But first White plays to stop the freeing . . . P–QB4, which is Black's main source of counterplay in such positions. This is the famous attack on the base of the pawn-chain that Nimzovich heralded a half-century ago.

Two points stand out concerning 10. P–QN4. It is overambitious, *but* it would have succeeded had Black routinely played 10. . . . B–K2 and 11. . . . 0–0. Black decided that he could defer kingside development as long as White is kept busy and does not have time for P–KB4–5, the attack on the base of Black's pawn-chain. The second point involves this question of logic: Why was it overambitious for White to take time out for P–QN4 but not for Black to play his next series? In part the answer is that Black is taking action on the side of the board on which he has strength. But White is shorthanded on the queenside, and his attempts to forestall Black's . . . P–QB4 before White is better developed are doomed to fail.

The game proceeded: *10. . . . P–QN3! 11. N–N3 P–QB4 12. P–QR3 N–B2 13. B–Q3 P–QR4!*. The opening of lines on the side where you are strongest is beneficial nine times out of ten. Black continued to delay . . . B–K2 and . . . 0–0: *14. PxRP PxRP 15. KN–K2 N–B3 16. 0–0 Q–N1!*, in order to add pressure on the QP with 17. . . . Q–R2.

Perhaps White was still unaware of Black's long-range plans.

He tried *17. BK–3 Q–R2 18. Q–Q2 P–B5! 19. B–QB2 P–R5! 20. B–B2,* and now *20. . . . N–R4 21. N–R5 0–0–0!* revealed Black's advantage. He was ready to plug the QN-file with . . . N–N6 and then work on the weak pawns on QR6 and QB6.

In the absence of kingside counterplay, White quickly went downhill: *22. B–R4 R–K1 23. Q–B4 N–N6 24. R–R2 N–N4 25. QxP NxBP 26. NxN QxPch 27. B–B2 QxN 28. Q–B4 B–B3 29. R–Q1 Q–R4 30. Q–N3 P–Q5 31. P–B4 P–Q6 32. BxP!? PxB 33. RxP B–B4* (first move by this piece) *34. BxB QxBch 35. Q–B2 Q–B8ch 36. Q–B1 QxQch 37. KxQ B–N4,* and *White Resigned.*

Steinitz was the master who introduced the idea of taking time out for strategic ideas before completing development. He laid down the principle that these structural improvements could be made provided the center was closed. Then, a loss of time through redevelopment and maneuver wouldn't count as heavily as in an open game:

Zukertort-Steinitz, match 1872—*1. P–K4 P–K4 2. N–KB3 N–QB3 3. B–N5 P–QR3 4. B–R4 N–B3 5. P–Q3 P–Q3 6. BxNch PxB 7. P–KR3? P–N3 8. N–B3 B–KN2 9. B–K3?* (9 *P–Q4!*) *P–B4! 10. Q–Q2 P–R3 11. R–QN1 N–N1! 12. N–R2 N–K2 13. P–B4 PxP 14. BxKBP P–N4! 15. B–K3 P–B4 16. 0–0 P–KB5,* and Black has a positionally winning game directly traceable to his last five moves. White forced open the queenside in the hope of obtaining counterplay: *17. B–B2 N–B3 18. N–Q5 0–0 19. P–QN4 PxP 20. NxNP NxN 21. RxN B–K3 22. B–Q4 BxBch 23. RxB P–B4 24. R–R4 Q–N3 25. P–B4 P–QR4 26. R–R3 P–R5! 27. R–QB3 KR–N1 28. R–QB2 Q–B2 29. R–N2 P–R6! 30. R(2)–N1 Q–KN2! 31. RxRch RxR 32. Q–R5 Q–Q5ch 33. K–R1 QxQP 34. Q–B7 R–N8 35. Q–Q8ch K–B2 and White Resigned.*

COOLNESS UNDER FIRE

Steinitz was also the first great player to make the transition from young attacking master to mature defensive master. And being one of the great chess thinkers, as opposed to players, he asked himself what made an attack succeed. It wasn't just the genius of the player marshaling the attack or the lack of skill of the defender. Even with the best defense, some attacks obtain major advantages.

Therefore, Steinitz concluded, there must be some form of superiority in the hands of the attacker before the first attacking move. An attack against a solidly positioned opponent cannot succeed. A successful attack is nothing more than the correct exploitation of (exploitable) weakness.

What this means to the practical player has more to do with faith than science. When an opponent opens up his pieces for assault he must theoretically be able to point to some advantages in the position to justify aggression. It may be kingside weakness in the opponent's camp or an edge in space or in development in a certain sector. Of course, this justification alone will not make the attack successful, but it is necessary for any real attack.

Therefore, the defender can think to himself that the attacker who advances from a position in which he has no superiority is doomed to failure—if correctly handled. "He is trying to beat me with a phony attack," you say to yourself, knowing that you can refute it with a careful response.

Here is an example of Steinitz himself applying the rule

of reason—and thereby placing absolute faith in the defensibility of his position—against Zukertort in their 1886 match.

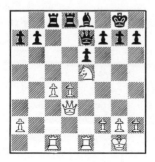

White has an obvious edge in space and an excellently posted knight. But Black's compensating chances include pressure against the hanging central pawns and the ability to drive the knight off with . . . P–KB3. Given time, White could gain a strong grasp on the center with KR–Q1, Q–N3, P–B5 and N–B4–Q6. But Black could anticipate this long-range threat with . . . P–QN3, the doubling of rooks on the QB-file and . . . P–B3. The position, as the analysts say, is theoretically equal—which is quite different from being drawish.

Zukertort played 23. R–K3? in the mistaken belief that a kingside attack could succeed. Steinitz "knew" it couldn't, even without calculating out his defensive chances. He had faith in his position.

Black responded 23. . . . Q–Q3 so that he could meet 24. R–R3 with the simple 24. . . . P–R3 25. R–Q1 P–B3, repulsing White's pieces. White brought additional defense to his QP with 24. R–Q1 and was embarrassed by 24. . . . P–B3. The White knight could retreat to KB3, but then 25. . . . Q–R3! 26. N–Q2 P–K4 or 26. Q–N3 RxBP 27. N–Q2 R(5)xP 28. RxP B–B2 would be very bad. So he made his only threat in the position, 25. R–R3.

Here Steinitz could take the knight and endure a lengthy attack, for example, 25. . . . PxN 26. QxPch K–B1 27. R–B3ch

B–B2 28. Q–R8ch K–K2 29. QxP R–B1 30. R–N1 or 27. R–KN3 B–B2 28. RxP R–B2 29. P–B5!. But there was a simpler road in 25. . . . *P–KR3!*.

Now White really had to move his knight, and N–B3 was no better than before. The interpolation of R–R3 and . . . P–KR3 allows 26. N–N6, but Zukertort rejected it because of 26. . . . BxN 27. QxB RxP! 28. RxP QxP!, e.g., 29. Q–R7ch K–B1 30. Q–R8ch K–B2 31. QxR QxQ!.

What actually happened was *26. N–N4*, and Black began to confuse White's pieces in the final stage: *26. . . . Q–B5! 27. N–K3 B–R5 28. R–B3 Q–Q3 29. R–Q2 B–B3* (even better is 29. . . . P–QN4) *30. R–N3 P–B4 31. R–N6 B–K5 32. Q–N3 K–R2*. The game ended with Black pieces running all over the board: *33. P–B5 RxP 34. RxKP R–B8ch 35. N–Q1 Q–B5 36. Q–N2 R–N8 37. Q–B3 R–QB1 38. RxB QxR and White Resigned.*

A different situation entirely is the attitude of a player who says, in effect, "Do what you will now—I'm lost on anything else I do." Here the defender has no faith in his position. He agrees it may be lost. There is point in calculating every variation possible. The defender recognizes he can just try to make the best move, one at a time.

This is a position from Fischer-Matanovic, Bled 1961. Besides the obvious danger to White from Black's active pieces, there was the additional pressure on Fischer of being the leader in one of his first powerful tournaments. But with White he was being outplayed, and this became apparent after *30. . . . QxRP!*, which makes 31. QxB unavailing because of 31. . . . N–N5.

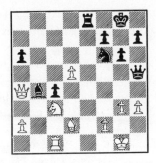

White is suddenly a pawn behind in an overextended position. He can expect to be pushed around in the next dozen moves. But you can only lose one game at a time. If the game is lost, there is nothing to do about it. Fischer coolly played *31. R–K1!*, a fine simplifying move which cannot be avoided without giving White better defensive play, e.g., 31. . . . R–N1 32. Q–Q1 N–N5 33. Q–B3.

Matanovic played the accurate *31. . . . RxRch 32. BxR B–B4*, and Fischer recognized the loss of his KNP and the removal of a very valuable protective pawn. His *33. QxBP!* was met by *33. . . . QxPch 34. K–B1 Q–R6ch 35. K–K2 Q–R4ch 36. K–B1 Q–R8ch 37. K–K2 Q–R4ch 38. K–B1* and finally *38. . . . B–B1*. Black still has a winning game, although there were superior queen checks previously.

But after *39. QxRP!* Black missed *39. . . . Q–B6!* (e.g., 40. K–N1 Q–N5ch 41. K–B1 N–R4) and allowed a further simplification, *39. . . . NxP 40. NxN QxN 41. P–R4*, which gave White's passed pawn great strength. Throughout all of this White saw that he could be checked around the board till doomsday, but it would not decisively improve Black's game.

The critical sequence came about via *41. . . . P–B4 42. B–B3 P–B5 43. Q–KB6 Q–R8ch 44. K–K2 Q–K5ch 45. K–Q2 P–B6 46. Q–R8ch K–B2* and now, *not* 47. QxPch?? K–K1, after which the threat of a queen check on K7 is decisive, but *47. Q–B6ch! K–K1 48. Q–K5ch!!*, which draws: *48. . . . QxQ 49. BxQ B–B4 50. K–Q3! P–N4* (or *50. . . . BxP 51. K–K4! winning the passed pawn*)

51. K–K4 P–N5 52. B–N3 P–R4 (otherwise *53. K–B5 P–R4 54. K–N5* wins the kingside pawns) *53. P–R5 K–Q2 54. K–Q5! B–R2 55. K–K4 K–B1 56. K–B5! B–N1 57. K–N5!*, followed by scooping up the Black pawns.

The condemned man can usually choose his paths simply. He just rejects the paths that lead to mate or decisive material loss. Knowing that your game is objectively lost often provides a psychological lift, ironically enough. You decide to go down fighting a hard game. And quite often this is the best way of confusing an opponent and saving a lost game. Facing a bad position in his first great tournament, José Capablanca allowed an obvious sacrificial line that saw his king kicked around the board. "As a matter of fact," he wrote, "I had already seen what was coming, but I also felt that my only chance was to weather the storm." He *won* the game and then the tournament.

THE SAVING GRACE

Chess players are not known for their belief in divine salvation. But at the board a successful defender can profit from faith in the inevitability of a saving tactical grace. To paraphrase an early argument in favor of believing in God, belief in the survival of your position is a sound bet. If there is no possible chance to save it, you haven't lost anything. But if you believe that tactical chances will appear at a later stage and those chances do exist, you will be in a better frame of mind to take advantage of them than the player who is convinced he will lose.

The trouble is that most defenders are dazzled by the surprise brilliant combination and become quickly demoralized. They ready themselves for resignation and fix blame on their failure to forecast the combination. But quite often the true source of blame is their failure to respond to brilliancy:

The diagram shows a famous offhand game played by the veteran coffeehouse player and occasional tournament champion Richard Teichmann. White's concluding combination is frequently cited by chess teachers as a model of tactical genius. Teichman played *1. RxP!!*, threatening mate on KR8. After *1. . . . NxR* he played *2. Q–N5*, threatening a check on Q8. And on *2. . . . N–B2* Teichmann continued with *3. Q–Q8ch!! NxQ 4. P–R6!*. Black resigned in view of the unstoppable 5. P–R7ch.

It is comforting to think such a series of sacrifices force resignation because of an impending check by a pawn. Chess can be a beautiful game, you say. But this isn't a good attitude for the defender. Millions of players have marveled at Teichmann's combination, but only a few years ago did an obscure analyst from Russia discover that Black wasn't lost at all. Black, he pointed out, can play 4. . . . Q–B1!! 5. P–R7ch K–B2! after which White will emerge with an extra queen, but Black may have sufficient material to compensate. Yet the psychological bias in favor of attack shrouded the tactical saving grace for more than half a century.

Leaf through any collection of great games and pick out a dozen kingside attacks with sacrifices. In almost every case the annotators have discovered that the defender could have held out much longer —in fact, should not have lost at all in some instances. Yet in the vast majority of these games, the defender misses his best chances.

Mikhail Tal became world champion because he won many of those games. Occasionally he was upended by a minor master who refuted his attack. But Tal made up for it by winning five or six extra games that might otherwise have been drawn.

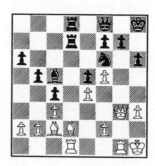

Here is Tal sliding into an inferior position with the White pieces against Dr. Miroslav Filip in the 1958 Interzonal tournament. The natural 28. B–K3 might hold the ending after a double trade of rooks. But Tal played 28. BxP!? PxB 29. QxP, objectively inferior but perhaps *practically* the best try.

His opponent played 29. . . . B–K2 30. R–Q4! RxR 31. PxR K–R2, and Tal answered with 32. R–Q1 in order to advance his central pawns and open up his bishop's diagonal. Filip allowed him to do just that: 32. . . . N–K1?? 33. P–B6! NxP 34. Q–B5ch K–R1 35. P–K5 and *Black Resigned* after 35. . . . Q–N2 36. PxN BxP 37. R–KN1 B–N4 38. P–B4.

Yes, Black's position is critical after 32. R–Q1, but if Filip had looked hard he would have found not only a saving defense but a winning defense: 32. . . . Q–N2!!, so that on 33. QxB Black mates with 33. . . . R–KN1, and on 33. R–KN1 he traps the White queen with 33. . . . B–Q3!!. It is reasonable to assume that Black overlooked this defense because he wasn't looking for it. That is, he didn't suspect that Black could use tactics to consolidate.

Max Pavey, a Scottish-born American who rose to the heights

of the chess and bridge worlds in the 1950s, formulated a theory (later embraced and perfected by grandmaster Larry Evans) that no matter how bad your position is—unless there is a forced loss or *zugzwang*—you will have an opportunity to fight off defeat. This may sound a bit far-fetched, but chess positions have a resiliency that never ceases to amaze. Take this Tal position:

The Latvian had White against Fridrik Olafsson of Iceland at Bled 1961 in a Sicilian Defense that developed: *1. P–K4 P–QB4. 2. N–KB3 N–QB3 3. P–Q4 PxP 4. NxP P–K3 5. N–QB3 Q–B2 6. B–K3 P–QR3 7. P–QR3 N–B3 8. P–B4 P–Q3 9. Q–B3 B–K2 10. B–Q3 0–0 11. 0–0 B–Q2 12. QR–K1 P–QN4 13. Q–N3 K–R1!? 14. NxN BxN 15. P–K5 N–N1 16. Q–R3 N–R3 17. P–B5! NxP 18. RxN PxR 19. BxBP P–N3 20. B–Q4.*

Black could have simplified his task earlier with 11. . . . NxN and 12. . . . P–K4. With his 13th and 15th moves he builds a defensive formation on the kingside popularized by Miguel Najdorf in the 1940s and '50s. But what concerns us is Black's ability to survive an apparently crushing Tal onslaught.

Olafsson played *20. . . . K–N1?* and lost soon after *21. P–K6! B–N4 22. PxPch RxP 23. BxNP! R–N2 24. Q–K6ch K–R1 25. B–K8!!.* The magic resources of defense would have appeared after 20. . . . Q-Q1!!, which allows him to block checks by inserting a bishop on his KB3.

The first critical possibility is 21. P–K6ch B–B3 22. Q–R4!, with a threat of P–K7. After 22. . . . PxP 23. RxP, Black cannot play either 23. . . . BxBch 24. QxBch K–N1 25. RxQP or 23. . . . K–N2 24. RxB RxR 25. B–K4!!. But he does have 23. . . . B–K4!!, killing the attack. Very nicely done.

But what about 21. PxPch B–B3 22. Q–R4, the second inspired try? Again 22. . . . K–N2 is refuted, this time by the ingenious 23. B–Q7!! (threatening BxB and R–K7) QBxB 24. N–Q5! BxBch 25. QxBch P–B3 26. R–K7ch or 25. . . . K–R3 26. R–K4 P–B3 27. R–K7. But again there is a defense: 22. . . . B–N2!!.

This game is an example of deep calculation which might have saved Black. But quite often just being aware of one-move interpolations and simple counterattacks makes the difference. To paraphrase Tartakover, the defensive coups are there, waiting to be played.

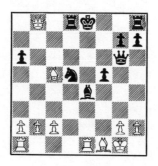

The occasion for the diagram above was the 1972 US Championship game between I. A. Horowitz and Orest Popovych. Throughout the middlegame White has been taking the Black position apart—first with kingside threats, then sharp queenside tactics, then a sacrifice or two and finally with a mating attack. Here White played 32. Q–K5ch K–B2 33. RxB PxR 34. B–B4 Q–QB3 35. R–B1ch, and after 35. . . . K–N3 36. QxKPch K–R3 37. B–K3ch, Black forfeited on time.

What is remarkable is that both White and Black were so carried away with the inevitability of White's victory that they overlooked 33. . . . . KR–K1!, a *zwischenzug* which turns a lost game into a real contest after 34. B–B4 RxQ 35. RxR Q–QB3 and . . . K–N3. Naturally, 32. Q–K5ch was bad and White could have obtained the same result with 32. RxBch and then 33. Q–K5ch. But that is the nature of the optimism—and for Black the pessimism—that takes over the minds of players during a difficult attack.

ILLUSTRATIVE GAMES
UKRAINIAN CHAMPIONSHIP 1957

STEIN   FLOHR

1. P–K4 P–QB3 2. P–Q4 P–Q4 3. N–QB3 PxP 4. NxP N–Q2 5. B–QB4 KN–B3 6. N–N5 P–K3 7. Q–K2 Q–K2? 8. B–Q2 P–QN3 9. 0–0–0 B–N2 10. KN–B3 P–KR3

11. B–N4!   . . .

This thunderbolt begins Black's time of troubles. He cannot easily take the bishop because of 12. NxBP!; e.g. 12. . . . KxN 13. QxPch K–N3 14. B–Q3ch and mates, or 12. . . . R–R2 13. QxPch Q–K2 14. Q–B5 Q–N5 15. KR–K1ch and 16. Q–K6. Best is 12. . . . QxB! It is easy to be jolted by a tactical shot like 11. B–N4!!. But even a series of sparkling moves is not enough to win against a determined defender. Salo Flohr, a veteran of many events and the victim of many brilliancies, never loses his will to survive in this game.

11. . . .	P–B4
12. PxP	PxP
13. BxBP!?	. . .

The most energetic consequence of his 11th move. Black must capture with his knight after which N–K5 threatens B–N5ch. White wins two pawns and a lengthy initiative for a piece.

13. . . .	NxB
14. N–K5	KN–Q2
15. N(N)xBP	NxN
16. NxN	Q–N4ch
17. P–B4!	. . .

Without a loss of time White opens the KB-file and gains control of KR5 for a queen check. So far everything has worked beautifully for White.

| 17 . . . | QxPch |
| 18. K–N1 | B–K5! |

Even in critical positions there are good moves and this one manages (1) to stop N–N6, (2) to minimize the effect of Q–R5ch, and (3) to threaten White's knight on the blocked K-file.

19. Q–R5ch	P–N3
20. B–N5ch	K–K2
21. NxPch	BxN
22. QxNch	. . .

A Russian eulogy to Stein after his premature death commented at this point, "Now was the time to switch over from romanticism to sober calculation and play the 'quiet' 22. QxB." That move would threaten KR–B1 strongly and would allow White to meet efforts to exchange queens with threats of his own, e.g., 22. . . . Q–K5 23. R–Q7ch! or 22. . . . Q–B4 (or B3 or B2) 23. Q–N3. But the Russian annotator doesn't mention 22. . . . Q–N4!.

22. . . .	K–B2
23. Q–B6	. . .

Apparently a winning move because of the dual threat against Black's QR and Q(KR–B1). But the attack can be just as difficult to handle as the defense if choice is forced upon the attacker. Here White could and should have looked longer at the alternatives such as 23. Q–B3 K–N1 24. KR–B1 Q–KN5 25. B–Q7.

23. . . .	Q–K5!

A saving move. That is, a move that prevents immediate collapse. It is interesting now that White begins to make bad moves in a position that is still very promising for him. Notice the psychological effect on the two players. Black maintains a "cheerful pessimism" even after 11. B–N4 and 13. BxBP, but White quickly does downhill after 23. . . . Q–K5.

24. Q–Q7ch	K–N1
25. B–Q3	Q–KN5
26. P–KR3	Q–N4
27. QxPch?	. . .

"Love of checking" is blamed here. 27. KR–B1! keeps strong chances in White's hands: 27. . . . R–R2? 28. QxPch or 27. . . . B–N2 28. QxPch K–R2 29. P–KR4.

27. . . .	B–B2
28. Q–QB6	R–N1

29. Q–B7	R–N3
30. B–B4?	. . .

Again 30. KR–B1 would have been strong, e.g., 30. . . . R–KB3 31. RxR QxR 32. R–KB1 Q–K3 33. P–QN3! (not 33. RxB Q–K8 mate) 33. . . . Q–K2 34. Q–B8 or Q–KB4.

30. . . .	R–R2
31. KR–B1	R–KB3
32. RxR	QxR
33. R–KB1??	QxRch

And *White Resigned* because of 34. BxQ BxPch and 35. . . . RxQ. It should be noted that even in 1957 Leonid Stein was a dangerous opponent. But as Tarrasch said, it's not enough to be a strong player—you must also play well.

CHAPTER TWO:

Defensive Weapons and Themes

The weapons of attack, such as the sacrifice, the line-opening pawn-break; the pin and the double threat, are well known. Every how-to-play primer introduces at least a few of them. The weapons of defense have suffered a bad press, however. The defender has a number of good points to his spear. But they are hardly as familiar as the attacker's, and we'll examine the following in this chapter:

(1) Keeping attack lines closed or under control
(2) Repairing weakness
(3) Trading pieces for endgame safety
(4) Elimination of the strong attacking piece
(5) Relieving pressure
(6) Confusing the opponent's pieces
(7) Maneuver and redeployment
(8) Breaking the attacking front
(9) Seizing a foothold in the center

OPEN LINES

Open lines are the canals of attack. If the player with the initiative has uncontested access to these avenues, he can write his own game plan. "The attack plays itself," as the annotators love to say. The tactics for success will suggest themselves. The defender should try therefore to do one of three things: (a) to

33

block, (b) to contest, or (c) to minimize the effect of the attacker's open lines. A fourth possibility is to ignore these lines completely and to try to scare up counterplay in another territory of the board. But counterplay is not always available, and, if the other side has control of key open lines, it may be felt several moves too late.

Recalling once again that Latvian game from the Introduction, we can see that Black would be in big trouble if just one of the major files had been open after a dozen moves. If the K-file, for example, were cleared of pawns it isn't hard to imagine Black's being mated swiftly.

Now evaluate this position from the Janowski-Lasker world championship match of 1909:

A cursory glance would indicate that White has a penetrating bishop and a pair of excellently posted rooks. One would guess that it only takes the addition of the White queen to force a decisive turn to the game. In actuality, Black holds the edge after 22. . . . *P–N3!*.

That move has the immediate effect of shortening the KN-file. It has the additional effect of threatening . . . P–KB4 with counterplay against the White center. All of a sudden it seems that White's rooks are sitting uselessly on a blocked file and that his KB could do much better service elsewhere.

In fact, White's next move was 23. *B–Q3* to stop 23. . . . P–KB4.

Lasker just prepared *23. . . . R–K2 24. P–B4 N–N2! 25. P–B3*
(25 QxP QxQ 26. RxQ N–K3 regains the pawn with an excellent
N-vs-B ending ahead) *N–K3*, and White was thrown into a
panic over the threatened *26. . . . N–N4* and the eventual
. . . P–KB4 and *. . . P–KN4–5*. White's once optimistic position
collapsed in a few moves: *26. B–B1 P–KB4 27. R(4)–N2 R–B3!
28. B–Q3 P–KN4 29. R–KR1* (to stop the threat of *28. . . .
QxPch!* and *29. . . . R–R3* mate) *P–N5! 30. B–K2 N–N4 31.
BPxP P–B6 32. R–N3 PxB* and *White Resigned.*

In reconstructing the collapse from the diagram we can see
that White's rooks are only effective as long as they are pressur-
ing the entire KN-file up to a weak dead-end point (KN7).
When that dead end is advanced a square and turned into a
strong point, the rooks suffer. The fact that White has a beautiful, clean line for his white-squared bishop is simply not
enough in a position with so many heavy pieces. By shortening
—and thereby minimizing the effect of White's control of—
the KN-file, Black turned the middlegame around.

Open lines are not enough for the attacker. But it is usually
in the defender's interest to undermine those lines (the KN-file
above) while trying to use the ones that the defender can
dominate (the K- and KB-files above). Here is a simple example of line-closing from the 20th USSR Championship. White
has just played *17. P–N5* (after *1. P–K4 P–QB4 2. N–KB3
N–QB3 3. P–Q4 PxP 4. NxP N–B3 5. N–QB3 P–Q3 6. B–KN5
P–K3 7. Q–Q2 B–K2 8. 0–0–0 NxN 9. QxN 0–0 10. P–B4 Q–R4
11. K–N1 P–KR3 12. P–KR4! R–Q1 13. P–KN4 P–K4! 14. Q–N1
PxP 15. BxN BxB 16. N–Q5 B–K4*):

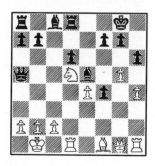

Black could, if he sought immediate counterplay, ignore the kingside temporarily and play 17. . . . B–K3 (and on 18. PxP play 18. . . . BxN 19. PxB Q–N5 or 19. . . . Q–N3). He has good survival chances on the kingside because of the strongly posted black-squared bishop.

But Black (Taimanov) played 17. . . . P–R4!, and his opponent, Byvshev, missed the correct continuation of 18. P–N6 (e.g., 18. . . . B–K3 19. B–B4 Q–B4 20. PxPch) when he at least opens a file for his pieces. White played 18. B–B4?, and after 18. . . . P–N3! Black had sealed off the kingside for the foreseeable future. The attack quickly turned to Black and he won systematically after 19. R–Q3 B–K3 20. R–QN3 QR–N1 21. R–R2 Q–B4 22. Q–KB1 K–N2 23. R–Q2 KR–QB1 24. B–K2 P–R3, followed by . . . P–N4. Black's kingside black squares were unexploitable weaknesses as long as he held his KB for protection.

What's good for the file is good for the diagonal. In another Soviet Championship two years later, Boris Spassky was being pressed sharply by Black in this position:

Black had been stymied on the long white-square diagonal by Spassky's previous P–Q5!. Now, before White has time for QR–N1, Black tried to open the line with 23. . . . PxP. But White played 24. P–B5!, keeping it closed and awaiting such variations as 24. . . . N–N4 25. PxP QxP 26. QxQ and 27. P–QR4 with an ending.

Black kept his hopes alive with 24. . . . K–R1, getting out of the pin which prevents the Black QP from moving. But after 25. PxP Q–Q3 26. R–B7 B–R3 27. P–N7 R–KN1 28. P–N8(Q) BxN 29. P–N3! NxPch 30. K–N2 B–B5 31. R–B8 QxQ 32. QxQ, Black had to surrender.

A further lesson is the defender's need to anticipate the forced opening of lines. In most cases this means the anticipation of pawn-breaks. Some pawn-breaks are inevitable and cannot be prevented. The solution is to minimize the effect. An interesting example of line-opening on two sides of the board was the Fischer-Larsen game in the 1970 Interzonal tournament:

1. P–K4 P–QB4 2. N–KB3 P–Q3 3. P–Q4 PxP 4. NxP N–KB3 5. N–QB3 N–B3 6. B–QB4 P–K3 7. B–N3 B–K2 8. B–K3 0–0 9. Q–K2 P–QR3 10. 0–0–0 Q–B2 11. P–N4 N–Q2 12. P–KR4? N–B4 13. P–N5 P–N4 14. P–B3 B–Q2 15. Q–N2 P–N5 16. N(3)–K2 NxBch 17. RPxN P–QR4

White's problems result from his 12th move. He has chosen a very sharp attacking variation of the opening and one misstep can be very harmful, if not fatal. His decision at move 12 was to attack via a general pawn advance on the kingside. This means he will play P–KN5 and P–KR5 in expectation of opening a line with P–N6 or P–R6. Actually, several other games have shown that White does better to continue 12. P–N5! followed by a direct piece-attack with ideas such as KR–N1–N3–R3 and Q–R5. In this case a piece-attack is more accurate than a pawn storm.

In the diagram we see that Black will play . . . P–R5 at a given point and force open the QR-file. White could have prevented this specific danger by recapturing on move 17 with his knight. But then Black would have played . . . P–QR4–5 anyway. He would actually be a tempo ahead of White's attack on the kingside, although both pawn formations would bear a great deal of similarity.

Fischer recognized that 18. P–R5 is too slow, e.g., 18. . . . P–R5 19. PxP RxP. In fact, if White eventually plays P–KN6, Black could just ignore it since PxRPch and . . . K–R1 would still deny White strong attacking threats. White's pawn blocks his own pieces. Therefore, White played *18. P–N6!?*, gaining a tempo on the 18. P–R5 idea after *18. . . . BPxP 19. P–R5*.

This pawn-sacrifice had succeeded in numerous other similar examples, since White opens two kingside lines after 19. . . . PxP 20. RxRP. But Larsen cleverly chose *19. . . . NxN 20. NxN*

P–N4!! 21. BxP BxB 22. QxB P–R3 23. Q–N4 R–B2, after which
his kingside was rock-solid. White could no longer restrain or
delay . . . P–R5 and he fell apart quickly: *24. KR–N1 P–R5!
25. PxP P–K4 26. N–K6 Q–B5!*, winning a piece.

A final example on the theme of anticipation of line-opening
is Palmer-Reshevsky, Western Open 1933, which began:

*1. P–Q4 N–KB3 2. P–QB4 P–KN3 3. N–QB3 B–N2 4. P–K4
P–Q3 5. N–B3 0–0 6. P–KR3 KN–Q2?! 7. B–K3 P–QB4 8. Q–Q2
N–QB3? 9. P–Q5 QN–K4 10. NxN NxN 11. B–R6 P–B3! 12.
B–K2 B–Q2 13. P–KR4 Q–B1 14. P–B3 P–R3 15. P–KN4?!
P–QN4 16. K–B2? PxP 17. BxB KxB 18. QR–KN1*

Out of a bad opening, Black began with his 11th move to restrain the P–K5 break and to create the possibility of meeting
P–KR5 or P–KB5 with . . . P–KN4 to keep matters closed. Now,
after erroneously delaying the forthright kingside attack, White
threatens 19. P–N5, and if 19. . . . P–B4 then 20. P–R5, clearing
the KR-file. Also threatened is 19. P–R5.

Though not decisive this would be unpleasant. So Black chose
18. . . . P–R3! which (a) allows him to meet 19. P–N5 with
19. . . . BPxP 20. PxP P–KR4!, keeping the most dangerous
file closed and (b) allows him to lock up part of the kingside
after 19. P–R5 P–N4!.

White needed time to prepare for the third breaking idea,

P–B4, and by the time he had played *19. N–Q1 R–QN1 20. N–K3 Q–N2 21. P–B4*, Black was in shape to sacrifice strongly with *21. . . . QxNP! 22. QxQ RxQ 23. PxN PxPch 24. K–K1 R–B5.* Black's rooks swept the board and claimed victory in six more moves. But it is Black's 18th move, not the knight sacrifice, which deserves the greatest appreciation because it made the later counterplay possible.

So far we have concentrated on pawn-breaks. Sometimes the defender must throw his pieces into the enemy onslaught or position them in such a manner to confuse the enemy pieces and blockade his forces. Two examples of this:

(a) Tal–Aronin, Riga 1954—*1. P–K4 P–QB3 2. N–QB3 P–Q4 3. N–B3 PxP 4. NxP N–B3 5. NxNch NPxN 6. B–B4 Q–B2 7. 0–0 B–N5 8. P–Q4 P–K3 9. R–K1 N–Q2 10. P–KR3 B–R4 11. BxP?! PxB 12. RxPch K–B2! 13. N–N5ch PxN 14. QxBch KxR 15. BxP*, and now the threat of R–K1ch appeared decisive. But Black blocked the file temporarily with *15. . . . N–K4! 16. R–K1 Q–N2!*, and this allowed him to escape and win quickly with his extra rook after *17. Q–N4ch K–Q3 18. PxNch K–B2 19. P–K6 R–KN1 20. B–B4ch B–Q3 21. BxBch KxB 22. R–Q1ch K–B2 23. Q–B4ch K–B1.*

(b) Taimanov–Sakharov, 31st USSR Championship 1963— *1. P–QB4 P–K4 2. N–QB3 N–KB3 3. P–K3 N–B3 4. N–B3 B–N5 5. N–Q5 P–K5 6. NxB PxN 7. N–Q5 PxP 8. BxP N–K4 9. Q–K2 P–Q3 10. P–Q4 N–N3 11. P–KR4! NxN 12. BxN P–QB3 13. B–K4 0–0 14. P–R5*, and now Black hit upon a strong idea to control the kingside lines which would normally pass into White's hands. Black played *14. . . . N–R5! 15. B–Q2 P–Q4 16. PxP PxP 17. B–Q3* (17. BxQP B–B4 18. P–K4 R–K1 is not unpleasant for Black) *Q–B3 18. 0–0–0 N–B6!*. This knight, buttressed by a white-square blockade begun in the next few moves, effectively reduces White's attack prospects through its inhibiting effect. The game continued *19. B–B3 B–N5 20. B–B2 Q–K3 21. Q–Q3 P–B4 22. P–R6 P–KN3*, and Black stood well.

REPAIRING WEAKNESSES

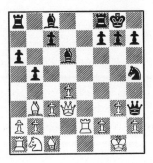

Consider White's position in this typical result of the Marshall Gambit in the Ruy Lopez. The first player has survived the initial assault but at the cost of P–KN3 which is about to be exploited by Black's white-squared QB (. . . B–N2 or . . . B–KN5–B6). White would like to repair his kingside by moving his KNP back a square. But since that's illegal he has another expedient: *16. B–Q5! B–KB4 17. Q–K3 QR–Q1 18. B–N2!.* Suddenly White has a newly fianchettoed KB and a solid kingside. In a Tal game from 1959 White consolidated and traded into a winning pawn-ahead endgame with *18. . . . Q–N5 19. N–Q2 Q–N3 20. N–B3 B–KN5 21. Q–N5!.*

Barring the movement of pawns backward or the magical additions of new pawns to the board, defenders will have to cope with weaknesses in the mechanical way—putting pieces on the right squares to mask those weaknesses. Another version of this theme may arise out of this opening: *1. P–K4 P–Q4 2. PxP QxP 3. N–QB3 Q–QR4 4. P–Q4 N–KB3 5. B–Q3.* Suppose Black becomes nervous about the attacking diagonal leading from the White KB to KR7? Suppose the player with the Black pieces has been burned once too often by the ancient BxKRPch sacrifice after he has castled?

One way of handling that danger and at the same time developing a piece is *5. . . . B–N5! 6. P–B3 B–R4* followed by . . .

B–N3 to neutralize the diagonal. For example, 7 KN–K2 P–B3 8. 0–0 P–K3 9. N–K4 QN–Q2 10. B–KB4 NxN and 11. . . . B–N3! with a fine game (Schiffers-Tarrasch, Leipzig 1894).

What is involved in these instances is the reparation of weakness through redevelopment. This is often done with bishops, but other pieces may serve as well. The special quality of a bishop is that it can serve as a "big pawn" in its new capacity. It can be a strong piece in its own right and yet also do repair work on squares that have been weakened by the advance of a pawn. The repairing piece must not be wasted, as our rule of economy indicates. Tal's KB in the first example and Black's QB in the second do valiant work for the defense beyond the simple function of repair.

A further example comes from one of Steinitz's most famous world championship victories (vs. Zukertort, St. Louis 1886). After *1. P–Q4 P–Q4 2. P–QB4 P–K3 3. N–QB3 N–KB3 4. P–K3 P–B4 5. N–B3 N–B3 6. P–QR3 QPxP 7. BxP PxP 8. PxP B–K2 9. 0–0 0–0 10. B–K3 B–Q2 11. Q–Q3,* Zukertort had begun a familar attacking formation behind his isolated QP. The formation usually includes B–KN5, N–K5 and B–QR2–N1, along with rooks placed at QB1 and K1. Black responded by putting pressure on the QP and queenside: *11. . . . R–B1 12. QR–B1 Q–R4 13. B–R2 KR–Q1 14. KR–K1 B–K1.*

Now White directed his attention at KR7 with *15. B–N1.* Steinitz might have thought twice about the black-square weaknesses incurred by *15. . . . P–KN3.* But he confidently made that move and continued *16. Q–K2 B–B1! 17. KR–Q1 B–N2.* Black's kingside has been weakened and repaired in three moves, and the result is that Black's position has improved sharply.

As it turned out, Zukertort sought to conjure up an attack with *18. B–R2? N–K2! 19. Q–Q2* (with a potential threat of N–Q5) *Q–R3 20. B–N5 N–B4 21. P–KN4?,* and Black soon achieved a winning position after *21. . . . NxQP! 22. NxN P–K4 23. N–Q5 RxR 24. QxR PxN 25. RxP NxN 26. RxN RxR 27. BxR Q–K7!.*

TRADE!

Exchanging off pieces is one of the most obvious and best-known defensive resources. With fewer pieces on the board—and especially with fewer pawns—the defender's task is lightened, the pressure on his weaknesses is lifted.

With one forced exchange all the dangers of a position can disappear:

Given time for . . . B–B1–N5 or –R6 in connection with . . . Q–R4, Black could have negated the central positional advantages of White. Black's tactical chances must be carefully contained. In this early game of Botvinnik's, White relied on 22. Q–B5!, forcing queens off the board (22. . . . QxQ? 23. N–K7ch and NxQ wins a pawn as well). In just a few moves Black's attacking pieces were revealed to be badly misplaced for the ending: 22. . . . Q–R4 23. QxQ NxQ 24. P–B4! R–K1 (24. . . . PxP 25. P–KN4!) 25. QR–K1, and so on.

Often the danger is not simply that of a kingside attack—which may be nullified by the exchange of one pugnacious piece—but of positional pressure over a whole sector of the board. Here it is usually wise to trade off the heavy pieces as long as (1) you don't exchange your most useful and active pieces for his passive ones, and (2) you don't allow your opponent time for an initiative as a result of the trades.

Take this 1963 Soviet Championship game:

Bondarevsky-Osnos—*1. P–Q4 P–KB4 2. N–KB3 N–KB3 3. P–B4 P–KN3 4. N–B3 B–N2 5. Q–B2?! P–B4! 6. P–Q5 N–R3 7. P–QR3?! P–Q3 8. P–KN3 N–B2 9. B–N2 R–QN1 10. 0–0 P–QN4! 11. PxP NxNP 12. NxN RxN 13. N–N5 0–0 14. R–N1 Q–N3*

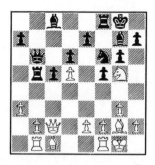

White has a good game, it appears. On closer inspection we see that he cannot exploit the hole on K6, but the weakness of his own QP and QNP are exploitable. The QP is artificially isolated. That is, attempts to support it with another pawn (P–K4) are easily stopped (. . . BPxKP).

Although there are other methods of defending this game— some of which offer White better chances of winning— Bondarevsky sought safety in the ending. He began with *15. P–QN4 PxP 16. B–K3! Q–N1 17. RxP!*. This, in effect, forced a liquidation of queenside pawns. This is almost always good for the defense because in many games the best drawing chance a player has is the elimination of all the queenside and center pawns . . . even at the cost of a kingside pawn. The reason this is sound is that most rook and pawn endings with, for example, two White kingside pawns opposed to three Black kingside pawns are drawn with proper play if both kings are on the kingside. Since rook endings are by far the most common ending type, this theme recurs frequently. The same principle holds for some other endings as well. Yet with both sides having three pawns on the kingside and Black enjoying an extra pawn on the queenside, the balance shifts sharply to Black's advantage. The ending may still be held, but the addition of a distant, passed pawn must greatly help Black.

Back to Bondarevsky-Osnos: *17. . . . RxR 18. PxR N–N5!* (wisely keeping queenside pawns on the board) *19. B–Q2 B–Q2 20. R–B1* (with a threat of Q–B7 with an endgame advantage, and thus forcing new trades) *20. . . . R–B1 21. Q–Q1 Q–N3 22. RxRch BxR.* White still had some pawn problems, but he solved the remaining center and queenside issues with *23. P–K3 Q–R3 24. B–KB1 Q–R7 25. Q–B1 B–N2 26. B–B4,* and after *26. . . . Q–R8 27. N–K6!* White drew comfortably.

The resiliency of a defensive position once pieces are traded off is remarkable. Trading is not just a method of achieving a draw. As pieces drop off the board, the overextended nature of the attacker's position may show through.

Above is an early Alekhine-Romanovsky game which arose from *1. P–Q4 P–Q4 2. N–KB3 P–QB4 3. P–B4 P–K3 4. P–K3 N–QB3 5. N–B3 N–B3 6. B–Q3 B–K2 7. 0–0 0–0 8. P–QN3 BPxP 9. KPxP P–QN3 10. B–N2 B–R3 11. R–K1 PxP 12. PxP R–B1 13. N–QN5?! BxN 14. PxB N–QN5 15. N–K5 N–Q2 16. R–K3!.* White has the makings of a lightning attack with BxPch followed by Q–R5ch and R–R3. Black averts this with a series of exchanges that concede White a large chunk of the board in space. But are the exchanges bad?

Black played *16. . . . NxB 17. RxN NxN 18. PxN Q–K1! 19. Q–N3 R–Q1 20. QR–Q1 RxR 21. RxR*, and after *21. . . . B–B4* it was clear that Black had protected all the squares he needed to work on the enemy weaknesses, chiefly the queenside and KP. The exchanges have left White with the appearance of strong control of territory, but this is illusory.

Play continued with *22. P–N3 P–KR3 23. P–QR4 Q–R1! 24. B–Q4 R–B1! 25. P–B3 Q–N1! 26. P–B4 Q–B2! 27. BxB QxBch*, and Black came within an inch of winning after *28. K–N2 Q–B8 29. Q–Q1 R–B7ch 30. K–B3 Q–N7 31. R–Q8ch K–R2 32. K–N4! RxP?* (*32. . . . P–R4ch 33. KxP RxPch 34. K–N4 Q–N7* wins) *33. Q–Q3ch P–N3 34. R–Q7 Q–N7 35. RxPch,* and *36. Q–Q8ch!* draws by perpetual check.

Having said that the exchange of pieces is good, we should realize that by trading off pieces at every opportunity a player is bound to lose. The mere exchange of pieces often serves to increase your opponent's control of the board. For instance, *1. P–K4 P–QB4 2. N–KB3 N–QB3 3. P–Q4 PxP 4. NxP* and now *4. . . . NxN? 5. QxN* is bad because it will take dynamite to remove White's Q from its excellent observation post. Like every good weapon, this one should be used only when appropriate.

ELIMINATE THE ATTACKING PIECE

Okay, suppose that trading everything off the board is counterproductive or impossible because of the blocked nature of the position. What you can still do is eliminate through exchanges the most dangerous opposition piece. That is, of course, provided that the piece you give up is not more vital to you.

Here is a position from the 22nd USSR Championship arising out of an Aronin-Simagin game:

1. P–K4 P–QB4 2. N–KB3 P–Q3 3. P–Q4 PxP 4. NxP N–KB3 5. N–QB3 P–QR3 6. P–B4 N–B3? 7. NxN PxN 8. P–K5

*N–Q2 9. B–B4 Q–N3 10. PxP? (10. P–K6!) PxP 11. Q–K2ch
B–K2 12. B–N3 N–B3 13. B–K3 Q–B2 14. 0–0 0–0 15. P–B5!
P–QR4 16. Q–B3 P–Q4 17. B–Q4 R–N1 18. P–QR3*

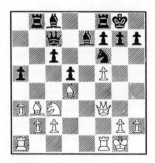

White threatens P–KN4–5 powerfully on the kingside. The
natural response in the center would be . . . P–QB4, but that
always fails to QBxKN followed by the capture of the QP.
Black looks for another method of meeting the threat.

What are the dangerous White pieces? Well, foremost the
bishop on Q4 is a problem. The other two minor pieces are
effectively shielded from the center of action by Black's center
pawns. Therefore *18. . . . N–Q2! 19. QR–K1 B–B3!* is indicated.

Off goes the obnoxious black-squared bishop and with it goes
most of White's attack. White continued with *20. BxB NxB
21. P–N4*, but he was trying to mate with a queen and two
pawns. That would be difficult, though not impossible.

However, the removal of the black-squared bishop also improved Black's counterplay chances on the queen side, and he
seized them with *21. . . . P–R5! 22. NxP B–R3 23. R–B2 KR–K1!
24. RxRch RxR 25. N–B5 Q–N3 26. NxB QxN*, after which
Black's control of the king file and his better minor pieces were
more than enough compensation for a pawn. Black was better.

The elimination of potential attacking pieces is a common
idea in the openings. In the French Defense, for example,
Black often trades off White's good KB, e.g., *1. P–K4 P–K3*

2. P–Q4 P–Q4 3. N–QB3 B–N5 4. P–K5 N–K2 5. P–QR3 BxNch 6. PxB P–QN3 and . . . *B–QR3, or 3. P–K5 P–QB4 4. P–QB3 Q–N3 5. B–Q3 B–Q2* and . . . *B–N4.*

Another version of this is Mudrov-Botvinnik, Odessa 1929: *1. P–Q4 N–KB3 2. P–K3 P–K3 3. B–Q3 B–K2 4. P–KB4 P–B4 5. P–B3 P–QN3 6. N–B3 0–0 7. 0–0 B–R3! 8. BxB NxB 9. Q–K2 Q–B1.* Here the removal of White's good piece, the white-squared bishop, can plague him all game because it leaves him with a bad black-squared bishop and weak white squares. White decided to offset his positional problems with *10. P–K4 Q–N2 11. QN–Q2 PxP 12. P–K5 N–Q4 13. NxP* (on the pawn recapture Black has . . . NxP) *P–B4!.*

This effectively closes much of the kingside to White's pieces and reinforces Black's positional advantage. White persisted: *14. R–B3? N–B4 15. N–B1 N–K5 16. R–R3 P–N3 17. P–KN4? K–R1 18. N–N3 NxN 19. PxN B–B4 20. B–K3 PxP 21. R–R4 P–KR4 22. N–B2 NxB 23. NxN Q–K5* (centralization) *24. K–B2 RxPch* and soon won.

And when speaking of the obnoxious attacking piece we must recall that the most irritating pain may be a pawn:

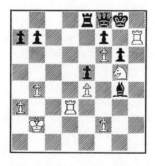

This is the case in one of Tal's unheralded early sparks of genius. It was unheralded because cool defense forced a draw. But it looks like Black is in grave difficulty in the diagrammed position because of the subtle threat of 29. P–B3!!. The attacked

Black bishop could then retreat either to KR4—blocking the KR-file but allowing R–Q7—or along the other diagonal to, say, K3—thus allowing the maneuver R–Q1–KR1!!. All of this despite the enormous material advantage in Black's hands.

Black (Lev Aronin) figured out what the real problem in the position was and proceeded to eliminate it: *28. . . . R–B1!* *29. P–B3 R–B3!*, intending to capture the pawn on his KB3. It is that soldier that provides the essential conditions for White's attack. Now on the 30th move White would lose if he takes the bishop because of 30. . . . RxP 31. QR–R3 R–B7ch and 32. . . . Q–Q3. So White had to force a drawish ending with *30. RxP QxR 31. NxQ KxN 32. PxB KxP 33. R–Q7 R–N3.*

Finally it should be noted that when the most offensive attacking pieces disappear they reveal some of the attacker's own weaknesses. Some opening systems, for example, depend for survival on the interaction of minor pieces. When those minor pieces are gone, the pawn structure doesn't jell with what is left. Several variations of the Sicilian Defense come to mind, including this one:

1. P–K4 P–QB4 2. N–KB3 N–QB3 3. P–Q4 PxP 4. NxP N–B3 5. N–QB3 P–Q3 6. B–QB4 P–K3 7. B–N3 B–K2 8. O–O O–O 9. K–R1?! N–QR4! 10. P–B4 P–QN3 11. P–K5 N–K1! 12. R–B3

Black would like time for 12. . . . B–N2 and then . . . NxB, but after 13. R–R3 NxB 14. Q–R5! P–KR3 15. NxN he has major problems facing his king (e.g., P–B5 and BxRP). So in Neikirkh-Botvinnik, Leipzig 1960, there followed *12. . . . NxB 13. N–B6* (uncomfortable, but hardly fatal) *Q–Q2 14. NxBch QxN 15. RPxN*, and now *15. . . . P–B3!*.

Surprisingly, Black is ready to open up the game. This would have been highly dangerous a few moves ago with two additional pairs of pieces in action. But now it is appropriate for Black because his remaining minor pieces are better than White's. White's pawn structure, furthermore, leads to the loss of time and the confusion of his pieces. (None of this would be true, for example, if White's pawns were at K4 and KB3 rather than K5 and KB4, the price of attack.)

The result was methodical: *16. PxQP NxP 17. R–Q3 N–B4 18. R–R4! Q–K1! 19. N–K4! P–QN4 20. R–R5 B–N2 21. N–Q6* (21. N–B5 BxPch!) *NxN 22. RxN R–Q1 23. Q–Q2 RxR 24. QxR Q–Q1!! 25. QxPch R–B2 26. Q–K1 R–K2*, and in face of *. . . RxQch* or *. . . Q–Q8ch* (or *27. Q–Q2 R–Q2*) *White Resigned*, his remaining pieces confused to the end.

RELIEVE PRESSURE AND PINS

One of the worst tasks for the defender is to survive a position under constant pressure. The pressure could be a massive assault of heavy pieces on the queenside or in the center, or it could be one painful pin on a vital file or rank. Pins especially are elements of pressure that cost the attacker little but are expensive for the defender to break.

We all know how dubious, for example, it is to break a kingside pin (opponent bishop on KN5 pinning your knight on KB3) with P–KR3 and P–KN4. It is a special case of eliminating the dangerous attacking piece which violates our economy principle through gross pawn weakenings.

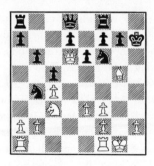

The above position occurred in the 1970 Match-of-the Century between Spassky and Larsen after *1. P–Q4 N–KB3 2. P–QB4 P–K3 3. N–KB3 P–QN3 4. N–B3 B–N2 5. B–N5 B–K2 6. P–K3 0–0* (immediate relief from the pin is available with 6. . . . N–K5, but Black wants a sharper game) *7. B–Q3 P–B4 8. 0–0 N–B3?! 9. P–Q5! N–QN5 10. P–Q6 BxP 11. BxPch KxB 12. QxB BxN 13. PxB.*

The last flurry of moves seem to have helped White. He has ready pressure against the enemy's backward QP. This pressure is abetted by the pin from KN5. Black can't even drive off the pinning piece with . . . P–KR3. And if he doesn't do something fast he will be forced into permanent passivity after 14. QR–Q1.

So Larsen found a tactical response which solved his problems, *13. . . . N–K1!*. One point is that on 14. Q–N3 or Q–B4, Black can break the pin with 14. . . . P–B3. This leads to consideration of two sacrifices of the Exchange which Black has raised. After 14. QxR QxBch 15. K–R1 Q–R4 16. R–KN1 QxBPch 17. R–N2 P–N3 and . . . N–Q6, Black has active play in the middlegame, and, on the other hand, after 14. BxQ NxQ 15. B–K7 NxBP 16. BxR RxB, Black has good ending chances. Black's extra pawn and strong center in both of these variations tend to equalize chances.

Thus, with one resourceful move, *13. . . . N–K1!*, Black's game brightens considerably. In the game, White played *14.*

Q–K7!? and held only a slight advantage after *14. . . . QxQ 15. BxQ R–KN1.*

Another version of the pin-break occurs in the Four Knights Game: *1. P–K4 P–K4 2. N–KB3 N–QB3 3. N–B3 N–B3 4. B–N5 B–N5 5. 0–0 0–0 6. P–Q3 BxN 7. PxB Q–K2. 8. R–K1 P–Q3 9. B–N5 N–Q1! 10. P–Q4 N–K3 11. B–QB1.* This is the so-called Metger Unpin, which seeks to remove the White QB from its post on the KR4–Q8 line through the redeployment of the QN. Note that on 11. B–KR4 Black would break the pin once and for all with 11. . . . N–B5 and 12. . . . N–N3.

This opening was once popular because of White's two bishops. But after the turn of the century it became questionable whether the bishops outweighed the stronghold of Black's central squares. For our purposes, an instructive 1941 game between Soviet grandmasters Bondarevsky and Lilienthal shows what happens when, through Black's misplay, White re-establishes a strong kingside pin:

11. . . . P–B4! 12. B–B1 (*12 PxKP PxP 13. NxP N–B2!*) *R–Q1? 13. P–N3 Q–B2? 14. P–Q5! N–B1 15. N–R4 N–N3 16. B–KN5 NxN 17. BxN(4) Q–K2 18. P–KB4 P–KR3 19. B–N2*

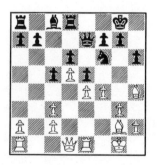

White's advantage is obvious. He is ready to increase the pressure by doubling rooks on the KB-file and bearing down on KB6, the weakest Black point because of the pin. Fortunately,

Black had prepared a challenging tactical response: *19. . . . PxP 20. PxP P–KN4!*.

The idea is to set up a profitable reverse pin after 21. PxP N–N5!, followed by . . . N–K4–N3. White's best, in fact, was 21. B–N3 so that he could better exploit the kingside after 21. . . . PxP 22. BxP N–N5 23. P–KR3 Q–B3 24. R–KB1 N–K4 25. Q–R5.

However, Bondarevsky played *21. PxP* and then saw that after *21. . . . N–N5* Black was in position to relieve the pin with . . . N–K4–N3. In the resulting position Black would be better because of the strength of his N on K4. The upshot was White's *22. P–K5!*, which led to a very difficult middlegame after *22. . . . NxKP 23. Q–R5 PxP 24. BxP P–B3 25. B–R4 Q–N2 26. B–N3 B–N5 27. Q–R4 K–B2!* (threatening . . . R–R1), and one that swiftly fell to Black's advantage.

These examples show that there are tactical and mechanical methods of unpinning pieces and relieving pressure. Pins, of course, are not the only kinds of pressure the defender tries to minimize, but they are among the easiest to understand. Aside from the pin, the defender must worry about an opponent who uses his space advantage to squeeze or, as Arthur Bisguier would say, to "massage" his opponent. But once again the defender can usually console himself with the thought that the aggressor pays a price for this pressure.

In the 1953 Candidates Tournament Miguel Najdorf obtained queenside pressure against Yuri Auerbach with a new, albeit double-edged idea in the opening: *1. P–QB4 N–KB3 2. N–KB3 P–K3 3. P–KN3 P–QN3 4. B–N2 B–N2 5. 0–0 B–K2 6. P–Q4 0–0 7. N–B3 N–K5 8. Q–B2 NxN 9. PxN?! N–B3 10. N–K5.* The idea of White's unusual 9th move is to support the center with an extra pawn even at the expense of doubled pawns.

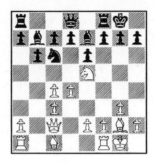

White's first benefit from his unusual 9th move is a diagonal pin from KN2–QN7. To relieve that pressure Black must make some critical judgments about his center. Black did this by way of *10. . . . N–R4! 11. BxB NxB* and then had to solve the problem of the attack on his QP after *12. Q–R4.*

He could have played what is sometimes called the "hedgehog defense"—that is, pushing up his pawns to the third rank with *12. . . . P–QB3* followed by *13. . . . P–B3* to drive the knight off and then *14. . . . P–Q3* and *. . . P–QB4.* This is solid but a bit slow. Auerbach concluded that he could just surrender his QB3 square and play *12. . . . P–Q3!.* If White had played 13. N–B6 he would find himself in a pin of his own creation after *13. . . . Q–Q2.* White could walk out of it with 14. NxBch, but then virtually all of White's pressure has been used up, and Black would seize the initiative with . . . Q–K1 followed by . . . P–QB4, . . . N–R4 and . . . QR–B1 to kill the White queenside.

Najdorf saw this and tried to liquidate his weak pawns before they became a problem: *13. N–Q3 N–R4 14. P–B5,* but after *14. . . . Q–K1! 15. QxQ KRxQ 16. R–N1 KR–QB1! 17. P–KR4 P–Q4 18. B–B4 P–KR3* and eventually *. . . N–B5* gave Black a winning endgame. The pressure White received from 9. PxN?! was not enough, and it ultimately cost Najdorf the game.

Another situation from the same tournament highlighted the problem of relieving central pressure. It was Geller vs. Keres and began with *1. P–Q4 N–KB3 2. P–QB4 P–K3 3. N–QB3 P–Q4*

4. N–B3 P–B4 5. BPxP BPxP 6. QxP PxP 7. P–K4! N–B3 8. B–QN5 NxP?! 9. 0–0.

Here White had a tremendous initiative for a pawn. Black saw that 9. . . . NxN 10. QxN or 10. PxN leaves him with big problems in completing his development. Keres chose instead the humble *9. . . . N–B3!*, which is best under the circumstances.

At this point White became overoptimistic and thought he could totally paralyze Black's pieces with *10. R–K1ch* (10. N–K5 is better) *B–K2 11. Q–K5*, thinking that only 11. . . . B–K3 12. N–Q4! was playable. But Black slipped away with *11. . . . 0–0!* (12 BxN B–Q3!). The game then proceeded toward a second crisis with *12. Q–K2 R–K1! 13. B–N5 B–KN5 14. QR–Q1 P–KR3 15. B–KR4.*

White still retains a degree of pull against the enemy central position, but Keres was able to reduce the position tactically into a favorable ending with just a few exchanges: *15. . . . N–K5!*, and now *16. B–N3* (16. BxB NxN 17. PxN RxB or 16. RxP? NxN or 16. NxP? BxB! is bad) *16. . . . NxN 17. PxN B–B3 18. QxRch QxQ 19. RxQch RxR 20. RxP R–QB1!*. The position then favors Black so greatly that a few inferior Geller moves cost him the game speedily: *21. R–Q3? N–N5! 22. R–K3 NxP 23. P–R3 BxN 24. PxB NxP 25. B–Q7 R–Q1 26. B–B5 P–KN3 27. B–Q3 N–Q8* and *White Resigned.*

CONFUSE THE OPPONENT'S PIECES

Confusing here does not mean complicating the position to a degree that your opponent does not understand the situation and makes errors through bewilderment. What is meant is the confusion sown into the harmonious interplay of his pieces. The Communication is cut and pieces are driven to bad squares. The attacker loses control of valuable territory. The well-oiled machine has its gears worn down.

A simple example of this is an old game of Sammy Reshevsky's (vs. Adams, US Championship 1936):

1. P–K4 P–K3 2. P–Q4 P–Q4 3. N–QB3 B–N5 4. B–Q3 PxP 5. BxP N–KB3 6. B–N5 P–KR3 7. BxN QxB 8. N–B3 0–0 9. 0–0 N–Q2 10. N–K2? B–Q3 11. P–B4 P–B4 12. R–B1 PxP 13. QNxP

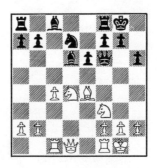

Despite the loss of the two bishops, White holds several apparent trumps in the diagrammed position. He has centralized pieces, a queenside majority and prospects of kingside attack. Black could easily be thrown into a very inferior late middlegame if he fails to recognize his opportunities.

Reshevsky began to stifle White's prospects with *13. . . . P–R3 14. P–QR3 N–B4 15. B–N1 B–B5!*. In a few moves he has kept a White knight off QN5 and started to push White's pieces around. Adams's QR and KB are momentarily disadvantaged and this helped Black to build threats in the center:

16. R–B3 R–Q1! 17. *Q–B2 P–KN3* (17. . . . RxN 18. NxR QxN 19. R–Q1 followed by Q–R7ch or R–Q8ch was too strong) *18. P–QN4 P–K4!.* Within another three moves the size of Black's superiority was clear: *19. PxN PxN 20. R–N3 B–Q2! 21. Q–N2* (21. RxP B–B3 is too strong) *B–B3 22. R–Q1 Q–K2!*, and Black won in 31 moves.

The important thing to remember here is that White's pieces were confused because of direct attacks against them in a position in which White just wasn't ready for that problem. Occasionally there will come a point, even late in the game, when the opponent allows you the chance to bother his pieces with a series of threats. As these pieces are driven from the mutual protection of one another the defense gains time and, in some cases, critical counterplay.

Another version of this comes from a 1932 consultation game of Alexander Alekhine's:

1. P–Q4 N–KB3 2. N–KB3 P–QN3 3. P–K3 B–N2 4. B–Q3 P–K3 5. QN–Q2 P–B4 6. 0–0 N–B3 7. P–B4 B–K2 8. P–QN3 PxP 9. PxP P–Q4 10. B–N2 N–QN5 11. B–N1 0–0 12. R–K1 R–B1 13. N–K5 N–B3 14. QN–B3

White's position certainly doesn't look passive. His bishops are aimed at the kingside. His knights are well posted, it appears. His center is solid and influential. The only problem is that tactically White is not ready for *14. . . . B–N5!.*

The first player could play 15. NxN and then R–K2 or R–K3, but Black stands well in any event. The White allies preferred 15. R–K3 and after 15. . . . N–K2! saw the prospect of . . . N–B4 on the horizon. White continued *16. N–N5 P–KR3*, but just before he played 17. R–R3 he noticed that 17. . . . N–B4! would be a simple way of avoiding the complications of accepting the knight sacrifice and of obtaining a strong game.

For this reason White played *17. N–R3*, and after *17. . . . B–Q3 18. Q–K2 N–B4 19. BxN PxB 20. R–QB1 R–B2 21. P–B3 Q–B1 22. KR–B3 R–K1 23. PxP NxP 24. RxR BxR* Black's pieces were so much better coordinated that he forced resignation by the 36th move.

Confusion of opposing forces is by no means limited to attacking his rooks with your minor pieces. You can harass an entire enemy camp, sometimes with one piece. An amusing commando mission is fought by Black's KN in Mikenas-Borisenko, 22nd USSR Championship, after *1. P–QB4 P–K3 2. N–KB3 P–Q4 3. P–QN3 P–Q5 4. P–K3 P–B4 5. P–QN4!? PxKP 6. BPxP PxP 7. P–Q4 N–KB3 8. B–Q3 N–B3 9. QN–Q2 P–KN3 10. B–N2 B–N2 11. Q–K2 N–Q2 12. P–KR4? P–KR3 13. N–K4 0–0 14. P–R5 P–B4! 15. N–Q6?.*

White's odd gambit was better suited for the conservative continuation of 12. 0–0 and P–K4. He retains some compensation here, however. But now Black sets off on a marauding adventure based on his KN's hops and the inability of White to extricate his QN: *15. . . . N–B3! 16. NxB NxP!.* Now *17. . . . N–N6* is a threat, and if *17. RxN PxR*, White must also lose his knight on QB8.

Mikenas then played *17. R–KN1 N–N6 18. Q–KB2* (better Q–QB2) and Black's knight eliminated further dangers with *18. . . . N–K5! 19. Q–B2 P–N6! 20. PxP N–N5 21. Q–N1 NxBch 22. QxN QxN 23. P–KN4 P–KN4.* Black's extra pawn and much better minor pieces won quickly. All due to the confusion created by Black's N.

The important element in each confusion campaign is the forcing nature of the threats. The most forceful threat, of course, is a check and that is illustrated in our last example, Euwe-Reshevsky, AVRO 1938: *1. P–Q4 N–KB3 2. P–QB4 P–KN3 3. P–B3 P–Q4 4. PxP NxP 5. P–K4 N–N3 6. N–B3 B–N2 7. B–K3 0–0 8. P–B4?! N–B3 9. P–Q5 N–N1 10. N–B3 P–QB3 11. Q–N3 PxP 12. NxP NxN 13. PxN N–Q2 14. B–K2.*

Black's *14. . . . Q–R4ch* offered White the choice of mis-placing one of three pieces. He decided against 15. N–Q2 N–N3 and 15. K–B2 N–B3! and in favor of *15. B–Q2.* Then Black played *15. . . . Q–N3*, inviting an ending in which White's QP would be quickly lost. White continued *16. B–B3 BxBch 17. PxB* (to support the QP with another pawn), and after *17. . . . Q–K6!* the Black queen interfered with all normal kingside play on White's side of the board. Euwe had to concede a pawn: *18. P–B4 QxP 19. 0–0 Q–B2 20. K–R1 N–B3 21. Q–K3*, after which Black eliminated the only dangerous kingside attacking piece and entered a winning position: *21. . . . B–N5 22. Q–R6 BxN! 23. RxB P–QN4! 24. PxP Q–K4 25. R–K1 NxP*, and so on. Confuse, divide and conquer.

MANEUVER AND REDEPLOYMENT

Maneuver is the trench warfare of chess. In simplest terms it means the movement of developed pieces to different squares, presumably better squares, behind closed lines. The ultimate effect of a maneuver, it is hoped, is to maximize the power and scope of your pieces. One redeployed piece can change the nature of a game drastically as is understandable from a study of master games. And, barring the appearance of open lines, maneuver is the key to most middlegame planning. Although redevelopment is considered in other chapters, a few points can be made here.

One redeployed piece can do wonders. Take this game from the 22nd Soviet Championship:

1. P–Q4 N–KB3 2. P–QB4 P–KN3 3. N–QB3 B–N2 4. P–K4 P–Q3 5. P–B3 P–K4 6. P–Q5 N–R4 7. B–K3 P–KB4 8. KN–K2 0–0 9. Q–Q2 N–Q2 10. 0–0–0 N–B4 11. K–N1 PxP 12. PxP N–B3 13. BxN PxB 14. P–KR3

In the absence of a black-squared bishop it would appear that White has no real attack chances on the kingside. Our theory of unexploitable weakness suggests that the black squares on the kingside are inviolate to White's plans. But White can work on the exploitation of white squares. If both white-squared bishops were traded off Black would be in trouble because his K6 would be vulnerable to a White knight, his black-squared KB would be a very bad bishop and there would even be mating prospects beginning with P–KR4–5.

In the game in question, Kan-Borisenko, Black hit upon a simple maneuver: *14. . . . N–K1!*, with the idea of shifting to

Q3 and perhaps KB2 to guard a number of good squares. On KB2 for example, the Black knight would permit Black's fianchettoed bishop to come to life at KR3.

But White was not asleep and he played *15. N–N1!*, another good maneuver with the idea of controlling KN5 from KB3. The game continued *15. . . . N–Q3 16. N–B3 N–B2! 17. B–Q3 B–R3 18. Q–KB2 P–N3 19. QR–KB1 Q–B3*, and Black had equalized the piece play. A draw soon ensued but Black could have played for more.

The maneuver can also be a method for the defender *to elicit new weaknesses from the opponent's pawn structure.* Consider Keres-Euwe, Zandvoort 1936: *1. P–K4 P–K3 2. P–Q4 P–Q4 3. P–K5 P–QB4 4. N–KB3 PxP 5. QxP N–QB3 6. Q–KB4 P–B4 7. B–Q3 KN–K2 8. 0–0 N–N3 9. Q–N3 B–K2 10. R–K1 0–0 11. P–QR3.* Here Black began a profitable knight maneuver with *11. . . . N–N1!*, heading for K5 via QR3 and QB4.

To avert this White played *12. QN–Q2 P–QR4 13. N–N3*, but then to keep his pieces in their places he had to make queenside concessions: *13. . . . N–R3 14. P–QR4 N–N5 15. N(B)–Q4 B–Q2 16. B–QN5 N–B3 17. P–QB4?.* By this time Black had a very good position indeed and was ready to seize the initiative with *17. . . . NxN 18. NxN B–B4 19. Q–Q3 BxB 20. NxB Q–R5 21. Q–B1 QR–Q1* and the advance of the QP. Black won a brilliant game.

A third form of maneuver is the *general reorganization of pieces for counterplay.* One excellent example of this is Unzicker-Taimanov, Stockholm Interzonal 1952:

1. P–K4 P–QB4 2. N–KB3 N–QB3 3. P–Q4 PxP 4. NxP N–B3 5. N–QB3 P–Q3 6. B–K2 P–K4 7. N–B3 P–KR3 8. 0–0 B–K2 9. R–K1 0–0 10. P–KR3 P–R3 11. B–B1 P–QN4 12. P–R3 B–N2 13. P–QN3 R–B1 14. B–N2

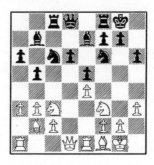

So far, all reasonable moves for both sides, although it must be said that White could have played more aggressively at several points. Black now borrowed a leaf from Richard Reti and maneuvered from the wings against the center: *14. . . . R–B2!*, with the idea of . . . Q–R1 and . . . KR–B1.

White also had an idea, but his choice, *15. N–N1?*, was too slow compared with the more natural 15. N–Q5. White failed to realize the extent of his problems and thought he could solve them by protecting several of his weak points such as K4 and QB2. But after *15. . . . Q–R1! 16. QN–Q2 N–Q1 17. B–Q3 N–K3 18. R–QB1 KR–B1 19. N–R2 N–Q2 20. KN–B1 N(2)–B4*, the bankruptcy of this strategy was evident. Black could play for a central break such as . . . P–Q4 while White could only wait.

The finish was in character. White continued to shift pieces around and was very soon in hot water: *21. N–N3 P–N3 22. N–K2 B–N4 23. N–QB3 N–Q5 24. N(3)–N1 P–Q4! 25. PxP NxB 26. PxN RxR 27. BxR BxP 28. P–B3 R–B7! 29. P–QR4 P–N5 30. K–R1 Q–B3* and *White Resigned.*

BREAKING THE ATTACKING FRONT

A more specialized tactic to round out this chapter is the advance of pawns to break or inhibit the attacking front (and to seize a foothold in the center). This can be the most subtle form of defensive weapon, can occur from early opening to early ending, and is appropriate on either flank or in the center.

We've seen many examples of a defender's shutting out the opponent's pieces with a pawn move. In most cases this is another form of controlling the open files. A clear instance is in the French Defense when Black plays . . . P–KB4 to restrain the line of White's KB: e.g., *1. P–K4 P–K3 2. P–Q4 P–Q4 3. N–QB3 N–KB3 4. B–KN5 B–K2 5. BxN BxB 6. P–K5 B–K2 7. Q–N4 0–0 8. B–Q3* and now *8. . . . P–KB4!* forces White to open up the game for his opponent's development and two bishops with 9. PxP e.p. or grant him counterchances with 9. Q–R3 P–B4 10. PxP N–Q2! 11. P–B4 NxBP (12. 0–0–0 P–QN4!?). White's KB is no longer a kingside attacker.

Another case is the defanging of the attacking wedge of pawns through tactical means. One example that springs to mind is a game between Petrosian and Alexander Kotov from a Soviet event in 1956. It began: *1. P–K4 P–QB4 2. N–KB3 P–Q3 3. P–B3 N–KB3 4. B–Q3 N–B3 5. B–B2 B–N5 6. P–Q3 P–K3 7. QN–Q2 B–K2 8. P–KR3 B–R4 9. Q–K2 P–Q4 10. P–R3 Q–B2 11. 0–0 0–0 12. P–KN4!? B–N3 13. N–R4,* and now Black finds a tactical hole in White's last move: *13. . . . NxNP!! 14. QxN P–B4,* and Black must regain the piece with a decided edge because even on the best line, 15. Q–N3 P–KB5 16. Q–N4 N–K4 17. QxPch B–B2 18. Q–B5 BxN 19. QxBP Q–K2, White's kingside pawn front has been ruined and he is vulnerable to a strong attack.

Petrosian actually played *15. PxBP? PxP 16. Q–R4 B–K1 17. N(4)–B3?,* thinking he could countersacrifice his queen for good compensation after 17. . . . N–Q5 18. PxN. He resigned after *17. . . . N–R4!.* But even 17. Q–N3 BxN 18. QxPch K–R1 is very bad for him because 19. QxQBP leads to a fast boomerang mate after 19. . . . B–R4, 20. . . . QR–K1 and . . . R–B3–N3.

By breaking the attacking front we mean the corruption of the opponent's fine pawn wedge before it gets within range of your defenses. This strategic idea can be very subtle if both sides appreciate the dangers. The incentive in most modern games is for the player to attack on the side on which he has the preponderance of material and the edge conferred by the pawn structure. To accomplish this a player has to advance some of his pawns. But if he does that he may face the kind of corruption that occurred in this 1968 Candidates Match game:

1. P–K4 P–QB4 2. N–QB3 P–Q3 3. P–KN3 P–KN3 4. B–N2 B–N2 5. P–Q3 N–QB3 6. P–B4 P–K3 7. N–B3 KN–K2 8. 0–0 0–0 9. B–Q2 R–N1, and now both sides prepare for queenside action with *10. R–N1 P–QN4 11. P–QR3*

Black (Larsen) may have concluded that White (Spassky) was preparing to subvert the queenside play with 12. P–QN4. This is exactly the idea with which Vassily Smyslov won many games two decades before. Larsen would like to stop that mechanically with . . . P–N5, but that leads immediately to 12. PxP PxP 13. N–K2, after which White is excellently placed. He can temporarily ignore the queenside because Black threatens none of his weak spots and can prepare his own thrust in the center with P–QB3 and P–Q4.

Therefore, Black seeks to play . . . P–QR4 which has the dual purpose of restraining P–QN4 and preparing for 12. . . . P–N5 13. PxP RPxP! so that Black can penetrate along the QR-file. With this major difference in mind, the game continued *11. . . . P–QR4* and now *12. P–QR4!!*.

This simple move is effective only because of Black's last. Black cannot support his QN4 square with a pawn because his QRP can't go back to QR3. Thus Larsen had to choose between separating his pawns and thereby allowing White to consolidate on the queenside (12. . . . PxP 13. NxP followed by P–N3) or to push on as he did with *12. . . . P–N5.*

White continued *13. N–N5 P–Q4* (or 13. . . . B–QR3 14. P–B4, killing all queenside play) *14. P–B4! PxP e.p. 15. NPxP*, and despite *15. . . . P–B5!*, which gave Black some counterchances, Spassky was much better after *16. B–K3! BPxP 17. P–K5!*.

A comparable kingside version of this corrupting pawn stroke came up in Petrosian-Hort, Oberhausen 1961:

1. P–QB4 P–K4 2. N–QB3 N–QB3 3. P–KN3 P–B4 4. B–N2 N–B3 5. P–Q3 P–KN3 6. R–N1 B–N2 7. P–QN4 P–Q3 8. P–N5 N–Q5 9. N–R3! 0–0 10. 0–0 P–KR3 11. P–B4! K–R2 12. P–QR4 R–QN1 13. N–B2 B–Q2 14. Q–Q2 N–R4 15. P–K3 N–K3 16. B–N2 P–N4

White's kingside restraint has been highly instructive. His knight maneuver N–KR3–B2 protects K4 and KN4 while allowing the P–KB4 advance which holds up . . . P–KB5, the opening shot to any Black aggression in that quarter. Since the success of this variation of the opening depends on whether White's queenside attack comes before Black's mating threats, this ounce of prevention is vital.

However, now Black confronts his opponent with the inevitable opening of some kingside lines. White cannot maintain his KB4 indefinitely. But Petrosian does have a powerful answer: *17. PxKP PxP 18. P–KN4!!*, crippling the Black phalanx of pawns. This useful move wins the K4 square for White's pieces and continues the blockade of dangerous files and diagonals around his king.

Black's only hope lay in the complications following *18. . . . PxP 19. NxP QN–B5*, which White handled with *20. B–K4ch K–R1 21. PxN BxN 22. PxNP N–B5* (*22. . . . PxP 23. RxRch* and *24. N–Q5* leaves a middlegame in which White is in command of the center and queenside while having nothing to worry about on the kingside) *23. PxP BxP 24. K–R1 Q–R5 25. Q–K1* followed by *Q–N3*, with a won game.

SEIZING A FOOTHOLD IN
THE CENTER

Even the newest player to the game learns quickly that an attack on the wings is best met by action in the center. Usually this takes the form of a pawn-advance which will upset the enemy's control of the center or clear away obstructions to your counterattack in the center. A slightly different motif is the pawn-advance that simply gains valuable space *before a wing attack is launched*.

This central action may serve several functions. Consider first the pawn-advance that denies the opponent squares for his pieces. In the King's Indian Defense we recall this position:

1. P–Q4 N–KB3 2. P–QB4 P–KN3 3. N–QB3 B–N2 4. P–K4 P–Q3 5. P–B4 P–B4 6. P–Q5 0–0 7. B–Q3 P–K3 8. KN–K2 PxP 9. KPxP

White's placement of his KB and KN indicates his intention to attack on the kingside with N–N3 and P–B5 followed by the use of the K4 square and the K- and KB-files. Although there are several other plans to counter this, the most effective is 9. . . . N–R4! (threatening to weaken White with a check on R5) 10. 0–0 P–B4!.

This advanced pawn mechanically stops P–KB5 or P–KN4 and denies White the K4 square he needs. Meanwhile, Black can turn to the queenside and to the K-file which he has just as much chance of exploiting as White.

The piece of the center that the advanced pawn controls may be a reward in itself. It provides a shield for counterplay while denying space to the opponent. A correspondence game of Tchigorin's comes to mind: *1. P–K4 P–K4 2. N–KB3 N–QB3 3. P–B3 N–B3 4. P–Q4 NxKP 5. P–Q5 N–N1 6. B–Q3 N–B4 7. NxP NxBch 8. QxN B–K2 9. 0–0 P–Q3 10. N–B3 0–0 11. P–B4 N–Q2 12. N–B3.*

Black has a fine game because of his two-bishop advantage and his control of good black squares such as his K4. He might, for example, begin his middlegame action by restraining White on the queenside with 12. . . . N–B4 13. Q–B2 B–B3 14. R–N1 P–QR4. But Tchigorin can afford to play more aggressively with *12 . . . P–KB4!.*

This is a surprise because White appears to have chances of sinking a knight on K6. But before he can exploit that with 13. N–Q4, Black can fight back with 13. . . . N–B4 and 14. . . . B–B3 or 13. . . . N–K4. The game proceeded with *13. R–K1 B–B3 14. B–K3*, and now 14. . . . N–K4 15. NxN PxN is not so strong because of White's 16 P–B4!, which restrains the pawn mass excellently.

Tchigorin played *14. . . . P–KN4!*, a move justified by his new-found strength in the center. The tactical justification was hidden in 15. QxP BxN 16. Q–K6ch K–N2 17. PxB N–B3! 18. NxNP (or 18. N–Q4) K–N3!!. Black soon had an overwhelming position on the kingside: *15. B–Q4 P–N5 16. N–Q2 B–K4 17. N–K2 P–B5 18. P–B3 BxBch 19. QxB N–K4!*. This lightning attack, however, was possible only because of the central control of Black's pieces and pawns beginning with his 12th move.

A simpler version of seizing a foothold in the center is the common theme of . . . P–K4 in the Sicilian Defense. For example, after *1. P–K4 P–QB4 2. N–KB3 N–QB3 3. P–Q4 PxP 4. NxP P–K3 5. N–QB3 Q–B2 6. B–K2 P–QR3 7. P–QR3 N–B3 8. B–K3 B–K2 9. 0–0 0–0 10. P–B4 P–Q3 11. Q–K1*, and now Black can equalize with *11. . . . NxN 12. BxN P–K4! 13. PxP PxP 14. Q–N3 B–B4! 15. BxB QxBch*.

Black has accomplished a great deal with his pawn-advance at move 12. White's remaining minor pieces don't work as effectively with a White pawn blocked at K4. A dangerous attacking piece, the QB, has been exchanged off. Black stands so well that after *16. K–R1 K–R1!* White's best chance to avoid a disadvantage is 17. RxN! PxR 18. Q–R4 R–KN1 19. N–Q5 or 19. QxBPch, with a draw most likely. If White doesn't sacrifice, Black can bolster his position with . . . B–K3 followed by . . . N–N1 or . . . N–Q2 and . . . P–B3. For example, Troianescu-Matulovic, Venice 1969, went *17. Q–R4? N–N1 18. B–Q3 N–K2 19. QR–K1 B–K3 20. Q–B2? QxQ 21. RxQ P–B3 22. K–N1 KR–Q1,* and Black soon had a winning endgame.

When Black plays . . . P–K4 in this situation, he is aiming at . . . PxKBP so that he can obtain K4 for his minor pieces. The fact that his QP becomes isolated is surprisingly insignificant. In most cases it is an unexploitable weakness.

In the above position, a game of the author's from the 1971–72 Reggio-Emilia tournament, White has a huge advantage in space plus the two-bishop edge. Black had lost several tempi in the late opening and now has to play very carefully. He chose *20. . . . N–B3*, an innocuous-looking move which White answered with *21. Q–Q2* to prevent 21. . . . B–N7. On the simple 21. QR–Q1! White's superiority would remain intact. But the text move allowed *21. . . . P–K4!*.

White could ignore this by playing 22. P–B5, but then 22. . . . N–Q5 grants Black good piece play. White assumed that 21. . . . P–K4 was a bad move because it allowed him to put direct pressure on Q6 and KB7. The game proceeded: *22. B–N4 R–R1 23. Q–KB2 PxP! 24. QxP N–K4!*.

Black's weak pawns are compensated by his strong K4-square. His position hangs together tactically on variations such as 25. QxB QxQ 26. RxQ NxB. The best White could do was 25. B–K2 B–N2 26. QR–Q1 Q–B2, after which a defensible position for Black has been secured. But White overoptimistically played 25. *QR–Q1?* and lost a pawn to 25. . . . *NxP! 26. B–QB5 Q–K2 27. B–K2? B–K4.* Black eventually won.

One final example—Gheorghescu-Stein, Bucharest 1960: *1. P–K4 P–QB4 2. N–KB3 P–Q3 3. P–Q4 PxP 4. NxP N–KB3 5. N–QB3 P–QR3 6. B–KN5 P–K3 7. P–B4 B–K2 8. Q–B3 Q–B2 9. 0–0–0 P–R3 10. BxN?! BxB 11. P–KN4 N–B3 12. N–N3 B–Q2 13. B–N2 0–0–0!? 14. P–KR4 P–KN3 15. P–N5 B–N2 16. Q–Q3,* and now it becomes difficult for Black because of his weakened QP.

However, Stein continued *16. . . . BxN! 17. QxB P–K4!* and had a superior ending after *18. PxKP NxP 19. RxP QxQ 20. PxQ PxP 21. R–Q5* (21. PxP RxRch and 22. . . . R–R1 is also bad) *QR–K1 22. PxP RxRch 23. BxR B–B3.* Black forced resignation in record time: *24. R–Q1 R–R1 25. N–Q4 R–R6 26. R–N1 RxP 27. B–N2 K–B2! 28. NxB KxN 29. B–B1 K–B4 30. B–Q3 NxBch 31. K–Q2 K–Q5 32. R–N3 N–B4!.* Black's pieces came alive after 17. . . . P–K4.

ILLUSTRATIVE GAMES
BYELORUSSIA CHAMPIONSHIP 1959

LITVINOV   SUETIN

1. P–K4 P–QB4 2. N–KB3 P–K3 3. P–Q4 PxP 4. NxP P–QR3 5. N–QB3 Q–B2 6. B–Q3 N–QB3 7. B–K3 N–B3 8. 0–0 N–K4 9. B–KB4 B–B4 10. N–N3 B–R2 11. Q–K2 P–Q3 12. K–R1 P–QN4 13. P–QR4?! P–N5 14. N–N1 0–0 15. N(1)–Q2 B–N2 16. B–KN5

Both sides have taken certain risks so far. Black's placement of his KB on QR2 rather than on the defensively useful K2 might have been punished with an earlier B–KN5 and P–KB4. But White preferred to provoke queenside weaknesses until Black had castled. Now Black's game looks critical because of the threats of BxN and P–KB4. If Black plays N(K4)xB he opens up the QB-file for White. And if he doesn't take that bishop, White will have a queen, his KR and three minor pieces for kingside attack.

16. . . .   **KN–Q2!**

Better than 16. . . . QN–Q2 17. P–KB4, after which White's attack proceeds unhindered. Black prepares to seize a foothold in the center with . . . P–B3 and . . . P–K4 just at the point when White plays P–KB4. Black's control of his interior lines, such as the second rank, will protect him.

17. P–KB4	**N–QB3**
18. Q–N4	**. . .**

Perhaps better was 18. P–B5 P–B3 19. PxP PxB 20. PxN QxP 21. N–B4, although 21. . . . R–B5 or 21. . . . N–K4 is fine for Black.

18. . . .	**K–R1**
19. R–B3	**P–B3!**
20. B–R4	**KR–K1**

Note the confusion of White's attacking pieces. The bishop on KR4 blocks the KR-file and serves only minor tactical duties (21. R–N3 N–B1? 22. BxBP). All of Black's kingside weaknesses will be covered after . . . N–B1, . . . P–K4 and . . . R–K2.

21. R–N3	R–K2
22. N–B3	P–K4

The White KB is shut out before an attack on KR7 can be manufactured from R–R3, B–B2 and P–K5. After 22. . . . P–K4 Black intends 23. . . . PxP and 24. . . . N(2)–K4, with magnificent centralized play.

23. P–B5	N–Q5!

Black wants to exchange off a few minor pieces so that his queenside counterattack will encounter no opposition. On 24. QNxN BxN 25. NxB PxN Black threatens 26. . . . N–K4 and 27. . . . P–N6!, cracking open the K-file by indirect play.

24. QNxN	BxN
25. R–KR3	BxNP
26. R–QN1	B–B6
27. B–B2	N–B1
28. N–R4	. . .

Finally another threat (N–N6ch) from White, whose pieces have been thrown into darkness by the change in central pawn structure. Black is ready for the final stage with . . . P–Q4 once the immediate threats are disposed of.

28. . . .	K–N1
29. Q–K2	. . .

Threatening the check on QB4. White loses a full rook after 29. N–N6 PxN 30. PxP B–B1 and doesn't get as much as a single threat in return.

29. . . .	P–Q4!
30. R–Q1	R–Q2
31. PxP	BxP

Black returns a pawn (32. BxP QR–Q1 33. B–Q3 P–N6) to coordinate his pieces for the winning breakthrough.

32. N–N6!?	**Q–B3!**
33. NxN	**BxPch**
34. K–N1	**BxR**
Resigns	

22ND USSR CHAMPIONSHIP 1955

SMYSLOV   ILIVITSKY

1. P–KB4 P–Q4 2. N–KB3 P–KN3 3. P–K3 B–N2 4. B–K2 N–KB3 5. 0–0 0–0 6. Q–K1 P–B4 7. P–Q3 N–B3 8. P–B3 B–N5!?

A logical idea. Black wants to play . . . P–K4 and first he must exchange off White's KN to reduce control of the K4 square. More significant is the exchange of a potential attacking piece. White's piece placement often leads to a mating attack with Q–KR4 and N–KN5. Without a knight, White's attack doesn't exist.

9. QN–Q2	**Q–B2**
10. N–N3!?	**P–N3**
11. P–Q4	**PxP**
12. KPxP	**N–K5**

White avoided . . . P–K4 by transposing into a stonewall pawn formation (P–KB4 and P–Q4). The drawback is Black's occupation of K4 with a knight which will be supported by . . . P–KB4.

13. B–K3	BxN!
14. RxB	P–B4

Black has equalized piece play and he needs only to ward off a kingside attack (R–KR3 and Q–R4) to begin thinking about an advantage. His center can be solidified with . . . P–K3 and . . . N–K2–B1–Q3. Then Black can launch the so-called Minority Attack on the queenside with . . . P–QN4–5 in order to weaken the White QP and QBP. White should drop his attacking plans in favor of 15. R–QB1.

15. R–R3?!	P–K3
16. R–B1	N–K2
17. Q–R4	K–B2!

This high-class move has two points. The first is 18. QxP R–R1, winning the queen. The threat against Black's weakest kingside square is thereby neutralized. But Black's king-move also prepares . . . N–N1–B3 to buttress his knight outpost. Black has no reason to fear P–B4 in such a position because White has removed two valuable pieces from the center.

18. N–Q2	NxN
19. BxN	N–N1
20. P–B4!	...

Black has an edge on the kingside and in the center after 20. QxP N–B3 21. Q–R4 R–R1 22. Q–N3 N–K5 and 23. . . . . RxR. Black stands much better in most endings because of the bad White QB. White's 20. P–B4 is a sharp attempt to exploit the position of the defender's king and queen: 20. . . . BxPch 21. K–R1 BxP 22. QxPch B–N2 23. B–QB3 N–B3 24. BxN KxB 25. R–N3 Q–B2 26. Q–R4ch.

20 ...	QR–B1!
21. PxP?	QxRch!

Black wins much more than enough material for the queen, and the win is mechanical:

22. BxQ RxBch 23. K–B2 BxPch 24. K–B3 PxP 25. QxPch B–N2 26. R–N3 N–K2 27. RxP (else 27. . . . R–KR1!) NxR 28. Q–R5 BxP 29. B–Q3 K–N2 30. P–N3 R–B6 31. K–K2 R–QB3 32. P–KR4 R–Klch 33. K–B1 R–K6 34. QxP N–K2 35. Q–R7ch K–B1 36. P–N4 B–N2 37. K–B2 P–Q5 38. P–N5 R–B6 39. B–K2 R–B4 40. P–R5 R–B4 41. P–R6 RxPch 42. K–K1 B–K4 43. K–Q1 and White Resigned.

STUDY EXAMPLES
(Answers on Page 259)

1. White threatens mate within a few moves along the KR-file. How does Black answer the threat?

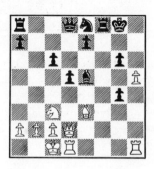

2. Black has considerable pressure against the queenside pawns of White (e.g., 1. PxP Q–R3 and . . . B–B3). How can White ease the pressure?

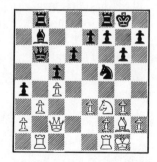

3. White ruined part of Black's kingside with 1. P–R5 PxP and then played 2. N–Q1. How does Black continue?

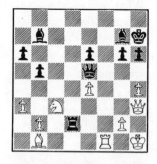

4. Does White threaten 1. BxRP? What is Black's most logical continuation if it is his move?

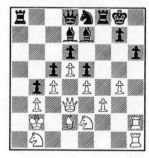

5. Black has problems on the kingside as White threatens R–K3 and N–R5. How does Black repair and redeploy best?

6. What makes White's game playable and what can Black do about it?

7. Black needs counterplay and the kingside looks like the easiest spot for it. But how can he drum up strong queenside action?

8. Black's position could be eased by trades. But which ones?

9. What can be done about Black's attacking wedge of pawns and pieces?

CHAPTER THREE:
Threats and Restraint

Threats are the building blocks of any attack. Whether subtly positional and aimed at the queenside or primitively tactical and concerned solely with mate, a player's aggressive intentions become real when hardened into threats.

In Lasker's words, a threat is "an intended combination" which "becomes an attack unless the threatened party parries, defends, prevents, forestalls, or defeats the intention." This takes in a lot of ground and would include, for example, an intended unsound combination which may seem sound to the attacker. But for our purpose a threat is *an attempt to exploit a weakness*.

Threats, from the attacker's point of view, can be distinguished according to the weakness they threaten to exploit (mating threats, threats to occupy weak squares, threats to weaken the pawn structure, etc.). But from the defender's point of view, the first point of departure is the threat's nearness to realization. What is the gestation period in terms of moves between a tactical trick in the back of your opponent's mind and the point when that trick wrecks your position?

We speak of immediate threats when he moves a knight to Q5 threatening our queen on K2. The gestation period is one move, and if we don't come up with sufficiently forcing diversion, the queen is going to disappear. At the same time, the move N–Q5 may have begun a plan to bring a pawn to KN5 and thereby support N–B6ch which would dislocate your kingside. This can be seen as an intermediate threat. And thirdly, the knight move may have a place in the scheme of things which reaches ten moves ahead. For example, the opponent hopes to exchange off the minor pieces by way of N–Q5 and thereby reach a heavy-piece ending that favors him because of material or pawn structure. This would be a long-range threat.

The first thing to do whenever there is a change in the position—it's a good habit to do it every move—is to ask yourself: Is there a threat? If so, what kind: immediate, intermediate or long range? If there is an immediate threat you have to respond on the next move. But if there is a more intricate danger lurking in the near future you must be aware of that too.

This is a 1943 game of Botvinnik's in which Black has defended a Ruy Lopez and White has played B-on-QN5-takes-N-on-QB6. A typical pawn structure has arisen. In theory, Black's two bishops compensate him for the damaged pawn structure, but this is a difficult point to prove in practice.

Black (Botvinnik) asks himself: Is there a threat? Yes, there is a clear and present danger in regard to his first QBP. White is preparing to play Q–KB2 and N–QR4, winning that pawn. (One of the unfortunate qualities of the "two bishops" is that they cannot be used to support the same square, in this case QB4). There is no immediate threat to take the pawn, but we can call White's intentions toward it an intermediate threat.

Furthermore, there is a more distant plan of exchanging rooks and queens along the queen file so that an easily won minor-piece ending is reached. Black can retain the heavy pieces only by moving them off the only open file, it would appear.

Once Black realizes the dangers to him he can take appropriately "desperate" action with the assurance that the position demands it. Botvinnik played 25. . . . *R–Q5!!*. This meets the intermediate problem of the attack on his weak pawn. It also solves the problem of exchanging several heavy pieces because now 26. RxR? BPxR corrects Black's pawn perfectly. By sacrificing the Exchange, Black will convert his weakest pawn into his most dangerous, a passed, advanced QP. Also, the closed nature of the position reduces the effect of White's rooks but actually strengthens Black's bishops.

White accepted the sacrifice with 26. *N–K2* (better to give up a knight than a bishop) *B–B1* 27. *NxR BPxN* 28. *B–B2*, but it was clear that Black had more than equalized when he shifted to kingside initiative: 28. . . . *P–QB4* 29. *R–KB1 P–B4* 30. *B–N3 B–Q2* 31. *QR–Q1 P–B5* 32. *B–B2 P–N4*. Black won in 53 moves.

These distinctions between immediate, intermediate and long-range threats tend to blur. For example, it should be noted that Black's Exchange sacrifice turned out to be sound only because he retained one pair of rooks on the board. (A good rule of thumb is that you want to preserve your other rook when you lose or sacrifice the Exchange because otherwise you can't compete adequately on files and ranks). Therefore, we could say that White had an immediate threat in 26. RxR because it would have made a subsequent . . . R–Q5 much less effective. In any event it is important to know what threats lie in the position and whether they are threats to your near future or your old age.

IMMEDIATE THREATS

Basically you can only do three things about immediate threats: (1) Prevent them physically from being played, e.g.,

exchange off the threatening piece, block the key file, occupy
the necessary square; (2) Divert the threatener's attention to
another area of the board (e.g., *Zwischenzug*, Chapter Five);
or (3) minimize the effects of the threat's realization. It's a
question of stopping, delaying or taking the sting out of the
danger.

In each case, however, the defender has to determine whether
the cure is worse than the disease—"Am I taking too great a
risk in defensive action to prevent something with which I can
easily live." The old story of the threat being stronger than the
execution has cost defenders hundreds—perhaps thousands—
of games.

The best guides to follow are the familiar principles of economy and exploitable weakness. Can the threat be met by a cheap
expenditure of force or by making a concession which can't be
exploited? If you can regularly answer that question correctly
you're certain to rise to grandmasterdom, for that is the most
difficult of all defensive skills.

For instance, here's a typical French Defense position:

    *1. P–K4 P–K3 2. P–Q4 P–Q4 3. N–Q2 N–KB3 4. P–K5
KN–Q2 5. B–Q3 P–QB4 6. P–QB3 P–QN3!? 7. N–K2 B–R3 8.
BxB NxB 9. 0–0 N–B2 10. N–KN3 B–K2 11. N–B3*

Should Black make the natural move of castling he will be
in for some kingside pressure after 12. N–R5!. How much of a

threat is the knight move? Botvinnik had this position once (vs. Tolush, USSR Championship 1952) and opted for *11. . . . P–KR4!? 12. N–K1 P–N3* (not *12. . . . P–R5 13. N–R5 P–N3 14. N–B4,* followed by *Q–N4* and *N–B3* to win the KRP).

Black's kingside pawn weaknesses were static and therefore not easily repairable. But White's pieces were cut out of action. White's best plan is the exchange of the black-squared bishop. Black tried to restrain that idea and work up his own counterplay at the same time: *13. N–Q3 Q–B1 14. B–K3 P–B5 15. N–B4 P–QN4 16. N–R3! Q–Q1! 17. Q–Q2 P–R4 18. P–R3 N–N1!,* and with *19. B–N5 N–B3* followed by *. . . N–K2–B4* after an exchange of bishops Black had a playable game.

But White had a better game. The World Champion was lucky to draw and the blame can be pinned on his experiment with his kingside pawns. The threat of *N–R5* wasn't so dangerous after all—at least when compared with the cost of prevention.

Besides the "threat-greater-than-execution" problem there is a corollary issue of secondary threats. A defender can be so concerned with the fire storm on the kingside that he allows his center to be uprooted. He takes so many precautions to avert one tactical disaster that he encourages another.

A recent example of this was Kuzmin-Mukhin, USSR Championship 1972:

1. P–K4 P–QB4 2. N–KB3 P–Q3 3. P–Q4 PxP 4. NxP N–KB3 5. N–QB3 P–QR3 6. P–B4 P–K3 7. B–Q3 Q–B2 8. 0–0 B–K2 9. N–B3 N–B3 10. Q–K1 0–0 11. K–R1

Quite plainly, White is aiming for P–K5 which will liberate one or two of his attacking bishops. For instance, 11. . . . P–QN4 12. Q–N3 B–N2 13. P–K5 PxP 14. PxP N–Q2 15. B–R6 or 13. . . . N–Q2 14. N–K4!. Black could stop the threat mechanically with 11. . . . P–K4, but then 12. N–Q5! is embarrassing. Best is 11. . . . N–QN5 which minimizes the threat by eliminating the strong attacking bishop on Q6.

But Black chose *11. . . . N–Q2? 12. Q–N3 R–Q1?*, a regrouping idea which makes P–K5 difficult if not impossible. The flaw, however, is allowing *13. P–B5!*. This attacking break is nearly as effective as P–K5, but in this case it is more so because Black has conveniently removed two kingside pieces from the defense. Now 13. . . . KN–K4 fails to NxN and P–B6. So Black tried *13. . . . B–B1*, but following *14. PxP PxP 15. P–K5!* (anyway) *KNxP 16. BxPch! KxB 17. N–N5ch K–N1 18. Q–R4 P–KN3 19. QN–K4* he had to resign. Preventing P–K5 only served to make P–B5 strong.

The simplest method of handling an immediate threat is to somehow stop it mechanically. This may involve a bit of tactics:

The diagram comes from Olafsson-Petrosian, Santa Monica 1963, the first Piatigorsky Cup event. White has a devilishly strong threat after *24. R–KB3* in 25. BxN PxB 26. N–N6ch or 25. . . . NxB 26. N–N6ch!. Black covered this first threat with *24. . . . R–Q1*, overprotecting the Q4 square and preparing to capture on it with a rook.

But White played *25. P–KN4*, with the devastating threat of pushing the pawn to the fifth rank. Black will not be able to move his KN away because the KBP would be loose. And 25. . . . P–KR3 does not stop the pawn advance at all. Black does have a simple defense, and it is a good exercise to stop here before going on to figure it out.

Petrosian's answer was *25. . . . P–KN4!*, which mechanically stops P–N5 and is based on this variation: 26. QxP R–KN1 27. Q–R6 NxP 28. NxN RxNch or 27. Q–R4 NxP! 28. NxPch QxN 29. RxQ RxR 30. K–B1 RxPch, with only a very slight edge for White in either case. Furthermore, White cannot reject this simplification by way of 26. Q–R6 because 26. . . . N–N1 27. Q–R3 N–B5! wins the QP. Olafsson, in fact, agreed to a draw here, perhaps surprised by the strength of *25. . . . P–KN4!*.

Another method of handling such threats is to develop countervailing tactical threats of your own. In double-edged modern openings such as the Sicilian Defense or Pirc Defense we frequently see one player with the White pieces preparing to drive the Black knight away from the kingside position with P–K5. But, just in time, Black has . . . P–QN5 which simultaneously attacks a White knight on QB3. If there is a mutual capture of knights it is often White who suffers most. And if White moves his knight away he may concede the loss of initiative (and often allow the Black knight to "retreat" to a glorious Q4–square).

The mechanism is so familiar that it will allow Mr. Nobody to defeat a future world champion:

Fischer-Munoz, Leipzig Olympiad 1960—*1. P–K4 P–QB4 2. N–KB3 P–Q3 3. P–Q4 PxP 4. NxP N–KB3 5. N–QB3 P–KN3 6. B–K3 B–N2 7. P–B3 0–0 8. Q–Q2 N–B3 9. B–QB4 P–QR3 10. B–N3 Q–R4 11. 0–0–0 B–Q2 12. K–N1!? QR–B1 13. P–N4? N–K4 14. B–R6 N–B5 15. BxN RxB 16. N–N3 Q–K4! 17. P–KR4 KR–B1 18. B–B4 Q–K3 19. P–R5 P–QN4 20. PxP BPxP 21. B–R6 B–R1!*

The opening has been very sharp, but White's failure to take advantage of the subtleties has given Black the edge. Notice that 12. K–N1 was good only if followed with 13. NxN! with the idea of 14. N–Q5!, simultaneously threatening QxQ and the *Zwischenzug* 15. NxPch. Later Black self-traps the queen but had prepared to meet 17. B–B4 Q–K3 18. N–Q4 with 18. . . . NxKP! and to pull off a clever countersacrifice involving 17. P–B4 Q–K3 18. P–B5 Q–K4 19. B–B4 QxN!! and 20. . . . NxKP. Finally, notice that Black has gained enough time with his counterplay to allow him to recapture with his KBP on KN3, thus keeping half the KR-file closed, and to avoid the trade of black-squared bishops after B–KR6.

All of this said, it is still critical for Black after *22. P–K5* in the diagram. Black loses quickly on 22. . . . PxP 23. P–N5 or 22. . . . QxKP 23. KR–K1. But Black is beautifully timed for *22. . . . P–N5!*. Since White's QN cannot run away without exposing his QB2 to disaster, White headed into *23. PxN PxN 24. Q–R2 QxBP 25. B–N5 Q–B2 26. Q–K2 PxP 27. QxP QxQ 28. BxQ* and lost rapidly after *28. . . . RxBP 29. RxQP B–R5!*.

Besides counterthreats from another side of the board there are tactical responses to be found when both sides have amassed strength in the center. Another example, from Karlsbad 1911, is worth study:

Alapin-Alekhine—*1. P–K4 P–K4 2. N–KB3 N–KB3 3. N–B3 B–N5 4. NxP Q–K2 5. N–Q3 BxN 6. QPxB NxP 7. B–K2 P–Q4 8. 0–0 0–0 9. N–B4 P–QB3 10. P–B4 PxP 11. BxP B–B4 12. Q–K2 R–K1 13. R–K1 Q–Q2 14. B–K3 P–QN4 15. QR–Q1 Q–B2 16. B–Q3 N–Q2 17. P–KB3 N–Q3 18. P–KN4? BxB! 19. QxB*

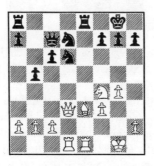

White's 18. P–KN4 was based on the idea that 18. . . . BxB would lose a piece to the pin on the Q-file and that 18. . . . B–K3? 19. Q–Q2 was almost as bad. Black needs a counter-threat and he must have had one in mind when he played 16. . . . N–Q2. The saver was *19. . . . N–K4!!*, which wins at least a pawn, because 20. QxN QxQ 21. RxQ NxPch and 22. . . . NxR costs an Exchange more. The game went *20. Q–B1 N(4)–B5 21. B–B1 Q–R4! 22. R–K2 QxP*, and Black cashed in forty moves later.

An even prettier example of counterthreats to seemingly crushing primary threats occurred in Vidmar-Yates, San Remo 1930, in the following position. White's *34. N–Q6* has all the earmarks of a game-ending dual threat: 35. N–B5ch and 35. RxPch being the ideas behind it. All serious protection of KB2 has been forgotten while Black maneuvered his rooks to the open file.

Yet Black, a top-flight player, is aware of the dangers because he can play *34. . . . NxP!!* which is justified tactically by 35. N–B5ch K–B1 36. NxQ RxRch 37. RxR (37. KxR allows mate) N–K7ch 38. K–B2 NxQ and . . . KxN. Black's passed pawns should win. And on 35. RxPch Black has the obvious 35. . . . QxR.

This so unnerved White that he made matters worse with *35. Q–N4 P–R4 36. Q–B8?* (better 36. Q–B3) *N–K7ch!*, and since 37. RxN Q–R5 38. P–N3 QxQPch 39. K–N2 RxR 40. KxR R–R8ch 41. K–N2 Q–N8ch 42. K–R3 Q–B8ch 43. R–N2 R–R7 loses to a trade of queens and the advance of the QBP and 38. R–KB2 RxRch 39. RxR QxQPch 40. K–R1 R–R8 invites mate, White had to settle for a bad middlegame after *37. K–R1*, which he eventually lost.

These examples show the defender responding with fireworks. The real difficulty is preparing the tactical ideas which will be available in such positions. That requires foresight and calculating ability. Both can be developed sufficiently through the study of hard-fought games. The moves of the masters are often totally inexplicable to the inexperienced eye. For example, what can you make of Black's 15. . . . QR–Q1 in this position?

Novopashin-Korchnoi, 31st USSR Championship 1963—
*1. P–K4 P–QB4 2. N–KB3 P–QR3 3. N–B3 P–K3 4. P–Q4 PxP
5. NxP Q–B2 6. B–Q3 N–KB3 7. 0–0 N–B3 8. B–K3 B–K2
9. K–R1 P–Q3 10. P–B4 0–0 11. Q–B3 B–Q2 12. QR–K1 P–QN4
13. P–QR3 QR–N1 14. NxN BxN 15. Q–R3!.*

Black's second move with his QR takes it away from a line that will breed counterplay after . . . P–N5 and puts it behind a pawn already overprotected. Korchnoi's point, however, is that 16. P–K5 PxP 17. PxP QxP 18. RxN is seriously threatened. Black can avert mate on KR2 with 15. . . . P–KN3 or 15. . . . P–KR3 but those responses are too weakening. Too "expensive."

The natural idea, in view of our subsection on seizing a foothold in the center, is 15. . . . P–K4, but that allows White a fine free hand for 16. PxP PxP 17. B–N5, intending N–Q5 or Q–R4 and R–K3–KR3. And there is clearly no way that 15. . . . P–QR4 16. P–K5 P–N5? can work.

The beauty of 15. . . . QR–Q1! is partly contained in the

possible line of play 16. P–K5 PxP 17. PxP QxP. Then 18. B–QN6 wins the Exchange but gives Black excellent play after 18. . . . Q–N4 19. BxR RxB: e.g., 20. R–K3? BxPch or 20. N–K4 NxN 21. BxN BxB 22. RxB Q–B3!. The second important element in 15. . . . QR–Q1! is revealed in the game continuation:

16. B–Q4 P–K4! 17. PxP PxP 18. N–Q5! BxN 19. BxP QxB 20. PxB QxNP, and now 21. RxN P–N3! 22. RxRP RxP 23. Q–B3 R–K4 Draw.

A third point, which didn't appear in the game or its main variations, was the possibility of Black's meeting P–K5 at some point with . . . QPxP and . . . RxB, an interesting Exchange sacrifice to kill White's attack on KR7.

This hardly exhausts the number of possible responses to immediate threats. But it suggests the nature of tactical play that the defender may be required to muster. A serious error for any chess student to make is thinking that tacticians attack and positional players defend. Examine game annotations by Sammy Reshevsky, for example, and you will see hundreds of little tactical points raised by the veteran grandmaster considered one of the great American positional players.

INTERMEDIATE THREATS

By intermediate we can have two meanings. One describes an involved threat that takes two, three or more moves to execute (but less than ten, for example). Another meaning, and perhaps a more significant one, includes threats which can be executed in one or two moves but only pay off several moves later. The second situation can be illustrated by the middlegame pawn-break.

Say that a point is reached after the first dozen or so moves when the attacker needs a new road. He prepares a breakthrough involving the advance of a pawn to a square where it will force an exchange of pawns and an opening of lines. The pawn-break does not give him any material or marked positional advantage so it is not properly called an immediate threat. But the break-

through will give him control of a key diagonal or file by eliminating a roadblock. The exploitation of this control is the next
step and may take several moves. But it is not something the
defender wants to look forward to. Therefore, the defender
should anticipate and judge the consequences of the threatened
break.

Again we have the choice among absolutely preventing the
threat, diverting attention, or minimizing the effect. Prevention
and restraint are the most important for the student.

Nimzovich found this case exceptionally instructive. The position is taken from Kupchik-Capablanca, Lake Hopatcong 1926.

By all rights Black should have a fine game because of his
better bishops and his prospects of queenside play with . . .
P–QR3, . . . P–QN4 and . . . P–N5. But before he does this,
Black is worried about R–KN1 (and R–R3) in support of
P–KN4. This would give White attacking counterplay which,
in connection with B–K1–KR4, may be annoying.

Capablanca chose *iron restraint: 19. . . . P–KR4! 20. R(1)–KB1
R–R3!*, and White was stymied, because even P–KR3 and P–KN4
has been denied him. Without kingside breaks, White tried to
force matters without them and was soon on the defensive on
the opposite wing: *21. B–K1 P–N3 22. B–KR4 K–B2 23. Q–K1
P–R3 24. B–R4 P–QN4 25. B–Q1 B–B3 26. R–R3 P–R4 27.
B–N5 KR–R1 28. Q–R4 P–N5*, etc.

Capablanca had to decide before 19. . . . P–KR4 that he could afford the kingside weaknesses (translation: they are unexploitable) and that he could carry off the pawn storm against White's exploitable queenside (which hardly seems so in the diagram).

A classic example of *fluid restraint* was Viacheslav Ragosin's victory over Andrei Lilienthal in the 1935 Moscow International tournament. The opening quickly created a tactical debate over whether White could engineer P–K4:

> 1. P–Q4 N–KB3 2. P–QB4 P–K3 3. N–QB3 B–N5 4. P–QR3 BxNch 5. PxB P–B4 6. P–B3 P–Q4 7. P–K3 (7. BPxP immediately is better) 0–0 8. BPxP KPxP 9. B–Q3 N–B3 10. N–K2 R–K1 11. 0–0 P–QR3 12. Q–K1 P–QN4 13. Q–B2

White's sixth, eighth and last two moves were geared for P–K4, which frees his second bishop and threatens to push the pawn to K5 as an attacking wedge. Since the fourth move, that QB is the key to success because it has no opposite number on the dark squares. Black, on the other hand, could have played loosely with 8. . . . NxP 9. B–Q2 N–QB3 10. B–Q3 PxP 11. BPxP P–K4!, as Botvinnik did in the same tournament. But Black chose instead to concentrate on stopping P–K4 and so played . . . BPxP and . . . R–K1.

Lilienthal threatens P–K4 immediately because if Black takes three times on K4 he is crushed on the open KB-file. So Black

played *13. . . . B–K3!*, which tactically prevents 14. P–K4: 14.
. . . QPxP 15. BPxP N–KN5 16. Q–N3 PxP 17. PxP NxP 18.
B–N2 NxNch 19. BxN Q–Q7! 20. BxN QxB.

Lilienthal put an end to the . . . N–KN5 idea with *14. P–KR3*
and was again threatening to push his KP. And once again
Ragosin stopped it with *14. . . . R–R2!*, which protects his
second rank laterally so he can play 15. P–K4 QPxP 16. BPxP
PxP 17. PxP B–B5! 18. BxB PxB 19. P–K5 N–Q4 and . . . P–B3.
Black's blockading knight and lack of weakness would make
his game preferable.

Now after *15. B–Q2 Q–N3* White had yet another chance
for P–K4, but this time it would be even less productive then
before, since Black would be able to play . . . N–K5! instead
of . . . N–Q4 as in the line cited above. The upshot of all this was
that Black had earned enough time to stop P–K4 for the course
of the middlegame. White turned to other spheres, and this
fascinating game continued: *16. KR–N1! QR–K2! 17. P–QR4 P–B5
18. B–B2 B–B1 19. N–N3 P–KR4.*

Black's last is further prevention of P–K4, because Black
will be able to play . . . P–R5 in response. The fixed queenside promises Black an outside passed pawn, and White
restrains those with his rooks while looking for counterchances
on the kingside with his queen: *20. N–K2 N–Q1 21. R–R2 B–Q2
22. PxP PxP 23. R(1)–R1 B–B1 24. R–N2 B–Q2 25. Q–R4! N–K3
26. K–R1.*

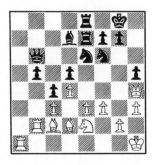

Better was 26. K–B2 to protect K3, as will be seen. Notice that once again P–K4 doesn't work (26. P–K4 PxP 27. PxP N–B1 28. P–K5 RxP or 28. N–N3 N–N3 29. Q–N5 P–R5 30. N–R5 NxP). There followed: *26. . . . N–B1 27. N–N3 RxP!! 28. BxR RxB 29. NxP NxN 30. QxN B–B3 31. Q–N5 RxQBP!! 32. Q–Q2 RxB 33. RxR N–K3.*

In the finale Black's passed pawns proved to be more potent than rooks: *34. R–Q1 P–N5 35. R–N2 P–N6 36. Q–B3 N–B2 37. R–K2 Q–R2 38. Q–N4 N–N4 39. R–K7 Q–R6 40. Q–K1! P–B6! 41. R–K8ch* (Hope of perpetual check springs eternal) *BxR 42. QxBch K–R2 43. QxP* (43. QxN P–B7 wins) *Q–R1 44. R–K1 N–Q3 45. Q–B7 P–B7! 46. QxN P–N7 47. Q–B4 Q–B3,* and *White Resigned.* One of the very best defensive games, a masterpiece of fluid, tactical restraint.

As usual, the defender must not worry about creating new weaknesses if he judges them to be difficult to exploit. One illustration that comes to mind is an early game of Alekhine's: *1. P–K4 P–K4 2. N–QB3 N–KB3 3. B–B4 N–B3 4. P–Q3 B–N5 5. B–KN5 P–KR3 6. BxN BxNch 7. PxB QxB 8. N–K2 P–Q3 9. P–Q4 B–Q2 10. QR–N1 N–Q1 11. 0–0,* and now Black decided he could afford to stop 12. P–B4 with *11. . . . P–KN4!.*

White was in no position to force the issue over Black's objections (P–KN3 and P–KB4) because his king position would be vastly more vulnerable. The strength of 11. . . .

P–KN4 had a bonus effect when 17-year-old Alekhine tried for too much undeserved central action: *12. Q–Q3 B–N5 13. N–N3 0–0 14. P–B3 B–B1 15. P–Q5? Q–N3 16. N–B5? BxN 17. PxB Q–N2 18. Q–K4 P–KB3 19. P–N3 P–QR4 20. K–R1 P–N3! 21. P–B4 N–N2 22. PxKP BPxP 23. B–K2 N–B4*, with a huge edge for Black.

Taking this one step further, restraining moves can do more than just stop pawn-breaks. They can be the sources of counterplay in themselves.

Schlechter-Nimzovich, Karlsbad 1907, began:

1. P–K4 P–K4 2. N–KB3 N–QB3 3. B–N5 P–QR3 4. B–R4 N–B3 5. N–B3 B–N5?! 6. N–Q5 B–K2 7. 0–0 0–0 8. R–K1 P–Q3 9. NxNch BxN 10. P–B3 P–R3 11. P–KR3 N–K2 12. P–Q4 N–N3 13. B–K3 K–R2 14. Q–Q2 B–K3 15. B–B2 Q–K2 16. P–Q5! B–Q2 17. K–R2?!

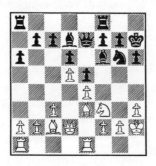

White's 16th move is the correct method of locking the center to begin a wing attack. But Schlechter indicates with his next move that he was looking at the wrong wing. Nimzovich correctly concluded that White was preparing for P–KB4–5 and a general pawn storm on the kingside instead of the dynamic P–QR4–5, P–QN4 and P–QB4 followed by breaking at QN5 or QB5. Nimzovich was proven right because after *17. . . . N–R1!?* Schlechter played *18. N–KN1.* Black established iron restraint with *18. . . . P–KN4! 19. P–KN3 N–N3 20. Q–Q1 B–N2.*

But that wasn't all. Nimzovich proceeded to take the sting out of Plan B, the queenside advance: *21. Q–B3 P–QR4! 22. N–K2 B–N4! 23. P–QR4 B–Q2.* Now White finds that P–KB4 is impossible to achieve and P–QN4–5 is unavailing. Black can begin to think about damaging counterplay.

He would like to play . . . P–KB4 but that would be difficult to carry off considering his weak white squares. The attack would have to be nearly decisive before it should be tried. What Nimzovich did was *24. R–R1 Q–K1!*, which has the dual effect of bolstering . . . P–KB4 and stopping the last kingside idea, P–KR4, once the queen gets to QB1.

Schlechter did play *25. P–R4? Q–B1 26. B–Q3 B–N5 27. Q–N2* and was capsized by a neat tactical flourish: *27. . . . PxP 28. P–B3 P–R6 29. Q–B1 P–KB4! 30. PxB PxKP 31. QxP PxB 32. BxP R–R1!! Resigns* (in view of . . . K–N1). All in all, Black had to restrain three pawn-breaks—P–KB4, P–QN4–5 or P–QB4–5 and P–KR4. And his counterplay built up with each prevention.

Besides restraint, there is a whole chapter to be learned about the exploitation of bad breaks. Again we'll take the typical case of a player trying to play P–KB4 in a double-KP game (both pawns on K4). But now let's see what happens if the other side allows it so that he can reap the advantages of the open lines and blockading squares.

Then P–KB4 may be the only kingside break but it may not be good at all. An early Tal game:

1. P–K4 P–K4 2. N–KB3 N–QB3 3. B–N5 P–QR3 4. B–R4 N–B3 5. Q–K2 P–QN4 6. B–N3 B–K2 7. P–B3 0–0 8. 0–0 P–Q3 9. P–KR3 N–QR4 10. B–B2 P–B4 11. P–Q4 Q–B2 12. P–Q5 B–Q2 13. N–R2 P–B5 14. P–KN4 N–N2 15. P–B4?

The trouble with P–B4 is the weak KP White gets and the excellent black-square play Black gets. Before Black can do anything with these advantages he must stop P–K5. Thus, his chore is additional restraint, minimizing the effect of the first break: *15. . . . . PxP 16. BxP N–B4 17. N–Q2 K–R1 18. QR–K1 QR–K1 19. Q–N2 Q–N3! 20. K–R1 B–B1!.*

A tactical trick here is 21. P–K5 NxQP! 22. QxN? B–N2. These tricks are not just footnotes; they are warnings to a player who is about to commit suicide by opening up his king position further. White pressed ahead nevertheless: *21. KN–B3 KN–Q2 22. Q–N3 P–B3! 23. P–N5,* and now *23. . . . . PxP 24. NxP BxN! 25. QxB N–K4* gave Black a sizable edge. Tal's Latvian opponent collapsed directly: *26. BxN PxB 27. RxRch RxR 28. QxP? Q–R3 29. Q–R2 BxP 30. N–B3 Q–R4 31. N–N1? B–N7ch!,* winning the queen.

Similar cases of exploiting the same break:

(1) Tarrasch-Tchigorin, Match 1893—*1. P–K4 P–K4 2. N–KB3 N–QB3 3. B–N5 N–B3 4. 0–0 P–Q3 5. P–Q4 N–Q2 6. N–B3 B–K2 7. N–K2 0–0 8. P–B3 B–B3* (Beginning a strange redeployment which is not satisfactory but shows what you can get away with.) *9. N–N3 N(2)–N1 10. P–KR3 P–QR3 11. B–QB4 N–Q2 12. B–K3 N–K2 13. Q–Q2 N–KN3! 14. QR–Q1 Q–K1 15. K–R2 K–R1 16. B–N3 B–K2 17. B–R4 P–QN4 18. B–B2 N–B3 19. N–K1 N–N1! 20. P–B4?! PxBP 21. BxP NxB*

22. *QxB* (not 22. RxB B–N4), and here Black cannot restrain P–K5 because of tactics.

22. . . . *N–R3* 23. *N–B3 P–KB3* 24. *P–K5! B–K3!* (24. . . . BPxP 25. Q–K4 is strong. White releases the tension too quickly now and gets a poor position.) 25. *PxBP? BxP* 26. *Q–K4 B–N1* 27. *Q–Q3 Q–Q2* 28. *QR–K1 P–N3!* 29. *Q–Q2 B–N2* 30. *P–N3 N–B2*. Black is safe and slightly better because of his two bishops. He won in 62 moves.

(2) Tartakover-Lasker, New York 1924—1. *P–QB4 P–K4* 2. *P–QR3 N–KB3* 3. *P–K3 B–K2* 4. *Q–B2 0–0* 5. *N–QB3 P–Q3* 6. *N–B3 R–K1* 7. *B–K2 B–B1* 8. *0–0 N–B3* 9. *P–Q4 B–N5* 10. *P–Q5 N–K2* 11. *P–KR3 B–Q2* 12. *N–R2 Q–B1* 13. *P–K4 N–N3!* 14. *P–B4? PxP* 15. *BxP NxB* 16. *RxN B–K2* 17. *QR–KB1 R–B1!* 18. *Q–Q3 B–K1* 19. *Q–N3 Q–Q1* (Black's KB2 has been repaired, and he is ready to go to work on the black squares) 20. *N–Q1 N–Q2!* 21. *N–K3 B–N4!* 22. *R–N4 P–KB3* 23. *Q–B2? P–KR4* 24. *R–N3 P–R5* 25. *R–N4 B–R4*, winning the Exchange and eventually the game.

(3) Hübner-Smyslov, Palma de Majorca 1970—1. *P–K4 P–K4* 2. *N–KB3 N–QB3* 3. *B–N5 P–QR3* 4. *B–R4 N–B3* 5. *0–0 B–K2* 6. *BxN QPxB* 7. *P–Q3 N–Q2* 8. *QN–Q2 0–0* 9. *N–B4 P–B3* 10. *N–R4 N–B4* 11. *P–B4?!*, and now 11. . . . *PxP* 12. *RxP P–KN3!* secures the better game, but 12. . . . P–KN4? 13. N–B5 PxR 14. Q–N4ch does not. After 12. . . . *P–KN3!* 13. *B–K3 N–K3*, White rejected 14. R–KB1 P–KB4! 15. PxP BxN 16. PxN BxP, which is better for Black, and played 14. *R–N4? N–N2!*, which is merely winning for Black. After 15. R–N3 P–KB4 16. N–B3 P–B5 or 15. R–B4 P–KN4, White loses a piece; so White went in for 15. *NxP BxR* 16. *NxBch QxN* 17. *QxB* and lost after 17. . . . *P–KB4!* 18. *Q–N5 QxQ.*

A third area—following restraint and exploitation—is minimizing the effects of a threat which cannot be stopped. If you can't stop it or exploit it, you may as well batten down the hatches.

Minimizing often means blockading, exchanging, uncovering

new targets, diverting attention, and so on. Almost anything we've considered earlier as a defensive weapon can be used to take the edge off a pawn-break—or off other intermediate threats as well. This can be one of the truly Herculean tasks of defense.

Here is Flohr (Black) against Keres in a 1957 USSR Championship game that began with *1. P–Q4 P–Q4 2. N–KB3 N–KB3 3. P–B4 PxP 4. P–K3 P–B4 5. BxP P–K3 6. 0–0 PxP?! 7. PxP N–B3 8. N–B3 P–QR3 9. B–K3 B–K2 10. P–QR3 0–0 11. N–K5 Q–B2 12. NxN QxN 13. B–R2.* There is no doubt that White's intention is P–Q5. That break will do several things, not the least of these being the exposure of the Black queen to further attack and the opening up of the K-file and QR2–KB7 diagonal. It would also eliminate the only static weakness in White's game, his QP.

Black will find it impossible to stop P–Q5 through iron restraint or through countervailing tactics. And he can't exploit new holes in the position. What he did was coordinate his pieces for the post-P–Q5 position: *13. . . . R–Q1 14. R–B1 Q–Q3! 15. Q–B3 B–Q2!,* which just allows him to survive the first crisis. White cannot win the QNP without handing the advantage over to Black (*16. QxNP QR–N1 17. Q–B3 RxP*).

Keres continued *16. P–Q5* and Flohr coolly began to blockade and trade down: *16. . . . P–K4! 17. P–R3 QR–B1 18. KR–K1 P–R3 19. B–Q2 R–K1 20. N–K2 RxR 21. RxR R–QB1 22. RxRch*

BxR. The dangerous file and diagonal were kept closed by bottling up the QP. There was still some chance for White in the ending but Black was alert: *23. N–N3 Q–Q2! 24. B–B3 B–Q3* (a more effective blockade) *25. B–N1 Q–B2 26. B–B5 B–Q2.* After some further excitement Black drew in 37 moves.

This case, however, pales by comparison to Black's agony in saving this position:

The game was Klaman-Korchnoi, also from the 1957 Soviet Championship, and it reached the diagram via: *1. P–Q4 N–KB3 2. N–KB3 P–B4 3. P–Q5 P–KN3 4. N–B3 P–Q3 5. P–K4 B–N2 6. B–KN5 0–0 7. N–Q2 QN–Q2 8. B–K2 R–N1 9. 0–0 N–K1 10. P–QR4 P–QR3 11. P–R5! N–B2 12. N–B4 Q–K1?! 13. N–R4 N–R1 14. P–QB3 N–K4?! 15. NxN BxN 16. B–R6 B–N2 17. BxB KxB 18. P–QN4! PxP 19. Q–Q4ch P–B3 20. PxP B–Q2 21. N–B3.*

What is White's threat? Pick one. His surest winning idea is P–KB4 and P–K5, although he would also have excellent chances by doubling rooks on the QB-file or by trying to exploit white-square weaknesses on the kingside with P–KB4–5xP and Q–KN3. But the P–K5 plan will rip open the center to expose bad pawns and a highly vulnerable king.

Positions like this require a subtle skill involving anticipation, exchanging and, most of all, waiting with good developing moves. Counterplay would be highly desirable but none exists. There are no immediate exchanges along the open file because

White can block the line with his knight. Black is weak enough —he can't create any pawn-breaks of his own like . . . P–KB4 or . . . P–K3.

Korchnoi began by redeveloping his most powerful piece to a square where it could influence events on his K4: *21. . . . R–B1 22. QR–B1 Q–Q1! 23. P–B4 Q–B2 24. B–Q3 Q–N1!*. Then, after *25. KR–K1*, he removed his most vulnerable piece from a line likely to be opened (*25. . . . K–N1*).

White could have prepared further for P–K5 but Black may obtain confusing counterplay if the break is delayed. For instance, if White doubles rooks on the K-file Black will play . . . Q–B2 at some point. Therefore, White played *26. P–K5*, and since Black can't live long with a pawn blocking in his bishop from K6, he played *26. . . . BPxP 27. PxP B–B4!*.

Here White made a slight slip. Best may have been *28. BxB* and *29. P–K6*, but White played *28. B–B4 R–QB2 29. P–N4*, an apparently strong thrust. But Black shot back with *29. . . . Q–B1!*, a saving tactical grace which attacks B and KNP.

This forced a new liquidation which Black sought to extend until there was nothing left to fight with: *30. N–K4 BxN 31. RxB Q–N1 32. QR–K1* (otherwise rooks are traded) *P–QN4! 33. PxP e.p. QxP 34. QxQ NxQ 35. BxRP PxP 36. RxP R–KB5 37. P–KN5 RxP 38. B–B1 R–N5ch 39. K–R1 R–KB5 40. B–R3!* (last try) *K–B1 41. R–QN1 N–B5 42. B–K6 K–N2 43. R–K2 N–Q3! 44. QR–K1 N–B2 45. BxN KxB 46. R–K5 R–Q2 47. R–Q1* and *Draw*.

That Black held such a position shot full of *static* irreparable weaknesses—the kind that require several fine anticipatory moves, constant vigilance and a little help from the opponent to save—is both instructive and a tribute to Korchnoi.

Another example of minimizing the danger of a pawn-advance —also involving P–K5 and again from the 1957 tournament:

Gurgenidze-Tolush—*1. P–Q4 N–KB3 2. P–QB4 P–K3 3. N–KB3 P–B4 4. P–Q5 PxP 5. PxP P–Q3 6. N–B3 B–K2 7. P–KN3 0–0 8. B–N2 N–K1 9. 0–0 N–Q2 10. N–Q2 B–B3? 11. N(Q)–K4 B–K2 12. P–B4 QN–B3 13. N–B2 N–N5 14. NxN BxN 15. P–KR3 B–Q2*

16. P–K4 B–KB3 17. R–K1 B–Q5ch 18. K–R2 N–B2 19. N–K2 B–KB3 20. N–N1!? R–K1 21. N–B3, and now Black found a clever way of provoking and then detoxifying a natural and apparently strong break: 21. . . . B–QN4 22. P–K5? B–K2! (threatening the QP via . . . B–B5 or simply . . . PxP) 23. P–N3 PxP 24. NxP (forced) P–B3! 25. N–B4 BxN 26. PxB B–Q3 27. B–K4 P–B4! 28. B–Q3 (28. BxP loses a piece to 28. . . . Q–B3) Q–B3 29. R–N1 RxR 30. QxR R–K1 and White sued for peace in a few moves.

LONG-TERM THREATS

The defender has a broader vista to consider when the threats are to be realized only in the long term. He doesn't simply look for immediate counterplay schemes but thinks about what he can conjure up. If he doesn't have an easy way of restraining a potentially dangerous pawn-break or the piling up of pressure, he can find flexible moves which keep his plans fluid. In short, the defender has more time to get his pieces onto good squares before he has to find an exact sequence of moves to respond to immediate dangers.

By long-term threats we also mean threats that you don't even see. You suspect that they exist. Capablanca had an uncanny ability to sniff out danger 10 to 15 moves in the future and to eliminate its vital elements sometimes even before the attacker was aware of the attacking ideas.

Former world champion Petrosian is another past master of this strategy. Witness his game with Spain's grandmaster Pomar from the 1970 Olympiad in Seigen: 1. P–Q4 P–KN3 2. P–QB4 B–N2 3. N–QB3 P–Q3 4. N–B3 B–N5 5. P–KN3 Q–B1 6. B–N2 N–KR3? 7. P–KR3 B–Q2 8. P–K4 P–KB3 (otherwise B–K3 and Q–Q2 will force Black to retreat his KN to KN1) 9. B–K3 N–B2 10. Q–Q2 P–QB4 11. PxP?! PxP 12. 0–0–0 N–B3 13. K–N1? (Best for both sides was 13. BxP QN–K4 14. NxN NxN 15. P–B4 QxB! 16. PxN 0–0–0 17. N–Q5! with a slight plus for White.) P–N3 14. P–N4.

Petrosian's sensors are out and he picks up signs of a general kingside advance with N–KR4 and P–KB4 or of a similar thrust in the center. Several moves from now he can see that his second rank will be vulnerable, especially his K2. And he still has the problem of keeping his king in the center to protect the bishop on Q2.

Petrosian chose a profound safety-move which covered key squares: *14. . . . R–QN1! 15. KR–K1 R–N2!.* Look around for an immediate threat to Black's second rank and you won't find it. But Black is thinking about the near future.

Black's opening, a form of provocateur chess, was too much for Pomar, who tried for the immediate knockout instead of preparing with 16. N–R4 and P–B4. The game continued: *16. P–K5? PxP! 17. N–KN5 0–0* (playable because . . . R–N2 protects the QB) *18. N–Q5 NxN 19. BxN B–K1! 20. B–R6 P–K3 21. BxB RxB* (second-rank harmony) *22. N–B3 N–Q5!,* and the game was decided for all practical purposes. White struggled on before forfeiting in a hopeless position: *23. RxP R(2)–KB2 24. N–K4? Q–B2 25. R–N5 R–B5! 26. Q–Q3* (26. P–QN4 P–K4) *P–KR3 27. N–Q6 PxR 28. NxB RxN 29. QxPch K–B1 30. QxNP Q–R2ch.*

Petrosian's rank-protection is an effective theme in long-term threats. It allows the minor pieces to function smoothly but also provides room for them to get out of the way and let the rook do its thing when appropriate. The need to protect a key rank is something you can figure out in advance and lends itself to long-term anticipation very well. Two examples from the games of Boris Spassky:

vs. Medina (White), Göteborg 1955—1. P–K4 P–K4 2. N–KB3 N–QB3 3. B–N5 P–QR3 4. B–R4 N–B3 5. 0–0 B–K2 6. R–K1 P–QN4 7. B–N3 P–Q3 8. P–B3 0–0 9. P–KR3 N–N1 10. P–Q3 QN–Q2 11. QN–Q2 B–N2 12. N–B1 N–B4 13. B–B2 R–K1 14. N–N3 B–KB1 15. N–R2?! P–Q4 16. Q–B3 P–N3 17. B–N5 B–K2! 18. P–KR4

Black's 17th move is better than 17. . . . B–N2, which allows White to maintain a pin. Even so, White has pressure against Black's KB3 and Spassky found an effective way of meeting it: 18. . . . P–QR4! 19. P–R5 R–R3!.

After a few mutual errors—20. B–R6 P–Q5 21. PxP N–K3? (best is simply 21. . . . KPxP) 22. RPxP RPxP 23. PxP N–Q5 24. Q–Q1 N–Q2 25. N–N4? (25. N–K2)—Black won quickly— 25. . . . B–N5 26. R–K3? Q–R5! 27. B–N3 NxP 28. NxN RxN 29. R–B3 QxB 30. RxP NxB 31. RxP NxR 32. RxB R–QB3 33. Resigns.

Ten years later vs. Tal in the Candidates match both sides repeated the moves of the Medina game until Tal varied with 15. P–QN4 QN–Q2 16. B–N3 P–QR4! 17. P–R3 PxP 18. BPxP P–R3 19. N–B5 P–Q4 20. N(3)–R4 P–B4 (rather than accept the sacrifice with 20. . . . BxP 21. PxB RxR 22. NxP or 21. NxP BxR 22. N(7)–B5, Black finds counterplay in the center) 21. R–K3 P–B5 22. R–N3! K–R2 23. B–B2 P–Q5 24. Q–B3.

Black's 24. . . . R–R3!! was an exceptionally perceptive anticipation because it took the sting out of all possible sacrifices on the kingside before Tal had played them. Black's protection of the third rank allowed him to fight off White's last stand easily: 25. *NxRP PxN* 26. *N–B5 Q–R1!* 27. *NxP BxN* 28. *Q–B5ch K–R1* 29. *BxB R–KN1*, and then to consolidate into an easily won middlegame: 30. *B–N5 Q–K1* followed by . . . *N–R2* and . . . *R(3)–KN3*.

Another fine example of anticipation in a difficult position occurred in the 1974 US Championship:

Commons-Evans—1. *P–K4 P–QB4* 2. *N–KB3 P–Q3* 3. *P–Q4 PxP* 4. *NxP N–KB3* 5. *N–QB3 P–K3* 6. *B–K2 P–QR3* 7. *0–0 B–K2* 8. *P–B4 0–0* 9. *B–K3 N–B3* 10. *Q–K1 NxN* 11. *BxN P–QN4* 12. *P–QR3 B–N2* 13. *Q–N3 P–N3?* 14. *B–Q3 P–Q4* 15. *P–K5 N–K5* 16. *Q–K3! NxN* 17. *BxN*

White's game is tremendous and his biggest drawback is having to choose between the mating attack that may occur on the kingside or the breakthrough on the queenside with P–QR4. It was to avoid mate threatened by P–B5 that Black played 14. . . . P–Q4 after his awful 13th move.

What to do as Black? It sounds simple when Black reasons out his difficulties. To avoid mate he will have to bid for space and counterplay on the kingside with . . . P–KB3. To avoid the loss of a queenside pawn or the control of key line on that side of the board, Black must place his pieces on protective squares there. Both ideas of anticipation can be forwarded by the same redeployment: *17. . . . R–B1 18. B–Q4 R–B3!! 19. P–B3 B–B1! 20. QR–K1 B–Q2.*

Now Black's KP will be solidly protected after . . . P–KB3 and KPxBP. Also, Black will be able to protect his QNP better with a B on Q2 if White should attack it with P–QN4 and P–QR4. Black is still inferior, but his survival chances have soared.

In the actual game White overestimated his chances in a rook-and-bishop-ending and then made several inexact moves: *21. R–B3 P–B4* (otherwise mate is in the offing) *22. PxP e.p. BxP 23. P–KN3 BxB 24. QxB Q–N3! 25. K–B2? QxQch 26. PxQ KR–QB1 27. K–K3 R–N3 28. R(3)–KB1 P–N5! 29. PxP RxP 30. R–B2? R–N6*, after which Black eventually won!

These examples of rook-maneuvers are not the last word on long-term threats but they are a common theme. The most important task is locating the threat and knowing that it exists before it becomes unstoppable.

ILLUSTRATIVE GAMES
LENINGRAD SPARTAKIAD 1963

CHEREPKOV   KORCHNOI

1. P–Q4 N–KB3 2. P–QB4 P–K3 3. N–QB3 B–N5 4. P–K3 P–B4 5. B–Q3 0–0 6. P–QR3 BxNch 7. PxB N–B3 8. N–K2 P–QN3 9. P–K4 P–Q3?!

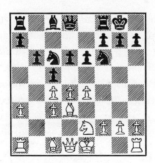

Since Johner-Capablanca, Karlsbad 1929, the recommended course in the position after 9. P–K4 is 9. . . . N–K1! followed by . . . P–KB4 in answer to P–KB4. The knight retreat does two things: stopping the threatened advance of the White KBP into Black territory and averting the pin that now irritates Black's kingside.

| 10. B–N5! | P–KR3 |
| 11. B–R4 | P–K4 |

Black's strategy is to fix the White pawn mass with pawns on black squares (to make up for the absence of a black-squared bishop). White needs a pawn-break and the only effective one is P–KB4. Black has discouraged it with his last two moves because, for example, 12. P–B4 leads to 12. . . . PxBP 13. NxP P–KN4.

A slower attempt at breaking open the kingside with P–KN4–5 is dubious: 12. P–B3 N–QR4 13. P–N4 B–R3, and neither 14. N–N3 P–KN4 nor 14. P–N5 N–R2 works.

| 12. 0–0 | P–KN4!? |

Sehr riskant, but necessary if P–B4 is to be stopped. If Black proceeds naturally with 12. . . . B–R3, White could try 13. P–B4! PxBP 14. NxP (or 14. BxN first) P–KN4? 15. N–R5 NxN 16. QxN PxB 17. QxRP, with mating threats of P–K5 and R–B4.

| 13. B–N3 | K–N2? |

Black wants an ironclad kingside with pawns at K4, KB3 and KN4 to restrain any kingside breaks by White. The text is a good preparatory move but it allows the sacrifice 14. P–B4! KPxBP 15. NxP! PxN 16. BxP, followed by Q–Q2 or Q–B3 with strong play for a piece. 13. . . . N–KR4 would lead to the same strategic setup without the risk. White overlooks the sacrificial idea, too.

| 14. P–B3? | Q–K1 |
| 15. B–KB2 | N–KR4 |

If he doesn't play this here White may continue with N–N3 followed by Q–Q2, B–K3 and P–KR4.

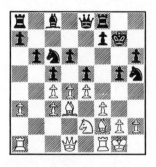

White should take stock at this point and decide (a) that P–KR4xNP leads to a self-mate on he KR-file, (b) that P–KB4 is too difficult to achieve because of Black's maneuvering, and (c) therefore he should think about defensive action on the queenside. He could play 16. N–B1 with the idea of meeting the 16. . . . N–R4 threat to his QBP with 17. N–N3. If Black plays 16. . . . BPxP White is happy to play 17. N–K2! sacrificing a pawn to open up the center.

But White doggedly presses on for P–KB4.

| 16. P–N3?! | N–R4 |
| 17. P–B4? | B–N5! |

And not 17. . . . KPxP 18. PxP PxP because 19. B–R4 would give White an excellent kingside attack. Black restrains the kingside pawns so that he can take over the initiative on the queenside whenever White slows down (e.g., 18. P–B5 N–KB3 19. Q–B2 P–N4! 20. PxNP P–B5!).

18. B–K3	**P–B3**
19. PxNP	**RPxP!**

Black has good reason to be optimistic about his own attacking chances and therefore avoids the exchanges along the KB-file that follow 18. . . . BPxP. Notice that Black has several "weak" squares and pawns but none of them can be approached by White's pieces.

20. P–Q5	**R–R1**
21. Q–K1	**Q–N3**

An effective square for this heavy piece. Black's first real threat in the game is 22. . . . NxBP 23. BxN QxP, winning two pawns.

22. B–B1	**B–R6**
23. R–B2	**NxBP!**
24. BxN	**QxP**
25. B–R2	**NxP!**

A sparkling concluding combination which mates or wins the queen.

26. PxN	**B–B8!!**

And 27. RxB R–R8ch and 28. . . . R–R7ch or 27. R–R2 RxR doesn't stop mate. The game concluded with speed:

27. KxB R–R8ch 28. N–N1 RxNch 29. KxR QxQch 30. K–N2 R–R1 White Resigns.

KARLSBAD 1923

BOGOLYUBOV   RETI

   1. P–Q4 P–Q4 2. P–QB4 P–K3 3. N–QB3 N–KB3 4. N–B3
B–K2 5. B–N5 QN–Q2 6. P–K3 0–0 7. R–B1 P–B3 8. P–QR3
P–QR3 9. Q–B2 R–K1 10. B–Q3 PxP 11. BxP P–N4 12. B–R2
P–B4 13. PxP NxP 14. 0–0 B–N2 15. N–Q4 QR–B1

The opening has been a familiar fight-for-the-tempo. Beginning with White's seventh move he tries to find developing
ideas that improve his position—aside from B–Q3. He doesn't
want to move his KB because Black will play . . . QPxBP eventually and White wants to capture on QB4 in one motion. But
Black also can wait (8. . . . P–QR3, 9. . . . R–K1).

Black has an excellent game due to his queenside activity.
But White has a threat in the distance. It is the common B–QN1
followed by BxKN and QxRPch theme. Black acts first with
his own threat of 16. . . . QN–K5 before White can bear on KR7.

| 16. P–B3 | Q–N3 |
| 17. B–N1 | P–R3!! |

Black determines that the threat isn't a threat at all. He
could easily stop the idea with 17. . . . P–N3. But Reti wants
the two-bishop advantage. The threat of Q–R7ch is not a threat,
he says.

18. BxN	BxB
19. Q–R7ch	K–B1

Oddly enough, White's queen is in as much danger on the kingside as Black's king. White doesn't have time for N–K4 because Black would win a pawn on Q4.

20. QR–Q1	KR–Q1
21. K–R1	K–K2!

And now 22. N–K4 is a threat but Black's 22. . . . R–KR1! would be an even greater one. White must retreat his queen and begin to worry about the queenside.

22. QN–K2	R–KR1
23. Q–B2	P–QR4
24. P–QN4!?	. . .

White appreciates that . . . P–N5 and . . . B–R3 is a strong threat to his queenside well-being. He mounts a counterattack on Black's QNP.

24. . . .	PxP
25. PxP	N–R5
26. Q–Q2	KR–Q1
27. B–Q3	P–N3

Now White is threatened with . . . P–K4, which will win material if allowed. To stop it White must concede his K4 square and the long diagonal. He resolves upon an Exchange sacrifice.

28. P–B4	B–Q4!
29. BxQNP	BxN
30. NxB	N–B6
31. B–Q3	NxR
32. RxN	R–QR1
33. Q–K1	. . .

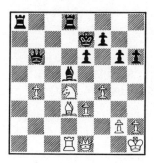

White's last chance is to capitalize on the weakness of Black's kingside by making a return trip with his queen. The irony is that Black's king can also make a return trip to answer the threats.

33. ...   **R–R7!**
34. Q–R4ch   **K–B1!**

The only move: e.g., 34. . . . K–K1 35. B–N5ch K–B1 36. NxPch! draws with queen checks, and 34. . . . K–Q2 35. B–N5ch K–B1 36. B–B1 and P–N5 gives White chances of holding out.

35. QxPch   **K–N1!**

Black is safe because 36. BxP PxB 37. QxPch isn't perpetual check after 37. . . . K–B1 38. Q–B6ch K–K1, and 38 NxPch QxN 39. QxQ fails to 39. . . . BxPch. The game drew to a close with:

36. R–KN1 BxPch! 37. RxB R–R8ch 38. R–N1 Q–N2ch 39. P–K4 RxRch 40. Resigns.

MOSCOW 1937

ALATORTZEV   PANOV

1. P–Q4 P–QB4 2. P–Q5 P–K4 3. P–K4 P–Q3 4. N–K2 N–KB3 5. P–KB3 B–K2! 6. P–QB4 0–0 7. B–K3 N–K1 8. Q–Q2 N–R3 9. QN–B3 QN–B2 10. P–KN4?!

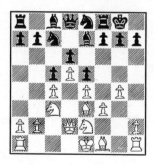

Black's Old Benoni system is exceptionally effective against White's arrangement of pieces. One explanation is that in the normal King's Indian setup with Black's KB on KN2 and his KNP on KN3, White could prepare a lightning attack with P–KR4–5 before Black is ready to create queenside diversions. But here there is nothing appealing about White's pawn storm on the kingside.

10. . . .	B–R5ch!

Especially after this mechanical prevention of P–KR4. In many cases White would be willing to sacrifice his KRP to obtain pressure against KR7. Now White's position appears unhealthy and he must complete development quickly before he's overrun by . . . P–B4 or . . . P–QN4, the two sources of Black's counterplay.

11. N–N3	B–Q2
12. B–Q3	P–KN3
13. 0–0	. . .

A sad concession but a necessary one. After 13. 0–0–0 P–QR3 or 13. . . . P–QN4 immediately White's king is in much greater danger than Black's.

13. . . .	N–N2

Now an interesting new stage begins with White working hard to restrain . . . P–B4 and Black missing opportunities to

attack the queenside directly with . . . P–QR3 and . . . P–QN4.
Notice that 14. B–R6 (to stop . . . P–B4) leads to an exchange
of black-squared bishops after 14. . . . P–B3! and 15. . . . B–N4.
That exchange would improve Black's game to the "won-game"
status.

14. K–R1!	P–N3?!
15. R–KN1!	Q–K2
16. R–N2	K–R1
17. QR–KN1	P–QR3
18. P–QR4	QR–N1
19. P–N3!	P–B3?!

Black is beginning to see shadows. The Benoni Jump (N–B5)
doesn't work as long as Black can cover his KN2 with a rook
on KN1. And he would be eager to see either 20. P–B4 PxP
or 20. P–N5 P–B3 because Black has better kingside piece play
despite the White rooks. Meanwhile, Black has delayed . . .
P–QN4 so long that White has consolidated his queenside and
can meet that advance with RPxP followed by turning his
attention elsewhere. Black would then have to try to win on
the QR-file.

20. KN–K2	P–QN4
21. RPxP	PxP
22. P–B4	P–N5

23. N–Q1	PxP
24. NxP	K–N1!

Since . . . P–KB4 is out of the question for the time being, Black eliminates some tactical ideas involving P–K5 and BxKNP. Black may also want to run to the queenside with . . . K–B2–K2. The fact that Black has played . . . K–R1 earlier doesn't mean that KR1 is the perfect square once the piece placement has been changed.

(For illustration, in Khassin-Tolush, 24th USSR Championship 1957, after 1. P–QB4 N–KB3 2. N–QB3 P–K3 3. P–Q4 B–N5 4. P–K3 P–B4 5. B–Q3 0–0 6. P–QR3 B–R4 7. N–K2 PxP 8. PxP P–Q4 9. 0–0 PxP 10. BxBP P–KR3 11. B–B4 B–B2 12. BxB QxB 13. B–R2 R–Q1 14. R–B1 N–B3 15. P–QN4 Q–N1 16. Q–B2 P–R3 17. KR–Q1 N–K2 18. N–K4 NxN 19. QxN B–Q2 20. N–N3 B–R5 21. R–K1 B–B3 22. Q–N4 Q–Q3 23. QR–Q1 Black saw there was a threat to his KN2 so he played 23. . . . K–R1! 24. N–R5 R–KN1. Later, after 25. N–B4 P–QR4 26. B–N1 PxP 27. PxP QxNP 28. N–Q3 Q–Q3 29. N–K5 he saw there was a threat to his KB2 so he defended it with 29. . . . KR–KB1! 30. P–KR4 K–N1. Black defended expertly and won after 31. R–K3 P–B4 32. Q–K2 N–Q4 33. R–KN3 N–B5 34. Q–Q2 N–R4 35. R–N6 B–K1 36. P–N4 BxR 37. NxB PxP 38. NxR RxN.)

25. Q–K2	R–R1
26. B–B1	B–KN4
27. R–B1	B–B1!

Black angles to bring a knight to K4 and wants Q2 free. Black need only ensure a closed kingside now for his victory. His QR-file is enough to win on the queenside.

28. B–N2	N–R3
29. Q–KB2	N–N1
30. P–R4	BxN
31. QxB	N–Q2
32. B–N1	N–K4
33. N–K3	B–Q2

34. R(2)–KB2	R–B2
35. Q–N3	

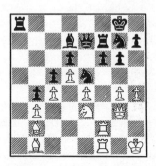

White's last move is a clever try for 36. P–R5 P–N4 37. P–R6! (otherwise 37. . . . . P–R3) to upset the kingside balance.

35. . . .	P–R3!
36. Q–B4	K–R2

Black plays this knowing that his KR3 cannot be protected easily by pieces other than his king. With White's next move he creates the chance for N–B5!? followed by QxPch, NPxP and doubling rooks on the KN-file. Black acts in time.

37. B–B1	R–R8!

So that on 38. B–Q2 he can simplify advantageously with 38. . . . RxB 39. RxR N–Q6 40. Q–B3 NxRch 41. QxN QxPch, as given by Panov in his memoirs.

38. R–QN2	P–R4!

Now the kingside is opened to Black's pieces. Panov need not fear 39. N–B2 R–R2 40. Q-R6ch K–N1.

39. PxP	NxRP
40. Q–B2	K–N1!
41. B–B2	R–KR2
42. R–QN1	RxR
43. BxR	P–KN4!

This cracks down White's last defense, e.g., 44. N–B5 BxN 45. PxB N–B5 46. BxN RxPch 47. B–R2 N–N5. Black finished off in style:

44. R–N1 N–N2 45. N–N2 N–N5 46. Q–N2 N–R4 47. R–K1 PxP 48. P–K5 P–R6! White Resigns.

STUDY EXAMPLES
(Answers on Page 260)

1. White has just played 1. B–B4 attacking a rook. If the rook moves off the file or if 1. . . . RxRch and 2. . . . QxB, White mates with a queen check. What does Black do?

2. What kind of threat does Black have on the kingside and what point does he threaten? Finally how do you protect that point (while meeting . . . BxN)?

3. Mate is the threat. What is the response?

4. What is White's major king-side threat and what is the best way of stopping it?

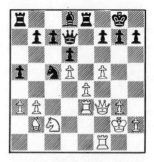

5. What does White threaten, how soon, and what can Black do about it?

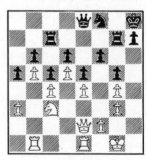

CHAPTER FOUR:

Counterplay

Counterplay is the cutting edge of defense. Without counter-chances—that is, countervailing threats against the opponent's weaknesses—the defender has to wage the lonely battle of parrying threats against his own position one at a time. His role is automatically passive and his best reward is respite from new threats. But with counterplay his reward is the turnover of the initiative. And the initiative, once in the hands of the defender, is the key to every defensive victory.

Having said that counterplay is highly desirable we have to point out what it's worth and under what circumstances you can take risks to obtain it. Seeking counterplay often means opening up the position in one sector of the board or maneuvering pieces from one theater to another. The newly opened position may expose the defender's targets to great pressure and the removal of defensive forces from one area to another may endanger the first area. Counterplay contains hidden costs and, as usual, a player has to determine whether a particular continuation is worth it.

A simple illustration of this would be the gamelet Letelier-Najdorf, Buenos Aires 1964, which began:

> 1. P–QB4 N–KB3 2. N–QB3 P–K3 3. P–K4 P–B4 4. N–B3 N–B3 5. P–Q4 PxP 6. NxP B–N5 7. NxN NPxN 8. B–Q3 P–K4?! (8. . . . P–Q4) 9. 0–0 0–0 10. P–B4 B–B4ch 11. K–R1 P–Q3 12. P–B5 P–KR3 13. P–KN4!

Black's game is secure in the center but threatened on the kingside. His choice is between restraint of the intermediate threat (opening the KN-file with 14. P–N5) or going for direct counterchances in the center. In other words, it is 13. . . . N–R2 vs. 13. . . . P–Q4. Either idea is valid in similar situations and so this becomes a major decision.

With 13. . . . N–R2 Black gives up the plan for . . . P–Q4 temporarily but holds up P–N5 for some time. White would have to play Q–B3–N3 and P–KR4 to prepare P–N5 and then Black could further restrain the break with . . . P–B3. On the other hand, the drawback of 13. . . . P–Q4 is that it allows P–N5 immediately. To decide in favor of the central counterplay Black must calculate the variations exactly.

But Black didn't. He played *13. . . . P–Q4? 14. P–N5 PxBP?* when the best he had available was the decidedly inferior 14. . . . RPxP 15. BxP PxBP 16. BxN QxB(3) 17. BxP. Najdorf was quickly crushed by *15. PxN QxB 16. PxP KxP 17. Q–N4ch K–R2 18. BxP! Resigns* (18. . . . KxB 19. Q–R4ch and 20. R–N1ch mates). Yet 13. . . . N–R2! should have held the position.

What lost the game for Black was a combination of the lack of force of his counterplay and the speed of White's mating attack. A little more strength to Black's . . . P–Q4 or a more easily defended kingside would change the judgment of Black's 13th move. The resilience of some positions is shocking. In a relatively closed position a player may be able to ignore development or impending mating attacks while he stirs up counterplay. The natural protection of his pieces does the rest.

For an entertaining example there was a 1952 consultation game between Russian grandmasters, Yuri Auerbach, Ewfim Geller, Tigran Petrosian and Mark Taimanov handling the White pieces opposed by Paul Keres, Alexander Kotov, Alexander Tolush and Isaac Boleslavsky. The game began:

> *1. P–Q4 N–KB3 2. P–QB4 P–K3 3. N–QB3 B–N5 4. P–QR3 BxNch 5. PxB N–B3 6. P–B3 P–QN3 7. P–K4 B–R3 8. B–N5 P–R3 9. B–R4*

Black could try to resolve the kingside issue a bit with 9. . . . N–QR4 10. P–K5 P–KN4!?, but the grandmaster quartet hit upon a highly original idea.The kingside was safe enough and there was nothing much to do in the center (9. . . . P–K4 10. PxP! NxP 11. P–B4 favors White). They were faced with the P–K5 threat anyway. So they sent the Q on a marauding adventure on the queenside.

The game went 9. . . . Q–B1 10. B–Q3 N–QR4 11. Q–K2 Q–N2!, intending to bring the Q to B3 where it would help win the QBP. The four grandmasters playing Black judged that 12. BxN PxB was nothing to worry about because they could always castle on the queenside. So the White quartet continued with the most natural move of aggression, 12. P–B4, and the game went 12. . . . Q–B3! 13. P–Q5 Q–R5 14. P–K5 Q–N6!.

This was the queen that sat quietly on its original square five moves ago. Black has ignored White's attack (15. PxN QxPch 16. K–B2 P–KN4! favors Black: e.g., 17. N–B3 PxB 18. PxP QPxP 19. N–K5 0–0–0), correctly judging that his counterplay was worth more. Now rather than 15. Q–Q2 N–N1 or 15. R–B1 QxRP, the White players chose *15. K–B2 QxP(B6) 16. N–B3 NxQP! 17. KR–QB1*, but after *17. . . . Q–N6 18. K–N3 NxKBP! 19. KxN P–N4ch* Black was winning.

Once again the story is the immediate exploitability of White's queenside versus the unexploitability of Black's kingside and center. Counterplay, like so much else in chess, is a matter of timing. Given a few extra tempi for White's attack, Black would be crushed.

The demand for counterplay frequently exceeds the desire for good-looking pawns. This is one of those lessons learned that distinguish the masters from average club players. The master knows, for example, that in a typical French Defense with queenside locked Black must try to break open the kingside for some counterplay with . . . P–KB3. For example, *1. P–K4 P–K3 2. P–Q4 P–Q4 3. N–QB3 B–N5 4. P–K5 P–QB4 5. P–QR3 BxNch 6. PxB N–K2 7. P–QR4 QN–B3 8. N–B3 Q–R4 9. B–Q2 B–Q2 10. B–K2 P–B5 11. 0–0 P–B3! 12. PxP PxP* and *13. . . . 0–0–0*, with an excellent game. A famous Smyslov-Botvinnik game (USSR Championship 1944) went *9. . . . P–B5 10. N–N5 P–KR3 11. N–R3 N–N3 12. Q–B3 B–Q2 13. N–B4 NxN 14. QxN N–K2 15. P–R4! BxP 16. P–R5 Q–N4 17. K–Q1 R–QB1 18. B–B1 R–B3! 19. B–K2 R–R3 20. K–Q2 0–0?! 21. P–N4*, and Black was virtually forced into *21. . . . P–B3 22. PxP RxP*, but his weak KP was perhaps the least significant aspect of a position crammed full of threat and counterplay.

Another version of this: *1. P–K4 P–QB4 2. N–KB3 P–Q3 3. P–Q4 PxP 4. NxP N–KB3 5. N–QB3 P–QR3 6. P–B4 Q–N3 7. B–K2 (7. P–K5!) N–B3 8. N–N3 P–K3 9. B–B3 B–K2 10. Q–K2 0–0 11. B–K3 Q–B2 12. P–QR4 P–QN3 13. 0–0 R–N1 14. K–R1? (14. P–N4 acts first)*, and in this position from a 1962 Soviet game the correct plan was *14. . . . N–QR4! 15. NxN*

PxN. Despite the worthlessness of Black's queenside pawns he has enough counterplay along the QN-file to compensate. White can only exploit the weak QRPs in the ending. But he can mate Black in the middlegame if there is no counterplay forthcoming from the defender.

In a sense, this is the paradox of counterplay. To offset the attack on some of your weaknesses you may have to create new weaknesses. The most difficult decisions a defender has to make are the choices from among moves of solid protection and of active, double-edged counterplay. And while there may be theoretically "correct" choices, the practical player must take into consideration such things as the opponent's style of play and the likelihood of catching him in an error.

Bronstein-Bagirov, 31st USSR Championship 1963, is a prime example:

1. P–K4 N–KB3 2. P–K5 N–Q4 3. P–Q4 P–Q3 4. P–QB4 N–N3 5. PxP BPxP 6. B–K3 P–N3 7. N–KB3 B–N2 8. B–K2 B–N5 9. QN–Q2 0–0 10. 0–0 N–B3 11. P–Q5 N–K4 12. NxN BxB 13. QxB BxN 14. N–B3 B–N2 15. QR–Q1 N–Q2 16. P–QN3 R–K1 17. N–Q4 P–QR3 18. P–B4

White's last move stops . . . N–K4 and prepares to play P–KB5xP opening up a good file. His restricting central position would then allow him good chances of carrying the attack off. Although P–KB5 may not be an immediate danger—since . . .

N–K4 would give Black an eased defense—White can build the attack with R-B3-KN3 or K-R1, N–B3 and B–Q4. Therefore, we can appreciate P–KB5 as a strong long-term threat.

Waiting tactics are not bad in themselves (see Chapter Seven). But Black should look for some more hopeful action. He can do battle on the KB-file with . . . R–KB1, . . . N–B3 and . . . Q–Q2. Or he can look for counterplay with . . . P–QN4 or . . . P–K3. The problems with the advance of the QNP are that it concedes QB3 to a White knight and that it isn't forceful enough to draw White's full attention from the kingside.

What about . . . P–K3 or . . . P–K4? White will naturally exchange his QP for the KP and leave Black with two weaklings on open files on the third rank. But it would also free Black's queen and rooks and stop P–KB5. Is it worth it? Bagirov thought so and played *18. . . . P–K4?! 19. PxP e.p. PxP 20. N–B3 N–B3 21. N–N5 P–QN4!.*

The QNP is indirectly protected since a double capture on QN5 would lose the White QRP. But, more importantly, this shot was the opening of queenside counterplay in a difficult position. Black had to act quickly before he was overrun in the center. The game proceeded: *22. B–Q4! PxP 23. QxP,* and now to break the center pressure and remove a dangerous piece Black played *23. . . . P–Q4 24. Q–Q3 N–R4! 25. BxB KxB.*

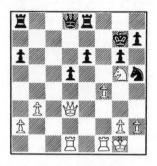

On the plus side Black's pieces are much freer than in the previous diagram. But they must defend a static pawn center which can be beautifully blockaded by a White Q on Q4 and N on K5. Black does have pressure against the White KBP and can try to bring his N to K5.

All in all, one might conclude that Black should have temporized at move 18. But Bronstein rewarded Bagirov's boldness by playing *26. QR–K1?? NxP! 27. Q–B3ch* (27. Q–Q4ch P–K4 or 27. RxN QxN) *P–Q5 28. Q–N3 P–K4 29. P–KR4 P–Q6,* and Black won. This leaves another irresolvable question: Since it is unlikely White would have blundered and lost the game had Black played 18. . . . Q–B2 or 18. . . . R–KB1, was Black justified in going for counterplay via 18. . . . P–K4? What if White had played more accurately at move 26 with 26. P–N3 or 26. Q–Q4ch and then obtained a decisive edge? Theoretically 18. . . . P–K4 is a dubious move but practically it has very definite merits.

For convenience, we'll consider the various forms of counterplay under the categories of counterplay in the center (to balance a wing attack), counterplay on the opposite wing, and counterplay in the same sector of the board. But a few pointers are appropriate beforehand.

We've so far concentrated on obtaining counterplay in much the same way that an attacker attacks—by bringing pieces to bear on one side of the board and then forcing a pawn-break. But even the most mundane defensive position with no available breaks can be given a modicum of vitality by a deft maneuver or shift of force. Awareness of these opportunities is another point that distinguishes the better players from the rest.

Consider this double-edged position from the 1963 Soviet Championship:

Korchnoi-Stein—*1. P–Q4 N–KB3 2. P–QB4 P–KN3 3. N–QB3 B–N2 4. P–K4 P–Q3 5. P–B3 0–0 6. B–K3 N–B3 7. KN–K2 P–QR3 8. P–QR3!? B–Q2 9. P–QN4 P–K4 10. P–Q5 N–K2 11. P–N4 N–K1 12. N–B1 P–KB4 13. N–N3 P–B3! 14. P–KN5! PxQP 15. BPxP*

Behind a closed center, White has mounted a double-flank attack and has a strong position. Black has played both of the normal freeing pawn-breaks, . . . P–KB4 and . . . P–QB3, that are recommended for this central structure, but his pieces still lack good squares. Black must do something quickly or else White will be able to choose between kingside attack (with P–KR5) or queenside (doubling rooks on the QB-file), with decisive effect in either case.

Black found an ingenious shift of pieces: *15. . . . B–R1! 16. Q–Q2 N–N2! 17. 0–0–0 N–B1! 18. R–N1 N–N3 19. K–N1 N–R4 20. N–R5! R–N1 21. R–B1 N–KB5*, and he had nearly equalized chances. His knights are the star players in a closed center and Black has used them well. The game saw more maneuvering— *22. P–KR4 R–B2 23. K–R2 B–N2 24. K–N3 B–K1 25. R–KR1 N–B1 26. R–R2 R–B2 27. K–N2 K–R1 28. N–N3 P–N4 29. N–R5 PxP 30. PxP N–N3*—and was drawn after 41 moves.

With just a few wary moves an entirely new wing attack can be sprung out of a colorless position. This always requires exact calculation of key variations and the weighing of consequences. A case in point is one of the Petrosian-Botvinnik world championship games:

1. P–QB4 P–QB4 2. N–KB3 N–KB3 3. N–B3 P–K3 4. P–K3 P–Q4 5. P–Q4 N–B3 6. BPxP KPxP 7. B–N5 B–Q3 8. PxP BxBP 9. 0–0 0–0 10. P–QN3 B–K3 11. B–N2 Q–K2 12. N–K2 QR–B1 13. P–QR3 KR–Q1 14. N(2)–Q4 B–KN5 15. B–K2 N–K5

16. Q–Q3 B–Q3 17. P–N3 N–B4 18. Q–N1 N–K5 19. Q–Q3 N–B4 20. Q–Q1 N–K3 21. R–K1 B–QB4 22. NxQN PxN 23. P–QN4 B–N3 24. Q–R4

White has a simple game to play. He just attacks the hanging central pawns by doubling rooks against them. The normal procedure for Black is to drum up a kingside initiative or dissolve his weak pawn complex. But the second option isn't available here because after either . . . P–QB4 or . . . P–Q5, White still has one very weak pawn to bombard.

As for kingside action, Black simply doesn't appear to have the pieces to exploit White's weaknesses around his king. Yet Botvinnik managed it in three moves: *24. . . . Q–K1! 25. QR–Q1 P–B3! 26. R–Q2 Q–R4.* In the guise of overprotecting his QBP at move 24 he initiated a transfer of force which gave him an excellent game after *27. Q–Q1 P–QB4* because then 28. PxP failed to 28. . . . B–R4. Petrosian correctly determined the size of the danger and played *28. N–Q4!*, exchanging pieces, which led to a draw at move 41.

CENTER VS. WING/WING VS. CENTER

One of the most repeated bits of chess advice is "a wing attack is best met by a thrust in the center." A corollary to this is that a closed center is highly desirable if you intend to attack on a wing. It is logical that if the attacker is using his force in one direction (e.g., toward the kingside) he is taking force away from the center. If the center can be penetrated effectively by the defender, the attack is doomed.

Even an apparently locked-solid center can be nudged into an avenue of counterplay through tactics. For instance, in Alapin-Burn, Karlsbad 1911, play went:

1. P–Q4 P–Q4 2. P–QB3 P–K3 3. B–B4 P–QB4 4. P–K3 N–QB3 5. N–Q2 N–B3 6. B–Q3 Q–N3 7. R–N1 B–Q2 8. B–N3!? B–K2 9. P–KB4 0–0 10. B–KB2 QR–B1 11. Q–B3 KR–Q1 12. N–K2 B–Q3 13. B–R4 B–K2 14. B–KB2 B–Q3 15. B–R4 B–K2 16. B–KB2 B–Q3 17. P–KR3 R–K1 18. P–KN4?

White refused the tacit offer of a draw through repetition of black-squared bishop moves when he chose 17. P–KR3 over 17. B–R4. Instead of peace, he launches a wing attack based on the premise that only Black's KN can compete with White's forces on the kingside. That is more or less true. But it is not sufficient to make the attack work. White also has to be safe on the queenside—which he is—and in the center, which he isn't. What happened was *18. . . . P–K4!! 19. QPxP RxP! 20. P–N5 N–K1 21. PxR NxP 22. BxPch KxB 23. Q–R5ch K–N1.*

Suddenly the center was opened to Black's pieces at the cost of the exchange. Burn took charge after *24. N–KB4* with *24. . . .*

B–B4 25. Q–Q1 N–Q6ch! 26. *NxN BxN* 27. *N–B3 P–B5* and won brilliantly in 41 moves.

The theme of attack in the center to counter kingside play is common in the Sicilian Defense when White begins a pawn storm against the Black K. As a general rule, pawn storms demand more than restraint. In the long run the eventual breakthrough will succeed for the attacker if there is no counterplay. This separates the pawn-storm attack from the piece-play attack. The latter can often be neutralized by the exchange of minor pieces. But behind a pawn army, the attacker has greater chance of carrying his forces into the vital area unimpeded.

A typical situation in the Sicilian is the . . . P–Q4 reaction by Black in response to P–KN4. When White advances his KNP two squares he is definitely announcing his intentions. But a well-timed . . . P–Q4 may expose him to a crossfire of Black's queenside force through the center. Take this 1936 Botvinnik-Ragosin game:

*1. P–K4 P–QB4 2. N–KB3 P–K3 3. P–Q4 PxP 4. NxP N–KB3
5. N–QB3 P–Q3 6. B–K2 P–QR3 7. B–K3 Q–B2 8. P–QR4
P–QN3 9. P–B4 B–N2 10. B–B3 QN–Q2 11. Q–K2 B–K2 12.
0–0 0–0 13. P–KN4*

Black's reaction depends on an evaluation of . . . P–Q4. If that is unappealing then he must agree to allow P–N5, which drives his KN back. (Note that 13. . . . P–KR3 has the drawback of allowing White to force open a file later with P–KR4 and P–N5.) Once White has P–N5 in he can proceed with several maneuvers: Q–N2–R3 or P–KR4–5. Ragosin's choice was *13. . . . P–Q4! 14. P–K5 N–K5!.*

It's true that Black has worsened his pawn structure but that's a kind of positional sacrifice. It now becomes impossible for White to continue with a routine kingside attack because then Black can fight back with . . . P–B3 or by doubling rooks on the QB-file. Botvinnik shifted gears and sought to exploit the apparent weakness in the center: *15. NxN PxN 16. B–N2 B–Q4 17. KR–B1 QR–B1 18. B–B2* (18. QxP B–B5 19. N–N5 Q–B3 and 20. . . . R–R1 is bad) *N–B4 19. P–N4.*

White could have played 19. R–K1 Q–Q2 20. P–N3, but his inferiority would have been apparent after 20. . . . P–B3. His 19. P–N4 appears to win the QP, but Black unleashed a tremendous counterattack with *19. . . . N–Q6!! 20. PxN QxRch 21. RxQ RxRch 22. B–B1 KR–B1*, after which White couldn't stop the threats of . . . B–B5 or the doubling of rooks on the first and second ranks. The finish was quick: *23. Q–N2 PxP 24. P–QN5 PxP 25. PxP R–Q8! 26. N–B6 B–B1 27. BxNP P–Q7! 28. Q–QB2 B–B6* and *White Resigned.*

Another case of this was Tarjan–Gheorghiu, Pasadena 1974: *1. P–K4 P–QB4 2. N–KB3 P–K3 3. P–Q4 PxP 4. NxP P–QR3 5. N–QB3 Q–B2 6. P–KN3 B–N5 7. N–K2 N–KB3 8. B–N2 B–K2 9. 0–0 0–0 10. P–KR3 N–B3 11. P–B4 P–QN4 12. B–K3 B–N2 13. P–KN4?*, and now with *13. . . . P–Q4!* Black offers a strong gambit to exploit the porous nature of the White kingside and the jumble of White pieces in the center. After 14. PxP PxP 15. NxQP NxN 16. BxN QR–Q1 or 16. QxN QR–Q1 (or 16. . . . N–R4), Black would have excellent play for a pawn.

White preferred *14. P–K5 N–Q2 15. N–Q4*, but after *15. . . . NxN 16. BxN P–N5! 17. N–K2 P–QR4* he had an inferior version of a pawn structure that often occurs in the French Defense. Before White can think further about mate he will be taken apart on the queenside. The game proceeded: *18. N–B1 KR–B1*

19. R–B2 N–B4 20. N–Q3 N–K5 21. R–K2 P–R5 22. R–B1 Q–B5 23. P–B3 B–R3, and White was quickly lost.

Besides the break in the center, the defender can take advantage of open lines that the attacker himself has sought. This pawn storm offers an illustration: *1. P–K4 P–QB4 2. N–KB3 P–K3 3. P–Q4 PxP 4. NxP N–KB3 5. N–QB3 P–Q3 6. P–KN3 P–QR3 7. B–N2 B–K2 8. 0–0 Q–B2 9. P–B4 0–0 10. P–KN4! N–B3 11. NxN* (otherwise 11. . . . NxN! will misplace the White Q for the coming kingside attack) *PxN 12. P–N5 N–Q2 13. P–B5.*

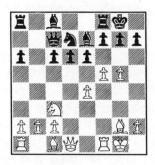

White's plan is to play P–B6 or P–N6 to force open some file or diagonal in the vicinity of the Black K. But simply keeping the lines closed is not enough for Black. In a game Fischer-Gligoric, Varna 1962, Black played 13. . . . R–K1 14. K–R1 B–B1 so that he could defend against P–B6xP with . . . BxP and . . . N–K4. Then his kingside squares would all be covered. But after 15. B–B4 N–K4 16. P–B6 P–N3 White can improve on Fischer's 17. P–KR4? with 17. BxN!, followed by a rapid attack on the KR-file without fear of counterplay.

The correct idea is 13. . . . PxP! 14. PxP P–Q4, to exploit the K-file and give Black's minor pieces, especially his QB, a better future. With the advance of his QP, Black shortens the diagonal of White KB and denies his N the K4 square.

The real test of the defense lies in specific variations. On the 15. P–B6 Black can play 15. . . . B–B4ch 16. K–R1 P–N3, so that on 17. Q–K1 B–N2 18. Q–R4 he can play 18. . . . KR–K1 19. Q–R6 B–KB1, with the better game. And against 15. K–R1 B–Q3 16. Q–R5 he can play 16. . . . R–K1 17. P–B6 P–N3 18. Q–R4 N–B4, also with a fine game. A third idea is 15. P–N6, e.g., 15. . . . RPxP 16. PxP PxP 17. NxQP!, but Black stands well with 15. . . . N–B3!.

The opposite side of the coin is the wing attack in answer to the opponent's domination of the center. It is, of course, highly desirable to have greater control of the center than your opponent, but this is not always possible. The wing attack versus the center is most effective when it drives the opponent's pieces and pawns away from defending the support points of the enemy center.

Perhaps the most famous instance of this was Vidmar-Nimzovich, New York 1927, in which White had an apparently potent hold on center squares after

1. P–Q4 N–KB3 2. N–KB3 P–K3 3. P–B4 B–N5ch 4. B–Q2 Q–K2 5. N–B3 0–0 6. P–K3 P–Q3 7. B–K2 P–QN3 8. 0–0 B–N2 9. Q–B2 QN–Q2 10. QR–Q1?! KBxN 11. BxB N–K5 12. B–K1 P–KB4 13. Q–N3 P–B4 14. N–Q2 NxN 15. RxN P–K4 16. PxKP PxKP 17. P–B3

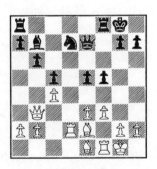

White's absolute control of the Q-file will be achieved after B–B2 and KR–Q1. He has regained control of his K4 square

with his last move. White's game looks highly promising until you see the next few moves. They were 17. . . . *P–KN4!!* 18. *B–B2 N–B3* 19. *KR–Q1 QR–K1* 20. *Q–R4 B–R1* 21. *R–Q6 Q–KN2!*.

Despite his Q-file and two bishops, White is in big trouble because of the kingside attack threatened via . . . P–KN5 or . . . P–K5. White should have tried 22. B–K1 with perhaps a defensible game, but he played 22. *B–B1* and lost after 22. . . . *P–K5* 23. *B–K1?! PxP* 24. *B–B3 Q–K2!* 25. *R(6)–Q3 PxP* 26. *BxP BxB* 27. *BxN Q–K5!* 28. *R(1)–Q2 B–R6* 29. *B–B3 Q–N5ch*.

In contrast to the previous Sicilian Defense example, this game shows that a wing attack can succeed swiftly if the center counterplay is mishandled. Black's attack succeeded in part because he won control of his K5 square and, in effect, won the Battle of the Center by attacking on his left. With better preparation such as 22. B–K1! (e.g., 22. . . . P–K5 23. B–B3! or 22. . . . P–N5 23. PxP NxP 24. BxN QxB 25. Q–B2), this could have been minimized.

WING VS. WING

Probably the most common counterplay model is one in which the defender scrapes up action on an opposite wing with the hope of breaking through there before his opponent succeeds on the other side of the board. White attacks the kingside so Black works the queenside. Or vice versa.

Although some pawn action is common in these examples, counterwing counterplay can also take place in static pawn structures. To wit:

Znosko-Borovsky vs. Alekhine, St. Petersburg 1913: 1. *P–K4 P–K4* 2. *N–KB3 N–QB3* 3. *B–N5 P–QR3* 4. *B–R4 P–Q3* 5. *P–Q4 B–N5* 6. *BxNch PxB* 7. *PxP PxP* 8. *Q–K2 B–Q3* 9. *B–K3 N–K2* 10. *P–KR3 B–R4* 11. *QN–Q2 0–0* 12. *P–KN4!? B–N3* 13. *P–KR4 P–B3* 14. *P–R5 B–B2* 15. *N–R4*

White's attack runs smoothly with N–B5 followed by P–KN5 (or NPxN if the outpost N is captured). The target is KN2, and that cannot be easily protected by Black. Ergo, he looks for counterplay. But where? He has blocked the Q-file. The QN-file is his, but it isn't worth that much after P–QN3. Black's minor pieces just aren't flexible enough to work up immediate threats.

Alekhine did the trick with heavier wood: *15. . . . Q–N1! 16. P–N3 Q–N5! 17. P–KB3 KR–Q1 18. K–B2 B–B4!*. After *19. N–B1 R–Q3 20. BxB QxBch 21. N–K3 QR–Q1 22. KR–Q1 Q–B6!* Black had seized a potent initiative in the center by way of queenside penetration.

But most counterwing play derives from the comingling of piece action with pawn-breaks. When the opponent depends on his *minor pieces* for success, the defender can rely on the familiar tacitcs of eliminating the dangerous piece, trading and applying pressure to weak points:

Dus-Chotimirsky vs. Bogolyubov, Moscow 1925—*1. N–KB3 N–KB3 2. P–Q4 P–K3 3. P–K3 P–B4 4. B–Q3 P–Q4 5. P–B3 QN–Q2 6. QN–Q2 B–Q3 7. 0–0 0–0 8. R–K1 Q–B2 9. P–K4 BPxP 10. BPxP PxP 11. NxP N–Q4 12. NxB QxN 13. N–N5 N(2)–B3 14. Q–B3*, and now Black swept through the queenside before White could make sufficient kingside progress: *14. . . . Q–N5! 15. R–Q1 B–Q2 16. Q–N3 KR–B1 17. Q–R4 P–KR3 18. N–B3 P–R3 19. P–N4 B–N4!*. Black won shortly after *20. P–N5 PxP 21. BxP BxB 22. RxB QxNP 23. R–K1 R–B6!*.

When the opponent launches a *pawn storm,* however, the

defender knows that his counterattack can afford a few extra tempi in preparation but that the mere exchange of pieces will not slow down the attacker. Timely, forceful counterplay is essential. But it is not just a case of getting there "fastest with the mostest." An ounce of prophylaxis has its place. Defenders rarely have time to apply a pound of cure.

For example, in this sharp King's Indian Defense position popular during the 1950s:

1. P–Q4 N–KB3 2. P–QB4 P–KN3 3. N–QB3 B–N2 4. P–K4 P–Q3 5. N–B3 0–0 6. B–K2 P–K4 7. 0–0 N–B3 8. P–Q5 N–K2 9. N–K1

Black must seek his counterplay on the kingside unless White makes a very grave slip on the queenside. This means the attack on the base of the pawn chain with . . . P–KB4. White, meanwhile, will be attacking another base with P–QB4–5. With this in mind Black plays *9. . . . N–Q2* instead of *9. . . . N–K1.* The former move restrains the P–B5 threat better.

Then after *10. B–K3* the counterwing action continues: *10. . . . P–KB4 11. P–B3 P–B5! 12. B–B2 P–KN4 13. N–Q3 N–KB3 14. P–B5 N–N3 15. R–B1.* Notice that Black has transferred the attack to a further point in the White pawn chain, the KN7 and KB6 squares. His 13th move lets go of his own QB4, but he could no longer safely restrain P–QB5. If he played . . . P–QN3, White would play P–QN4 and have good chances of opening *two* queenside files. The same goes for a possible P–KR3 by White on the kingside: it makes an open kingside inevitable.

For many years it was thought that White's queenside action was faster than Black's mating ideas. But at the 1953 Candidates Tournament Najdorf scored a stunning win over Taimanov of the Soviet Union after *15. . . . R–B2! 16. R–B2 B–B1! 17. PxP PxP 18. Q–Q2 P–N5 19. KR–B1 P–N6! 20. PxP PxP 21. BxNP N–R4 22. B–R2 B–K2 23. N–N1 B–Q2 24. Q–K1 B–KN4 25. N–Q2 B–K6ch 26. K–R1 Q–N4,* and decisive threats forced resignation soon thereafter.

The instructive preparation for . . . P–KN6 also forestalled White's queenside play. Notice that 15. . . . R–B2 and 16. . . . B–B1 not only allow Black to move his rook to the KN-file but, more significantly, they cover his weaknesses at QB2 and Q3.

Now, let's look at the corresponding mixture of restraint and counterplay on the other side of the board. Our model for study is Bisguier-Gligoric, Bled 1961:

1. P–K4 P–QB4 2. N–KB3 P–Q3 3. P–Q4 PxP 4. NxP N–KB3 5. N–QB3 P–QR3 6. B–K2 P–K3 7. 0–0 Q–B2 8. P–B4 QN–Q2 9. B–B3 B–K2 10. K–R1 N–B1?! 11. P–KN4! P–R3 12. P–B5 P–K4 13. KN–K2 B–Q2 14. P–QR4 B–B3! 15. B–K3 N(1)–Q2 16. N–N3 R–QB1 17. Q–K2

Black's exotic knight maneuver at move 10 was a popular idea of Petrosian's. The Armenian had employed it earlier in the Bled tournament and equalized quickly through the familiar idea of seizing a foothold in the center (11. Q–K1 N–N3 12. B–K3 0–0 13. R–Q1 P–K4! 14. PxP PxP 15. N–B5 B–N5 16. R–Q3 QBxN 17. PxB P–K5 18. BxP NxB 19. N–Q5 BxQ 20. NxQ QR–B1). But White's 11. P–KN4! throws Black on the defensive on the kingside because of the threat of P–KN5. And his 14. P–QR4 was necessary to stop Black's natural bid for play with . . . P–QN4–5.

But P–QR4 also creates weaknesses on White's queenside, and that is what Black hopes to exploit while he watches his KN4. He played *17. . . . Q–N1*, intending *18. . . . P–QN4*, and White continued *18. P–R5 Q–B2 19. P–N4!?* with the idea of playing P–QN5 at some time. As an immediate threat, 20. P–QN5 PxP 21. NxP BxN 22. QxB or 21. . . . Q–N1 22. P–B4 would be strong. So Black again played *19. . . . Q–N1* with the idea of meeting 20. P–QN5 with 20. . . . PxP 21. NxP P–Q4!, opening up the center.

The next stage is delicate. Black anticipates the White kingside build-up by safeguarding his king—but not by castling. After *20. R–B2 N–R2 21. N–R5* Black played *21. . . . K–B1!*, which allows him to keep his KR in the immediate vicinity and helps discourage P–KN5. There followed *22. R–Q1 B–KN4 23. BxB NxB 24. B–N2?* (better 24 P–R4!) *N–R2!*.

Black retreats, so that on 25. Q–Q2 he can play 25. . . . KN–B3 26. QxPch QxQ 27. RxQ NxNP 28. KR–Q2 N(2)–B3 29. R–Q8ch K–K2. White was consistent in playing *25. P–R4*, but then *25. . . . QN–B3! 26. N–N3* (26. NxN NxN 27. K–R1 P–R4! gives White troubles on the kingside) *B–Q2* gave Black excellent queenside counterplay. White was weak on his QB3 and QB4 and now he had to protect these squares. These weaknesses only become significant now that White's P–KN5 has lost its immediacy.

Rather than 27. R–Q3 R–B5, White went into *27. N–Q5 NxN 28. PxN?* which was worse: *28. . . . B–N4 29. Q–B3 N–B3 30. B–B1 BxB 31. NxB R–B5! 32. N–K3 RxQNP 33. P–B4 Q–R2! 34. K–N1 R–N6 35. R–K1 Q–Q5*, and Black won in a few moves.

Despite the absence of Black queenside play and the obviousness of White's P–KN5 threat, an opportunistic combination of restraint and counterthreats—plus an inexact 24. B–N2?—turned the tables.

There are instances when a flank attack may be even more desirable than a central break. The sensational 1969 game between the young Italian master Mariotti and veteran grandmaster Gligoric was a case in point:

> 1. *P–Q4 N–KB3 2. P–QB4 P–KN3 3. N–QB3 B–N2 4. P–K4 P–Q3 5. P–B4 P–B4 6. P–Q5 0–0 7. B–K2 P–K3 8. PxP!? PxP 9. P–KN4*

Clearly White is going for a quick mate by way of a pawn storm. As usual, a pawn storm cannot be satisfactorily met by mere piece play. Black needs pawn action and he must choose between . . . P–Q4 in the center or . . . P–QN4 on the queenside. Gligoric's defeat was blamed on his preference for the center but that isn't fair. He could have obtained good play immediately with 9. . . . P–Q4!?: e.g., 10. BPxP PxP 11. PxP NxNP! 12. BxN Q–R5ch, or 10. BPxP PxP 11. P–K5 NxP 12. QxPch QxQ 13. NxQ N–QB3, or 10. KPxP PxP 11. P–N5 N–K5.

Black played 9. . . . N–B3 10. P–KR4 N–Q5, although again 10. . . . P–Q4! would have opened the game to his satisfaction. But Gligoric's critical mistake was answering 11. P–R5 with 11. . . . P–Q4?, which allowed White an unimpeded attack:

12. P–K5 N–K5 13. RPxP RPxP 14. Q–Q3! P–QN4 15. NxN
NPxP 16. Q–KR3! PxN 17. Q–R7ch K–B2 18. P–B5! KPxP 19.
R–R6!, and White won. It's true that Black could have taken
greater precautions by exchanging off pieces and vacating the
danger area with 14. . . . NxN 15. PxN NxB 16. NxN K–B2,
but his game was still inferior.

The correct plan for Black once he has brought his N to
Q5 is 11. . . . P–QN4! with the idea of sacrificing pawns to seize
the initiative. On 12. RPxP Black continues 12. . . . P–N5! 13.
PxPch K–R1 with a degree of kingside safety. Black then wins
the KP and brings his QB to power on the long diagonal. And
if White takes time for 12. BPxP B–N2 13. B–Q3, Black can
play 13. . . . P–Q4 14. P–K5 N–K5 with the White queen un-
able to reach the vicinity of Black's king so easily. (A game
between two British schoolboys in 1974 went 15. N–B3 P–N4!
16. BxN PxB 17. NxNP P–KR3 18. NxP(6) NxN 19. Q–N3 Q–Q6
20. QxNch K–R1 21. N–K2 B–Q4 22. Q–R6 B–B5 23. R–R2
QR–Q1 24. Q–R4 BxKP! 25. B–K3 KBxNP 26. R–Q1 B–B6ch 27.
NxB Q–B8 mate. Black had even better chances with 17. . . .
BxP! 18. PxB P–K6 19. KN–K4 P–K7!.)

SAME SIDE COUNTERPLAY

When the defender chooses—or is forced—to do battle on
the same side of the board that the attacker has chosen, the
game often turns into a battle for space. The defender may
concede his opponent more terrain only if he is sure he can
establish an impregnable line of protection.

In the following position, which arose from the game Smyslov-
Auerbach, 22nd USSR Championship, after *1. N–KB3 N–KB3
2. P–KN3 P–KN3 3. B–N2 B–N2 4. 0–0 0–0 5. P–Q4 P–Q4 6.
P–B4 P–B3 7. N–R3 P–K3? 8. B–B4 P–N3 9. Q–B1! B–N2 10.
B–R6 QN–Q2 11. BxB KxB 12. P–N3 R–B1 13. Q–N2 Q–K2 14.
QR–B1 K–N1*, Black is denied kingside play and he hasn't
enough force to make . . . P–K4 or other central play work.

For example, 14. . . . PxP 15. NxP P–B4 16. Q–R3 is uncomfortable. So, he waits for White to make a decision about
his own middlegame plans. An alert defender can often choose
the perfect time to make consolidating moves (e.g., 14. . . . K–N1
to get the king off a diagonal that might later be opened) when
it forces the opponent into a difficult decision. On 15. N–B2 or
15. N–N1, to reposition the N, Black has 15. . . . PxP 16. PxP
KR–K1 and . . . P–K4 without the usual problems. And 15.
KR–Q1 KR–K1 or . . . KR–Q1 delays a decision.

Smyslov played *15. P–QN4*, with the dual purpose of gaining
queenside space (stopping . . . Q–N5 or . . . P–QB4 in certain
cases) and threatening P–B5 or P–N5 after some preparation.
White has a considerable advantage because of his better
minor pieces. He only needs superior heavy pieces, more terrain and an opening to make his edge felt.

Black subtly played *15. . . . R–N1!*, threatening 16. . . . P–B4
to take advantage of the placement of the White Q opposite
his rook. Now 16. P–B5 PxP 17. NPxP B–R3 would have been
excellent for Black and 16. R–B2 P–B4! 17. NPxP NPxP 18.
Q–B1 KR–B1 certainly equal. White preferred *16. PxP BPxP
17. R–B2*.

Again Black had to play actively or he would be squashed
by KR–B1. Auerbach chose *17. . . . P–QR4!* and, to avoid the
opening of Black's file, White allowed *18. P–N5 Q–N5! 19. KR–B1
QxQ 20. RxQ KR–B1*. In the ensuing endgame Black protected
his weak spot at QN3 and drew after *21. R(2)–B2 RxR 22. RxR*

R–QB1 23. RxR BxR 24. N–Q2 K–B1 25. N(3)–N1 K–K2 26.
N–B3 N–K1 27. P–B3 B–N2 28. K–B2 N–Q3 and another nine
moves.

The trick to obtaining counterplay on the same side as the
attack is to catch the aggressor at just the point when he is
least prepared for it. For illustration there is a common theme
of kingside play when White advances with P–KN4 and Black
responds . . . P–KR4!. If White plays P–N5 he allows Black
the choice of when to open the kingside later with . . . P–KB3.
And on NPxRP White may have ruined his kingside pawn
structure for the dubious sake of a half-open file.

This is a typical instance in the Sämisch Variation of the
King's Indian Defense: *1. P–Q4 N–KB3 2. P–QB4 P–KN3 3.
N–QB3 B–N2 4. P–K4 P–Q3 5. P–B3 0–0 6. B–K3 P–K4 7. P–Q5
P–B3 8. KN–K2 PxP 9. BPxP P–QR3*, and now after *10. P–KN4*
Black has *10. . . . P–KR4!*.

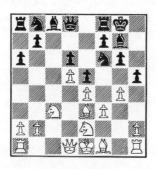

Black's action stops the natural attack deriving from P–KR4–5
and B–R6 while at the same time threatening . . . PxP. On 11.
P–N5 N–R2 Black has a fine game on both sides of the board.
White's kingside assault is halted. And the alternative, 11.
PxP NxP with . . . P–KB4 coming up, is worse.

White's best chance is 11. P–KR3 to maintain the tension.
But with the kingside in balance, Black can seize the initiative
on the opposite wing with 11. . . . P–QN4!; e.g., 12. B–N2 QN–Q2
13. B–N5 Q–R4 and . . . P–N5.

The weakness of . . . P–KR4 is often much less than P–KN4, an advance that Tarrasch liked to call the "hari-kari-zug." An amusing exploitation of this occurred in Steinberg-Tukmakov, USSR 1966: *1. P–QB4 P–QB4 2. N–QB3 N–QB3 3. P–KN3 P–KN3 4. B–N2 B–N2 5. N–B3 P–K3 6. 0–0 KN–K2 7. P–Q4?! NxP 8. NxN PxN 9. N–N5 N–B4 10. P–KN4 P–QR3! 11. Q–R4 N–R5 12. N–Q6ch K–B1 13. NxB? QxN! 14. Q–N4ch K–N1 15. BxP Q–N1 16. Q–N3,* and Black offered a fine sacrifice with *16. . . . P–KR4!* which would have led to a smashing attack if accepted (*17. BxR QxB 18. Q–N3 PxP*). White refused the offer with *17. P–N5* but was quickly lost anyway after *17. . . . R–R2.*

PASSIVE VS. ACTIVE CENTER

Here is a typical middlegame situation from a Queen's Gambit Declined (*1. P–Q4 P–Q4 2. P–QB4 P–QB3 3. N–KB3 N–B3 4. P–K3 P–K3 5. B–Q3 QN–Q2 6. QN–Q2 B–Q3 7. 0–0 0–0 8. P–K4 PxP 9. NxP NxN 10. BxN N–B3 11. B–B2 P–KR3 12. Q–K2 P–QN3 13. P–QN3 B–N2 14. B–N2 Q–K2 15. QR–Q1 QR–Q1 16. B–N1*):

It's easy to imagine Black's being mated quickly in the next dozen moves after, say, *16. . . . Q–B2 17. N–K5 N–Q2 18. P–B4 KR–K1 19. Q–N4 N–B1 20. R–B3* and a timely *P–Q5* or *P–KB5*. But Black has a perfectly good game in the diagram. The **reason he** can lose quickly is because his position demands counterplay. The only way to obtain it is to turn his passive center formation into an active one.

In this situation, a familiar one in Queen's Pawn games and the Caro-Kann Defense, Black needs either . . . P–K4 or . . . P–QB4 to liberate his pieces. This is just what happened in Duras-Alekhine, Karlsbad 1911, after *16. . . . P–B4! 17. KR–K1 PxP 18. NxP B–N5! 19. R–KB1 KR–K1*.

Suddenly Black's bishops were as menacing as White's pair. And Alekhine was ready to create threats of . . . Q–B4 and . . . P–K4 or . . . Q–KN4. White's weak play led to a speedy downfall: *20. K–R1 Q–B4 21. P–B3 Q–KN4 22. N–N5 N–R4! 23. B–K5? P–B3 24. B–B7 RxR 25. RxR P–R3 26. N–Q4 P–K4 27. N–B5 P–N3 28. N–K3 B–B4 29. N–B1 N–B5 30. Q–QB2 BxP!* and wins.

Back at the diagram we might lodge a number of criticisms of the . . . P–QB4 break. It grants White a queenside majority of pawns. And it opens up the long diagonal of White's QB. But these considerations pale before the dynamic demand for piece play. Black simply has to strike in the center or be swamped.

Another instance comes from the 9th USSR Championship in 1934:

Ilyin-Genevsky vs. Ryumin—*1. P–K4 P–QB3 2. P–Q4 P–Q4 3. N–QB3 PxP 4. NxP N–Q2 5. N–KB3 KN–B3 6. N–N3 P–K3 7. B–K2?! B–Q3 8. 0–0 0–0 9. P–QN3 Q–B2 10. B–N2*

If Black doesn't break in the center, his minor pieces will never see life. He could prepare for the break with . . . P–QN3 and . . . B–N2, followed by putting rooks on K1 and Q1 or on Q1 and QB1 depending on whether he wants . . . P–QB4 or P–K4. Or he could play 10. . . . P–B4 immediately.

But Ryumin's *10. . . . P–K4!* is most effective because it carries its own threat (. . . P–K5) and secures developing squares for Black's QB and QN. He is not afraid of 11. N–B5 P–K5 12. NxB PxN! 13. NxB PxB 14. N–K7ch K–R1 15. QxP QR–K1, with the knight trapped on K7.

White obtains nothing from 11. PxP NxP 12. NxN BxN 13. BxB QxB except a slightly inferior game. The best he can do is 11. PxP NxP 12. R–K1, but 12. . . . R–K1 then offers easy equality. White actually played *11. P–B4 P–K5 12. N–Q2 R–K1 13. P–B5* and quickly lost the initiative after *13. . . . B–B5 14. N–B4 P–QN4 15. PxP e.p. PxP 16. B–B1 BxB 17. QxB B–R3.*

White threw himself into a desperate kingside attack and went down after *18. Q–N5 P–R3 19. Q–R4 N–B1 20. N–B5 N–N3! 21. NxPch? K–B1 22. Q–N3 N–B5!* (not 22. . . . QxQ 23. BPxQ) *23. B–Q1 PxN 24. N–K5 N(3)–Q4 25. R–K1 P–B3 26. RxP PxN.*

A strong center, even if arranged totally for defense and restraint, can be converted to an active center with a few deft touches if the defender is alert. For example:

(1) Moll-Teichmann, Berlin 1907: *1. P–K4 P–K4 2. N–KB3 N–QB3 3. N–B3 N–B3 4. B–N5 B–N5 5. 0–0 0–0 6. P–Q3 P–Q3 7. B–N5 N–K2 8. N–KR4 BxN 9. PxB N–K1! 10. P–Q4 P–KB3 11. B–B1 B–K3 12. P–N3 P–QB4 13. B–K2 N–B2 14. B–K3 P–QN3,* and now, after *15. P–KB4?* Black ended his black-square blockade strategy in order to exploit White's square weaknesses: *15. . . . KPxQP! 16. PxP P–B4 17. B–B3 PxKP 18. BxP B–Q4! 19. B–Q3 P–B5 20. B–K2 N–N3!,* and Black won with the aid of his central control and queenside majority.

(2) Ivkov-Spassky, Piatigorsky Cup 1966: *1. P–Q4 N–KB3 2. P–QB4 P–K3 3. N–KB3 P–QN3 4. P–KN3 B–N2 5. B–N2*

B–K2 6. 0–0 0–0 7. N–B3 N–K5 8. NxN BxN 9. N–K1 BxB
10. NxB P–Q3 11. P–K4 N–Q2 12. B–K3 Q–B1 13. N–B4 P–QB3
14. R–B1 R–K1 15. N–Q3. White has maneuvered his pieces
to stop . . . P–Q4 and Black has played to anticipate P–Q5
(which would be met by . . . KPxP and . . . P–QB4). But
White's piece placement left him vulnerable to another action: *15. . . . P–QB4 16. P–B3 Q–R3 17. P–QR4? B–B3 18.
N–B2?* (18. PxP may be best) *PxP 19. BxP BxB 20. QxB
N–B4 21. QxQP QxRP,* with a winning ending.

PLAY ON BOTH SIDES

On those infrequent occasions in which the chances are so
complex that the defender can work on both sides of the street
at once he must consider himself fortunate. Usually when a
player watches both wings it is because he is trying to calculate
whether he can break through on one before getting mated on
the other. But it can also mean that the defender is sniping at
two extended flanks:

Kholmov-Ragosin, 21st USSR Championship 1954—*1. P–QB4
N–KB3 2. N–QB3 P–Q3 3. P–KN3 P–KN3 4. B–N2 B–N2 5.
P–K3 0–0 6. KN–K2 P–B4 7. 0–0 N–B3 8. P–N3 B–B4 9. P–Q4
PxP?! 10. NxP NxN 11. PxN Q–Q2 12. R–K1 KR–K1 13. B–N2
QR–N1 14. Q–Q2 B–R6 15. B–R1 P–KR4!? 16. P–Q5 B–B4 17.
R–K2 P–QR3 18. P–QR4 Q–B2 19. N–Q1 Q–N3 20. P–QN4
B–N5! 21. B–Q4 Q–B2 22. P–B3 B–Q2 23. N–K3*

White clearly has the lion's share of the center and a strong queenside game. Given time for P–R5, Q–N2, R–QB1 and P–B5, White will be winning. Black's counterplay could come from . . . P–K4, but Ragosin found an intriguing alternative: 23. . . . P–R5! 24. P–R5 N–R4 (eliminating the strong piece) 25. BxB NxB 26. Q–Q4 P–N3!.

Black's idea is to exchange pawns along the QN-file, play . . . Q–B4 and then occupy the file with doubled rooks. It is worth the sacrifice of his KRP. White's best plan, in fact, is 27. PxP QxNP 28. P–B5! QxNP 29. QxQ RxQ 30. P–B6 B–B1 31. P–N4, although as Ragosin pointed out in his notes, Black has good chances then with 31. . . . P–K3.

The combination of attacking White's queenside at its base and the kingside at KN3 is highly original. Black was further rewarded when White played 27. R–QN2? overlooking 27. . . . PxP 28. RxP RxP!, after which 29. RxRP (29. RxR QxR) RxR 30. QxR R–N1 31. Q–Q4 R–N8ch 32. N–B1 N–B4 put Black on top. White's pawns fell like plums: 33. R–R8ch B–B1 34. Q–B2 QxP 35. B–N2 K–N2 36. P–N4 B–N2! 37. R–R2 N–Q5 38. R–Q2 N–N6 39. R–K2 BxP 40. RxP N–Q5 41. P–R3 B–K3 42. Q–K3 N–K7ch 43. K–B2 N–B5 44. N–Q2 N–Q6ch and *White Resigned.*

ILLUSTRATIVE GAMES
USA VS. USSR MATCH 1954

BISGUIER   PETROSIAN

1. P–Q4 N–KB3 2. P–QB4 P–B4 3. N–KB3 PxP 4. NxP N–B3 5. N–QB3 P–K3 6. P–KN3 B–B4 7. N–N3 B–K2 8. B–N2 0–0 9. 0–0 P–Q3

White has a small positional advantage due to his greater control of space. Black's modest arrangement of minor pieces indicates he will play against the QBP as in a Sicilian Defense. Since that is Black's main hope of counterplay, White should continue with something like 10. N–Q4 and 11. P–N3.

10. P–K4?!	N–K4
11. Q–K2	Q–B2
12. N–Q2	P–QR3
13. P–N3?	P–QN4!

This assures Black of queenside activity since on 14. P–B4 N–B3 15. PxP White loses a piece to 15. . . . N–Q5 and 16. . . . QxN!.

14. P–B4	N–B3
15. B–N2	. . .

Black has won a minor tactical battle to get . . . P–QN4 in but now faces a problem. He cannot support his QNP (15.

. . . N–R2 16. P–K5) and he doesn't like 15. . . . PxP 16. NxP,
followed by QR–B1.

15. . . .	**P–N5!**

An excellent decision. This would appear to give up the
queenside play Black strove for with . . . P–QN4. But Black
directs his attention now to the QR-file which he will open
with . . . P–QR4–5. In coordination with . . . N–Q2–B4 Black
can pose serious problems to the White queenside. And if White
mechanically stops the break with 16. N–QR4, Black plays
. . . N–Q2–B4 and capitalizes on the opening of the Q-file after
NxN.

16. N–Q1	P–QR4
17. N–K3?!	P–R5
18. QR–N1	PxP
19. PxP	R–R7

Black has a fine game due to his QR-file. To dislodge the
Black rook White should have brought his knight to Q3 via
KB2. Then with R–R1 or N–B1 he could force the rook away,
as Hans Kmoch noted. Failing to do this White threw himself
into a mating attempt. This game is reminiscent of another
Petrosian masterpiece—vs. Donald Byrne (White) at Majorca
1969: 1. P–QB4 P–KN3 2. N–QB3 B–N2 3. P–KN3 N–KB3 4.
B–N2 0–0 5. P–K4 P–Q3 6. KN–K2 P–B3 7. 0–0 P–QR3 8.
P–Q4 QN–Q2 9. P–KR3 R–N1 10. P–Q5? P–B4 11. P–QR4 N–K1
12. P–B4 N–B2 13. Q–Q3 N–B3 14. B–Q2 B–Q2 15. P–R5 P–N3!
16. PxP RxP 17. Q–B2 Q–N1 18. N–Q1 N(3)–K1 19. B–QB3
BxB 20. N(2)xB R–N5 21. Q–K2 P–K4! 22. P–B5 N–B3 23.
R–B2 K–R1 24. K–R2 P–N4! 25. N–K3 R–N1 26. B–B3 R–QN3
27. K–R1 K–N2! 28. P–R4 P–R3 29. R–KN1 K–B1 30. N–N4 NxN
31. BxN N–K1 32. P–B6 BxB 33. QxB R–N3 34. R(1)–KB1 PxP
35. QxP RxQNP 36. P–N4 RxR 37. RxR Q–N6 38. R–B3 K–N1!
39. P–N5 PxP 40. Q–N4 NxP *White Resigns.*

20. P–N4	N–Q2!
21. P–N5	R–K1
22. K–R1	N–B4
23. P–R4	Q–Q1
24. R–B3	B–B1

Black has covered his kingside neatly and now prepares a thrust in the center to make decisive inroads. Black never relinquishes the initiative.

25. R–N3	P–K4!
26. P–B5	N–Q5!

In addition to . . . NxQ there is a . . . N–Q6 threat. White loses a pawn or two after 27. BxN PxB and 28. . . . . BxP.

27. Q–B1	N(5)xNP
28. NxN	NxN
29. Q–K1	N–B4!

Another star move which gives him time to pile up on the KP and on the uncoordinated White pieces on both wings.

30. QxP	B–N2
31. N–Q5	R–R5
32. Q–Q2	BxN

Last chance for White was 33. N–B6ch PxN 34. PxPch
which Black stops.

33. QxB   **R–N5!**

Black wins a piece now because of the pin on the QN-file.
Petrosian's play was a model of sharpness and ingenuity from
a cramped opening. The game ended:

*34. B–KB3 Q–R1 35. Q–Q2 Q–N2 36. R–N2 R–N1 37. B–Q1
QxP 38. B–B2 QxQBP 39. P–N6 RxB 40. PxRPch K–R1 41.
QR–N1 QxPch 42. R–R2 Q–KB5 White Resigns.*

13TH USSR CHAMPIONSHIP 1944

RAVINSKY   SMYSLOV

*1. P–Q4 N–KB3 2. P–QB4 P–K3 3. P–KN3 P–Q4 4. B–N2
PxP 5. Q–R4ch B–Q2 6. QxBP B–B3 7. N–KB3 B–K2 8. N–B3
0–0 9. 0–0 QN–Q2 10. B–KN5 P–KR3 11. BxN NxB 12. QR–Q1*

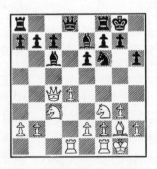

Black has won the two bishops and has good lines and squares
for his minor pieces. Surprisingly enough he must still play
accurately to equalize. The problem he faces is bringing his
pieces, especially his queen and rooks, into active play. There
is a temporary traffic jam in his center, and he has to avoid
White's tactical tricks involving N–K5 and P–Q5; e.g., 12. . . .

N–K5 13. N–K5 NxN 14. NxB or 12. . . . N–K1 13. P–K4 N–Q3 14. Q–Q3.

12. . . .   **Q–Q3!**

This greatly eases Black's game because an exchange of queens with . . . Q–N5 would put White's center under attack immediately. Black also readies . . . KR–Q1 and . . . B–K1 so that he can follow with . . . P–QN3 and . . . P–QB4. This last thrust is the key to Black's counterplay but it requires great caution in execution. A model game was Junge-Alekhine, Munich 1942, which diverged from this same opening with 7. . . . QN–Q2 (instead of 7. . . . B–K2) 8. N–B3 N–N3 9. Q–Q3 B–N5! 10. 0–0 0–0 11. B–N5 P–KR3 12. BxN QxB 13. P–K4 KR–Q1 14. QR–Q1 B–K1! 15. P–QR3 B–B1 16. Q–K3 QR–B1 17. B–R3 R–N1 18. KR–Ḱ1 N–R5! 19. P–K5?! Q–K2 20. NxN BxN 21. QR–B1 P–QN3 22. B–B1 (22. P–QN4 P–QR4!) P–QB4, with a moderate edge for Black.

13. Q–Q3	Q–N5
14. Q–B2	Q–R4
15. P–K4	KR–Q1

Now that White can play N–K5 wihout exchanging off his strong bishop, Black allows his QB to retreat to K1 without locking in a rook. Smyslov notes that Black is happy to see 16. N–K5 B–K1 17. N–B4 Q–R3 18. P–N3 P–B3 because of his threats against the center involving . . . P–QN4 and . . . Q–N3.

16. KR–K1!   **B–K1!**

Now Black has anticipated 17. P–Q5, which he could meet with 17. . . . PxP 18. PxP B–N5 19. N–Q4 B–Q2 followed by . . . BxN and . . . R–K1 or . . . B–N5. White's QP can become a major liability then.

In the next stage White takes advantage of the position of the Black Q to establish what appears to be iron restraint of . . . P–QB4. Whether Black can succeed in making that break will determine the course of the game.

17. P–QR3	P–B3
18. N–QR4	QR–B1
19. P–QN4!?	Q–B2
20. Q–N3	P–QN3
21. R–QB1	P–B4!

This succeeds because in the simplified position that follows Black's bishop and use of the Q-file grant him a slight pull. White's problems stem from P–K4. If his KP were on the third rank so that his KB2 wouldn't be easily attackable and his KP would be easily defended, the game would certainly lead to a draw.

22. QPxP	BxN
23. QxB	PxP
24. B–B1	Q–N3
25. P–N5!	. . .

A good defensive idea involving the blockading move B–B4.

25. . . .   P–B5!

But the diagonal is worth a pawn to Black, e.g., 26. BxP N–N5 27. R–K2 R–Q6! or 26. RxP N–N5 27. Q–B2 RxR 28. BxR NxP! (best is 26. RxP N–N5 27. R–K2 RxR 28. QxR B–B4 29. Q–B2 QxP 30. P–R3).

26. P–R3?	P–B6
27. Q–N3	B–B4
28. R–B2	R–Q7!

Now 29. NxR leads to the pretty variation 29. . . . BxPch 30. K–N2 BxR 31. N–B3 Q–K6 32. R–K2 QxRch! and 33. . . . P–B7. Black just marches over the first three White ranks now:

29. *RxR PxR* 30. *R–K2 BxPch!* 31. *K–N2 R–B6!* 32. *Q–Q1 B–K6* 33. *NxP Q–Q5* 34. *Q–K1 NxP* 35. *NxN QxNch* 36. *K–R2 Q–Q5* 37. *R–KN2 R–B8* 38. *Q–K2 Q–R8* 39. *QxB RxB* 40. *P–N4 R–K8* and *White Resigned* in face of threats to his queenside pawns and his king.

CHAPTER FIVE:

Sacrifice

A brilliant sacrifice, the wise man once said, only proves that someone has blundered. What Savielly Tartakover meant is that flashy offers of queens and rooks can only be sound if the sacrificer has already accumulated several positional pluses. Then, when he has a manifest advantage, he can cap the middle-game with a dazzling sacrifice and submit the game-score to the anthologies.

This kind of "practical" or "sham" sacrifice is simple to understand. It is the inconclusive sacrifice, the one with no immediate follow-up to force resignation, that is the real challenge for the defender. There is not much to be done about the pseudosacrifice mentioned above: your game is probably hopeless anyway. But the inconclusive or speculative sacrifice demands great attention.

Should I take the offered material? Can I refuse? From a practical point of view, would refusal of the sacrifice confuse my opponent more than acceptance? If I accept, can I defend against his immediate threats? What about the long-range threats following acceptance? How much material do I need to win? When should I return the sacrificed material? How much material is worth the risk? These are only a few of the problems.

In this chapter we'll take a look at some of the major questions involving sacrifices. From a practical standpoint there is not much difference between (a) a sacrifice deliberately planned by the other side, (b) a loss of material overlooked by the opponent, and (c) your provoking his sacrifice by making the alternative to it an inferior position. In each case material is won and lost, and the merits of the material change often have little to do with the motivation. But for our purposes we'll leave provocation and pawn-grabbing for the next chapter.

ACCEPT OR REFUSE?

There have been a number of fine textbooks written from the point of view of the sacrificer. In these works, the authors, such as Spielmann, Vukovich and Shamkovich, take pains to distinguish between the functions that different sacrifices serve. Some "sacks" are made to open lines, others to secure an advantage in time, still others to denude the opponent's kingside, and so on.

From the defender's point of view, however, these distinctions are secondary. The first line the defender draws is between forcing and non-forcing sacrifices. In other words, must I accept or is this an offer I *can* refuse?

Miguel Najdorf recalled another Tartakoverism when the Argentine grandmaster annotated his first game with Unzicker from the 1966 Piatigorsky Cup. The position was a common product of the Nimzo-Indian Defense:

1. P–Q4 N–KB3 2. P–QB4 P–K3 3. N–QB3 B–N5 4. P–K3 0–0 5. B–Q3 P–Q4 6. N–B3 P–B4 7. 0–0 N–B3 8. P–QR3 BxN 9. PxB PxBP 10. BxBP Q–B2 11. B–Q3 P–K4 12. Q–B2 R–K1 13. PxKP NxP 14. NxN QxN 15. P–B3 B–K3!? 16. R–K1? QR–Q1 17. R–N1 Q–Q4! 18. B–B1 B–B4 19. P–K4

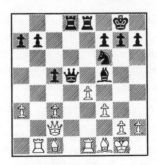

Black's last idea was revealed in *19. . . . NxP!*, a relatively direct sacrificial idea which would have given him a winning position after 20. PxN RxP! 21. RxR BxR 22. Q–N2 BxR 23. QxB Q–Q8, followed by . . . Q–K8 and . . . R–Q8.

"Luckily I did not lose my head and remembered the saying of my old master Tartakover," Najdorf wrote in the tournament book, "that in order to lose a game it is not enough to make only one mistake."

To make things difficult, White played *20. Q–N3!!*, an unexpectedly strong refusal. If Black now exchanges material and preserves his pawn advantage he winds up in a bad endgame: 20. . . . QxQ 21. RxQ N–Q3 22. RxRch RxR 23. B–KB4 or 22. . . . NxR 23. RxP R–Q8 24. R–N8 K–B1 25. B–K3!.

Unzicker decided to win a second pawn temporarily with *20. . . . NxP*, but after this White's active pieces secured a standoff in the ending. The game concluded quickly with *21. RxRch RxR 22. QxQ NxQ 23. RxP K–B1 24. K–B2 R–K2 25. R–N8ch R–K1 26. R–N7 R–K2 Draw.* Najdorf caught himself just in time—before making the second mistake of accepting Unzicker's sacrifice.

The simple act of refusal has been known to confound more than a few opponents, even very strong ones. The sacrificer has prepared his position for this moment and has calculated all the lines emanating from acceptance. But has he given adequate consideration to refusal? A sharp demonstration of this came about in a Russian team championship game between Boris Spassky and Alexei Suetin in 1963:

1. P–Q4 P–Q4 2. P–QB4 PxP 3. N–KB3 N–KB3 4. P–K3 P–K3 5. BxP P–B4 6. 0–0 P–QR3 7. Q–K2 P–QN4 8. B–N3 B–N2 9. R–Q1 Q–B2 10. N–B3 QN–Q2 11. P–K4 PxP 12. P–K5!? PxN 13. PxN NxP 14. N–K5 B–B4! 15. B–KB4 Q–N3 16. NxP

Black could try to save himself after 16. . . . KxN, but Suetin appreciated the impossibility of survival after Spassky's intended followup, 17. R–Q6!!. Even if this weren't convincing, Black might have preferred the riskless *16. . . . 0–0!!* which Suetin played.

Yes, it is quite legal to castle in this position. But Spassky, no doubt, had overlooked this when he began the complications with 12. P–K5. Now the future world champion should have tried 17. N–Q6. But, perhaps jarred by the castling surprise, he simply ran out of steam and lost shortly after *17. N–N5? PxP 18. QR–N1 QR–K1 19. RxP Q–B3 20. N–B3 N–K5!*.

One of the reasons sacrificial gambles pay off so often is that defenders tend to believe that ancient saw, "the only way to refute a sacrifice is to accept it." Amos Burn, for many years the strongest English player, was peculiarly vulnerable. He accepted all sacrifices "on principle." One notorious example of this was his fiasco versus Frank Marshall (White) at Ostend

1907. The American began with *1. P–Q4 N–KB3 2. N–KB3 P–Q3
3. B–B4 QN–Q2 4. P–K3 P–KN3 5. B–Q3 B–N2 6. QN–Q2 0–0
7. P–KR4?! R–K1 8. P–R5 NxP 9. RxN? PxR 10. BxPch.* Here
the simple 10. . . . K–B1! would end Marshall's attack before
it has begun. Black could then take over the initiative with
. . . P–K4. But, true to form, Burn played *10. . . . KxB??* and
was mated in 11 moves beginning with *11. N–N5ch K–N3
12. QN–B3 P–K4 13. N–R4ch K–B3 14. N–R7ch.*

But perhaps the most notorious example of this was Karl
Schlechter's most celebrated tournament victory. He had White
against Salve at St. Petersburg 1909:

*1. P–K4 P–K4 2. N–KB3 N–QB3 3. B–N5 P–QR3 4. B–R4
N–B3 5. 0–0 B–K2 6. R–K1 P–QN4 7. B–N3 P–Q3 8. P–B3
N–QR4 9. B–B2 P–B4 10. P–Q3 N–B3 11. QN–Q2 0–0 12.
N–B1 Q–B2 13. B–N5 N–K1 14. N–K3 BxB 15. NxB N–K2 16.
P–QR4 R–N1 17. PxP PxP 18. Q–Q2 P–R3 19. N–B3 B–K3 20.
P–Q4 N–KB3 21. R–R6 R–R1*

Here Schlechter played 22. PxKP!?, a sacrifice which, world
champion Emanuel Lasker noted, was advantageous whether
accepted or declined. On *22. . . . PxP 23. KR–R1 RxR 24. RxR
B–B1* White now has time for 25. Q–Q6!, with a big endgame
edge. And on *24. . . . R–Q1* White would play 25. Q–B1 to
double on the QR-file. His superiority would be clear.

Therefore Salve chose *22. . . . RxR 23. PxN PxP 24. N–Q5!*

BxN 25. PxB K–N2 26. N–R4, with a lost position. White won in classic style after *26. . . . R–K1 27. P–R3 Q–Q1 28. R–K3 N–N3 29. N–B5ch K–B1 30. R–K6!!*.

After the game won the brilliancy prize and after Lasker extolled it in the tournament book, it was discovered that *22. . . . NxP!* would simply have refuted the sacrifice because on *23. BxN RxR* Black's kingside remains rock solid.

PROBLEMS AND VIRTUES OF REFUSAL

What makes these sacrifices refusable is that they are non-forcing. It is one thing if an opponent plays *RxN* and you must play *. . . PxR* if you don't want to remain a knight behind. It is an entirely different story when he plops down a rook in the middle of the board, as in Smyslov-Makaganov, USSR Championship 1944:

The position is reminiscent of the Botvinnik game mentioned in Chapter Three. Black has just played *24. . . . R–K5!*, with the intention of bringing a knight to Q4 after *25. BxR QPxB*. Then, with the dangerous K-file closed, he can breath more easily. From a material point of view, Black is virtually equal because of a pawn he grabbed early in the opening.

White, however, is not forced into any action. In fact, Smyslov simply improved his position with a queen penetration. The exchange offer was not going to run away. White played 25. Q–N3! R–N1 26. Q–N5! B–K2 27. Q–R6 B–B3 28. Q–R7 R–N2 29. Q–R8ch N–B1 and now 30. BxR QPxB 31. Q–B8. Black's knight can't get to Q4 as easily now and his pieces are much less well coordinated. Not only was Black's sacrifice non-forcing but there was no time limit attached to the offer. White eventually won a long hard struggle.

How forcing is forcing? When we speak of a forcing sacrifice we mean one in which the concessions made by the defender in refusing it are too great. Often, this issue is a matter of judgment: "If I don't take his knight now, he will move it away next move and remain a pawn ahead. Is it worth it to me to lose a pawn?" Yet sometimes it is more a question of calculation than judgment.

This was the case in the critical game of the 1953 Candidates Tournament. Paul Keres, trailing young David Bronstein by one point, went all out for mate in a late round:

1. P–QB4 N–KB3 2. N–QB3 P–K3 3. N–B3 P–B4 4. P–K3 B–K2 5. P–QN3 0–0 6. B–N2 P–QN3 7. P–Q4 PxP 8. PxP P–Q4 9. B–Q3 N–B3 10. 0–0 B–N2 11. R–B1 R–B1 12. R–K1 N–QN5! 13. B–B1 N–K5! 14. P–QR3 NxN 15. RxN N–B3 16. N–K5 NxN 17. RxN!? B–KB3 18. R–R5 P–N3 19. R(3)–R3!!?

As Bronstein quoted him in the tournament book, Smyslov wanted very much to take the offered rook "the more so because I did not see how White could win." In retrospect the decision to refuse the offer must be applauded because subsequent analysis has shown that White has a devastating attack after 19. . . . PxR 20. QxP R–K1 21. P–R4!! (to bring a B to QR3) Q–Q3 22. P–B5!. (On the other hand, it would also be fair to ask whether Keres would have found his way through the complications as well as Smyslov.)

But Black remained exceptionally cool after the astounding 19th move by his opponent. Of course, the doubling of rooks against his KRP means that White pieces will penetrate his castled position. But how dangerous is that? A bit of hard thinking convinced Smyslov that he could safely refuse the offer with *19. . . . PxP!!.*

The first reason this is strong is that White cannot routinely recapture with 20. PxP because then Black can accept the sacrifice and beat off the attack by bringing his QB to K5. The second reason is that White was under the gun. He had to find an equally strong rejoinder from among the several candidates such as 20. R–R6, 20. Q–N4 and 20. RxP. Requiring a choice to be made is the ultimate defense weapon.

The last possibility, 20. RxP, was critical because it also answers the question of whether White's 19th move was forcing or not. Keres played *20. RxP P–B6 21. Q–B1!*, intending to bring his queen to KR6. However, Smyslov had calculated in advance that he could bring his queen to the defense with *21. . . . QxP!*, covering KN2 and KR1. This was crushing. The game ended with *22. Q–R6 KR–Q1 23. B–B1 B–N2 24. Q–N5 Q–B3 25. Q–N4 P–B7 26. B–K2 R–Q5 27. P–B4 R–Q8ch 28. BxR Q–Q5ch* and *White Resigned.*

When the defender says to himself "I can afford to refuse that sacrifice" he is also making an offer of his own. Sometimes it means sacrificing his pawn structure and sometimes it means giving up a piece or pawn temporarily, or even permanently.

Here is a 1952 USSR Championship game between Korchnoi

(Black) and Goldenov. Black has skillfully defended his kingside and is ready to take the initiative with 27. . . . R–K7. The trouble with White's game is indicated by 27. R–K3 B–B5! and by 27. Q–N5 P–B3! 28. BxP P–R3 29. Q–N6 Q–K3!.

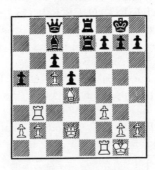

In view of this, Goldenov took refuge in the time-honored try for perpetual check: 27. *BxP*, with the idea of interminable checks on KB6, KN5 and KR6. Is this forcing, Korchnoi asked himself? White does threaten 28. B–B6 or 28. Q–N5 if Black plays something other than 27. . . . KxB.

But Black does have 27. . . . *Q–B4!*, which serves the dual function of threatening to take the bishop now that perpetual check is impossible and also of supporting a vicious counterattack with . . . R–K7 and . . . B–B5.

To stop this last idea, White played 28. *B–R6*, but then 28. . . . *R–K7!* 29. *Q–N5ch QxQ* 30. *BxQ B–K4!* resulted in a superior endgame for Black. The manner in which Korchnoi forced his edge home was interesting: 31. *R–Q1 BxP* 32. *K–B1 R–B7* 33. *R–Q2? R–B8ch* 34. *K–B2 B–B6!* 35. *R–K2 B–K8ch!* 36. *RxB* (36. K–B1 is met by 36. . . . B–Q7ch followed by 37. . . . RxRch and 38. . . . BxB) *R(8)xR* and wins.

Black was making a gamble of his own with 27. . . . Q–B4!. He believed his counterattack was stronger than a pawn. Another illustration of this was the key Olafsson-Tal game from the 1959 Candidates Tournament:

1. P–K4 P–QB4 2. N–KB3 P–K3 3. P–Q4 PxP 4. NxP P–QR3
5. P–QB4 N–KB3 6. N–QB3 B–N5 7. B–Q3 N–B3 8. N–K2
Q–B2 9. 0–0 N–K4? 10. P–B4! NxBP 11. K–R1! B–K2 12. P–QN3
N–N3 13. P–K5 KN–Q4 14. N–K4 P–B4! 15. PxP e.p. NxP(3)
16. N(2)–N3 QN–Q4 17. B–N2 0–0 18. R–B1 Q–Q1 19. Q–K2
P–QN4 20. NxNch BxN 21. Q–R5.

Black had taken a very dubious gambit pawn, and despite
his fine bid to control kingside space (14. . . . P–B4) it is White
who still stands better. In fact, there are several improvements
for White earlier. Here, however, Black has little choice, because
21. . . . P–R3 22. B–R3 followed by Q–N6 or P–B5 is too strong
for White.

Therefore, Black chose an ingenious countersacrifice of a pawn,
returning the material he had won in the opening: *21. . . .
P–N3!* 22. BxKNP, and now not 22. . . . PxB 23. QxPch K–R1
24. N–B5! followed by R–B3–R3, but *22. . . . Q–K2!*.

Now examine White's position. He can renew the attack
on KR7 and the other kingside targets only with great difficulty.
The biggest problem is untangling his pieces which are under
threat of capture or exchange. To get his pieces back into coordination White had to lose time. This gain of time for Black
is what saved him.

This happened: *23. BxB NxB 24. Q–B3 R–N1 25. B–Q3 B–N2
26. Q–K2 K–R1 27. QR–K1 QR–K1*, and here White should have

played for simplicity with 28. N–K4. He erred with 28. *N–B5?*
Q–N5 29. *Q–N2 R–B1* 30. *N–N3 Q–B6* 31. *Q–K2 R–KN1* 32.
N–K4 Q–Q5, and it was clear that Black had taken over the
initiative. Tal won shortly.

Refusal also may call for the countersacrifice of non-material
values such as the health of your pawn structure, the activity
of your pieces, or the like. A typical example of this arises out
of a Queen's Gambit variation that was the scourge of the mid-
1930s:

> 1. *P–Q4 P–Q4* 2. *P–QB4 PxP* 3. *N–KB3 N–KB3* 4. *P–K3*
> *P–K3* 5. *BxP P–B4* 6. *0–0 N–B3* 7. *Q–K2 P–QR3* 8. *R–Q1*
> *P–QN4* 9. *B–N3 P–B5!?* 10. *B–B2 N–QN5* 11. *N–B3 NxB*
> 12. *QxN B–N2* 13. *P–Q5!?*

Several crushing wins for White had been scored after 13. . . .
PxP 14. P–K4!, as the center was ripped open and Black tried
to make up for lost development. But at Nottingham 1936
Salo Flohr introduced an excellent defense against Reshevsky:
13. . . . Q–B2!.

Black is willing to accept a weak KP after 14. PxP PxP
because then 15. P–K4 is stopped by way of 15. . . . P–N5.
Black can continue with . . . B–K2 or . . . B–Q3, . . . 0–0 and
. . . QR–Q1. The KP, once again, is an unexploitable weakness
in the complicated middlegame.

So, in the game cited, White continued *14. P–K4* instead of 14. PxP, and this allowed *14. . . . . P–K4!*, keeping the center closed. Black stood very well after *15. B–N5 N–Q2*—actually a bit better because of his queenside majority and minor exchange.

Finally it should be noted that a non-forcing sacrifice can be costly even if the defender cannot accept or launch an immediate counterattack. The attacker may have also cut off his options by making the sacrificial offer. For example, in a match game between Najdorf and Reshevsky in 1952, the Argentine grandmaster played:

1. P–Q4 N–KB3 2. P–QB4 P–K3 3. N–QB3 B–N5 4. Q–B2 P–B4 5. PxP 0–0 6. P–QR3 BxBP 7. N–B3 N–B3 8. P–QN4 B–K2 9. P–K3 P–Q3 10. B–N2 P–QR4! 11. P–N5 N–N1 12. N–N5 QN–Q2 13. B–K2 P–R3 14. P–KR4

The novice is apt to lose several games to players who don't retreat their pieces when attacked by P–KR3. Their opponents play P–KR4 in response. The novice captures the piece and gets mated in a few moves along the newly opened KR-file.

But this is one of the oldest non-forcing sacrifices. Black is not eager to play 14. . . . PxN? 15. PxP N–K1?? 16. Q–R7 mate. If he doesn't have to play . . . PxN, then P–KR4 is a naive move. Not only naive but expensive because instead of a knight White has actually given up the possibility of playing a quiet positional middlegame with the option of castling into a safe kingside. His pseudosacrifice is refused, but the loss of the option of positional play is irretrievable.

Black responded *14. . . . Q–B2 15. QN–K4 P–K4!* (meeting the threat of NxN and BxN) with the idea of developing his pieces for a murderous . . . P–Q4. Then White's forces will be exposed as misplaced and by that time his KN may be capturable.

The one-idea attack crumbled after *16. N–N3 R–Q1 17. R–QB1 N–B1 18. KN–K4 B–K3 19. N–KB5 QR–B1 20. NxBch QxN 21. NxNch QxN 22. Q–K4* (to stop . . . P–Q4) *P–QN3 23. P–R5 N–Q2 24. P–B4 B–B4 25. Q–B3 N–B4! 26. PxP PxP 27. 0–0 B–Q6!*, and White forfeited on time in a hopeless position a few moves later.

ZWISCHENZUG AND COUNTERSACRIFICE

A few special cases—which, nevertheless, occur surprisingly frequently—are those involving "in-between moves" and counter-sacrifices before and after acceptance.

The word *Zwischenzug* denotes the interruption of the normal sequence of events with an unexpected move. This extra move is of such a forcing nature that the other side must respond to it before resuming the sacrificial theme. The *Zwischenzug* hopefully introduces a new set of circumstances which upset the basis for the sacrifice's soundness.

An early game of Alekhine's, versus Olland at Scheveningen 1913, provides an excellent example:

1. P–K4 P–K4 2. N–KB3 N–QB3 3. B–N5 N–Q5 4. B–K2? NxB 5. QxN P–Q3 6. P–B3 P–QB3 7. P–Q4 Q–B2 8. B–K3 N–B3 9. QN–Q2 B–K2 10. P–KR3 P–QN3 11. 0–0 P–QR4 12. P–B4 P–B4! 13. P–Q5 P–R3 14. P–R3 P–KN4! 15. P–QN4 P–N5 16. RPxP BxP 17. PxBP NPxP 18. Q–Q3 Q–Q2

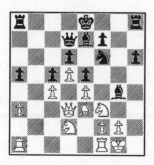

Olland (White) appreciated that he was drifting into a playless middlegame in which he could be wrecked by Black's simple assault on the KN-file. He took proper measures beginning with *19. BxBP!*, intending to continue after 19. . . . PxB with 20. NxP and P–B3–4, with a powerful center in return for a relatively small amount of sacrificed material. Then White's kingside dangers are made less significant and Black's lag in development is made more.

But there is no rush to accept. Alekhine calculated a fine series of "in-between moves": *19. . . . BxN! 20. NxB R–KN1!*. This amounts to a pseudocountersacrifice of a pawn because White could retreat his bishop from QB5 now. However, the sacrifice by Black could not be accepted because of brutal threats such as 21. B–K3 RxPch! 22. KxR Q–N5ch 23. K–R2 QxN, followed by the crushing entrance of a Black knight on N5 and a Black rook on KN1.

There was, of course, more to the game. White realized the dangers and continued *21. NxP! PxN 22. BxB* so that on the routine recapture on K7 he could consolidate the kingside with P–B3 and R–B2. In that case White would still have some middlegame chances with two passed queenside pawns ready to march.

But once again Black had a *Zwischenzug*, *22. . . . Q–N5!*, after which Black retained both his extra piece and the kingside initiative needed to offset the White center pawns.

The game continued with *23. P–N3 KxB 24. P–Q6ch K–B1*

*25. KR–K1 P–R4 26. QR–Q1 R–Q1 27. P–B5 P–KR5 28. R–K3
PxP* and *29. . . . N–R4*, with a decisive position for Black. Quite
a different kind of game from the one that would have followed
19. . . . PxB.

Another example of the confusion that a *Zwischenzug* can
sow into the smooth lines of a sacrificial attack occurs in a
recently controversial variation of the Najdorf Sicilian. It begins
with:

> *1. P–K4 P–QB4 2. N–KB3 P–Q3 3. P–Q4 PxP 4. NxP
> N–KB3 5. N–QB3 P–QR3 6. B–KN5 QN–Q2 7. B–QB4 Q–R4
> 8. Q–Q2 P–K3 9. 0–0–0 P–QN4 10. B–N3 B–N2 11. KR–K1
> N–B4? 12. P–K5! PxP 13. BxP! PxB 14. NxKP!*

There are much safer ways of playing the positions which
arise after *6. . . . QN–Q2.* (*11. . . . 0–0–0* is one that comes
to mind.) The diagrammed position is highly interesting in
itself. It occurred in the great Bled tournament of 1961 between
Boris Ivkov and Tigran Petrosian. Ivkov took more than two
hours for his first 14 moves and after *14. . . . QN–Q2 15. BxN
NxB* he accepted Petrosian's draw offer because of his time
shortage. Later it was pointed out that *16. RxP K–B2 17.
Q–B4* or *17. Q–K3* was very strong.

Black could improve also, the post-mortem analysis revealed.
Not with *14. . . . NxN* because of *15. BxN* threatening death on
Q7. But consider the *Zwischenzug 14. . . . P–N5!*

The point of the move is not just that another White piece is attacked. The White QN has no comfortable jump, it is true. But the move 14. . . . P–N5 also puts the Black queen on an indirect line with the KP. This is felt after, say, 15. RxP N–Q6ch! 16. QxN QxR or 15. NxN PxN 16. RxPch K–B2. Since RxKP cannot be played immediately and is not deadly later, Black's 14. . . . P–N5 is a key improvement.

The appearance of such *Zwischenzug* ideas not only occurs in forcing lines but also in speculative sacks. For an illustration, we recall another Alekhine game, this time with the future world champion on the receiving end. It occurred in his game with Teichmann from Karlsbad 1911: *1. P–K4 P–K4 2. N–KB3 N–QB3 3. B–N5 P–QR3 4. B–R4 N–B3 5. P–Q4 PxP 6. 0–0 B–K2 7. P–K5 N–K5 8. NxP 0–0 9. P–QB4 N–B4.*

Here White chose a speculative sacrifice of the KP to preserve his good bishop: *10. B–B2?! NxP 11. Q–R5 N–N3 12. P–B4.* Obviously White has a strong threat of 13. P–B5 N–K4 14. P–B6 (mate at KR7 threatened) P–N3 15. PxB winning a piece. The natural defense would be 12. . . . R–K1 13. P–B5 N–B1 and this is satisfactory only because on 14. P–B6 Black can capture the pawn with his bishop—14. . . . BxP 15. QxN Q–K2 16. Q–Q5 P–B3, regaining the piece.

Teichmann found an even simpler defense: *12. . . . P–Q3 13. P–B5 B–B3!,* with the in-between threat of . . . BxN *check.* The added feature of this move—the one that makes 12. . . . P–Q3 playable—is that now Black's KB3 is occupied and P–B6 is physically impossible. After *14. B–K3 N–K4* Black was quite safe and, in fact, he added to his extra pawn in the next few moves: *15. N–Q2 R–K1 16. K–R1 KN–Q6! 17. N–K6 BxN 18. PxB RxP 19. QBxN P–KN3 20. Q–B3 NxB* and wins the ending easily.

One further example shows how a countersacrifice can be a form of *Zwischenzug* to upset the sacrificial theme: *1. P–Q4 N–KB3 2. P–QB4 P–KN3 3. P–KN3 B–N2 4. B–N2 0–0 5. N–KB3 P–Q3 6. 0–0 QN–Q2 7. N–B3 P–K4 8. P–K4 P–B3 9. P–KR3 Q–R4 10. B–K3 PxP 11. NxP N–N3!? 12. Q–Q3 Q–R3 13. P–N3 P–Q4,* and now, to prevent the pin on the White queen from giving Black a dangerous initiative, the opening analysts of the early 1960s recommended *14. Q–B2 P–B4 15. KPxP*. The point is that on 15. . . . PxN 16. BxP White has excellent compensation in the form of two central pawns. An early game went on 16. . . . R–Q1 17. KR–Q1 B–B4 18. Q–Q2 N–K1 19. P–KN4! BxB 20. QxB B–Q2 21. P–B5 N–B1 22. P–Q6 B–B3 23. N–K4, with a winning position.

However, this judgment was eventually overthrown with subsequent discovery of the in-between countersacrifice *15. . . . KNxKP!*, which obtains Black the advantage in every case: 16. NxN NxN 17. PxN PxN, followed by taking control of the QB-file, or 16. N(4)–N5 NxB, etc.

IF YOU MUST ACCEPT

The forcing sacrifice removes one of the defender's options —refusal—and thus is a more dangerous animal. The first priority for the defender is to be aware of all the various sacrificial ideas that are possible in this or that kind of middlegame. On the Black side of a French Defense, for example, you must recognize that with a White bishop on the QN1–KR7 diagonal and a White pawn on K5, there lurks the danger of the ancient BxKRPch-N–KN5ch-Q–R5 mating sacrifice. On the Black side of a Sicilian Defense, you look for piece sacrifices for pawns on your QN4 and K3. These possibilities don't arise in every game, but the defender has to recognize that they exist and might come about. All it takes is a minor slip to make the sacrifice real.

Here we should draw a further distinction between sacks of heavy material with little immediate material return (bishop for pawn, rook for two pawns, queen for two pieces) and sacks that are properly considered, in Spielmann's phrase, a form of business transaction (bishop for two or three pawns). In the former case the defender is faced with immediate threats which the attacker believes to be insurmountable. The defender can console himself with the thought that if he survives the crisis of the next few moves, he will win with his material advantage. In the latter case, the threats tend to be less immediate but the material difference is smaller.

A diligent reader of game anthologies will sometimes conclude that certain sacrifices always win. After all, every time he sees a particular sack played, it leads to mate. For some reason unknown to him, the same sacrifice just never works when he tries it. For those players, a few examples like this can be a tonic:

Dus-Chotimirsky vs. Levenfisch, Karlsbad 1911:

1. P–Q4 P–Q4 2. N–KB3 N–KB3 3. P–K3 P–B4 4. PxP P–K3
5. P–QR3 BxP 6. P–QN4 B–K2 7. B–N2 P–QR4 8. P–N5 QN–Q2
9. B–Q3 P–QN3 10. N–K5 NxN 11. BxN 0–0 12. 0–0 N–Q2
13. B–Q4 B–N2 14. P–KB4 N–B4

Black could also block the attacking line QN1–KR7 with 14. . . . P–B4 and then contest the QN2–KN7 line with 15. . . . B–KB3 (cf., Open Lines, Chapter Two). But the text move is sound because the two-bishop sacrifice doesn't work. This sacrificial idea was first made famous, ironically, by one of the great defensive minds, Emanuel Lasker. But White thought the combination worked here and he played *15. BxPch KxB 16.*

Q–R5ch K–N1 17. *BxP*. The usual sacrifice mechanism continues with . . . KxB, a White queen check on the KN-file to force the Black king to the KR-file, and the decisive rook-lift, R–B3, followed by R–R3 mate.

Unfortunately, Dus-Chotimirsky was embarrassed to find himself simply a piece behind after *17. . . . KxB 18. Q–N4ch B–N4! 19. PxB N–K5 20. P–KR4 Q–B2! 21. N–Q2 Q–N6.*

Here is another case in point, a slugfest between two unknown Russians two decades ago: *1. P–K4 P–QB4 2. P–QB3 N–KB3 3. P–K5 N–Q4 4. P–Q4 N–QB3 5. PxP P–K3 6. N–B3 BxP 7. QN–Q2 Q–B2 8. N–B4 0–0 9. B–Q3 P–QN4.* Now that White has everything in place, Black provokes him: *10. BxPch KxB 11. N–N5ch K–N3* (not *11. . . . K–N1??* 12. Q–R5 and mates) *12. Q–Q3ch P–B4 13. Q–N3.* As in countless published examples before, White has played the bishop sack and is ready to discover a strong check against the Black king.

But things like this don't happen every day, and this time Black covered himself with glory: *13. . . . P–B5! 14. BxP BxPch! 15. KxB RxBch 16. K–K1 K–R3.* Black's king was safe now that the black-squared White QB was off the board. The finish was *17. Q–R3ch KxN! 18. Q–R7 NxKP 19. QxPch N–N3 20. P–R4ch RxP 21. RxR Q–N6ch 22. K–K2 QxR 23. N–Q2 N–B5ch 24. K–Q1 B–N2,* and *White Resigned.*

In these cases of serious material's being sacrificed for direct threats, the defender's friends are the same tactics we discussed earlier—counterthreats, exchanges, *Zwischenzug*, elimination of the dangerous attacking pieces and repairing weaknesses. An additional friend is the return of material through countersacrifice. This can mean giving back exactly the same material as was originally sacrificed in order to break the attack and obtain a positional advantage in the materially equal middlegame. Or it can mean creating a material disequilibrium by giving back other pieces—giving back a piece to weaken the effect of his queen-for-rook sacrifice, countersacrificing the exchange to end the attack begun by his piece sack, and so on.

Here is a classic example of returning material for profit:

Ahues-Carls, Hamburg 1921—*1. P–K4 P–QB3 2. P–Q4 P–Q4 3. PxP PxP 4. P–QB3 N–QB3 5. B–Q3 P–K3 6. N–B3 B–Q3 7. 0–0 KN–K2 8. Q–K2 N–N3 9. N–N5 QN–K2 10. P–KB4 0–0!.* White is lured into a very appealing pseudosack: *11. Q–R5 P–KR3 12. NxBP KxN! 13. P–KN4*

White threatens P–B5, regaining his knight. There is little that Black can do to extricate himself from the pin on his king. Presumably this early spurt of fireworks has helped White because Black's kingside is overexposed. However, Black showed that it is White who is in trouble after material equality is reestablished:

13. . . . Q–K1! 14. P–B5 PxP 15. PxP BxP! 16. BxB K–N1! 17. B–Q3 RxRch 18. KxR Q–B2ch 19. K–N1 R–KB1. In a few moves Black has taken over the kingside lines and the initiative. He reduced White's hopes to rubble with a few finishing strokes: *20. B–K3 B–B5! 21. Q–K2 Q–B3 22. K–R1 Q–N4 23. B–N1 B–B8!! 24. BxN NxB*, and *White Resigned* in face of the . . . N–B5 threat.

Now consider a material imbalance arising out of a countersacrifice. A simple case is *1. P–K4 P–K3 2. P–Q4 P–Q4 3. N–QB3 N–KB3 4. B–KN5 B–K2 5. P–K5 KN–Q2 6. BxB QxB 7. Q–N4 0–0 8. N–B3 P–QB4 9. B–Q3 PxP 10. BxPch KxB 11. Q–R5ch K–N1 12. N–KN5*, and now the only way to prevent mate, *12. . . . QxN!*, turns out to be perfectly O.K. after *13. QxQ PxN*. Black has three minor pieces and excellent prospects along the

QB-file and against the KP. White's attack is over, and once the Black pieces are coordinated, White will be on the defensive.

Countersacrifices are among the most challenging chess themes that develop. And among the most exciting. To cite a few examples:

(1) Robatsch-Tal, Leipzig 1960: *1. P–K4 P–QB4 2. N–KB3 P–Q3 3. P–Q4 PxP 4. NxP N–KB3 5. N–QB3 P–QR3 6. B–QB4 P–K3 7. P–QR3 B–K2 8. B–R2 0–0 9. 0–0 P–QN4 10. P–B4 QN–Q2 11. R–B3! B–N2 12. R–R3 R–B1 13. B–K3 Q–B2.* White has a potent attack here beginning with *14. NxKP! PxN 15. BxPch K–R1 16. B–Q4 B–Q1* and, in fact, missed a very strong 17. B–KB5!. The strength of White's opening assault, by the way, is such that in subsequent games Black deferred castling until he had gained a considerable leverage on the queenside. White was then not as well prepared to open up the center as he was in this game to open up the kingside.

The game continued *17. Q–K2? Q–B3 18. K–R1 B–N3 19. KBxN!*, and Black could not preserve his extra piece because 19. . . . NxB loses to 20. Q–R5. But Tal uncovered an ingenious countersacrifice—*19. . . . QxB 20. BxB R–B5! 21. P–QN3 QxR!! 22. PxQ RxN 23. K–N1 BxKP,* which not only beat off the White attack but nearly won for Black. A draw was the fair result.

(2) Pachman-Fischer, Bled 1961: *1. P–QB4 N–KB3 2. N–KB3 P–KN3 3. P–KN3 B–N2 4. B–N2 0–0 5. 0–0 P–Q3 6. N–B3 N–B3 7. P–Q4 P–K4 8. PxP PxP 9. N–Q5 B–K3 10. N–N5 B–B4 11. P–KR3 P–KR3 12. P–KN4?! B–B1! 13. NxNch QxN 14. N–K4 Q–R5 15. N–B3 P–KB4 16. N–Q5 PxP!?.* Black is justified in his decision to offer the queen rook because of the porous White kingside. Fischer missed better chances in the ensuing play, but even after *17. NxP PxP 18. B–Q5ch K–R2 19. NxR N–K2? 20. B–K3 P–R7ch 21. K–R1 B–R6* it appeared that Black was winning.

Pachman rose to the occasion by thwarting the threats of . . . N–B4xB and . . . P–K5 with a fine countersacrifice: *22.*

N–B7! N–B4 23. N–K6! R–B3 24. NxB NxB 25. PxN! RxRch 26. QxR BxQ 27. RxB, and after *27. . . . . KxN* White gave perpetual check along the KB-file.

(3) Geller-Euwe, 1953 Candidates Tournament: *1. P–Q4 N–KB3 2. P–QB4 P–K3 3. N–QB3 B–N5 4. P–K3 P–B4 5. P–QR3 BxNch 6. PxB P–QN3 7. B–Q3 B–N2 8. P–B3 N–B3 9. N–K2 0–0 10. 0–0 N–QR4 11. P–K4 N–K1! 12. N–N3 PxP 13. PxP R–B1 14. P–B4! NxP 15. P–B5 P–B3!* (to stop P–B6 and to keep the Q3–KR7 line closed) *16. R–B4? P–QN4! 17. R–R4 Q–N3 18. P–K5! NxKP 19. PxP NxB 20. QxN QxP! 21. QxPch K–B2 22. B–R6.*

White's attack should not be underestimated. The counter-sacrifice chosen by Euwe had great effect because it threw White off balance psychologically. He had to turn from attack to defense and immediately missed his best chance. The game continued *22. . . . . R–KR1!! 23. QxR R–B7! 24. R–QB1?? RxPch 25. K–B1 Q–N6! 26. K–K1 Q–B6 27. Resigns.*

How should White defend the final attack? The indicated idea to stop immediate mate is *24. P–Q5!!*, which forces Black to capture on Q5 with one of two pieces. If the bishop takes, the queen cannot easily penetrate to QN6. If the queen takes on Q4, White can block the long diagonal with N or R–K4.

These examples should indicate the breadth of countersack possibilities—sometimes to avert mate, sometimes to secure perpetual check, sometimes to begin one's own mating attack.

PAWN SACRIFICES

When the attacker is not going for the immediate kill but is instead hedging his bets by sacking only a pawn or a similar material minimum, a new set of attitudes is required by the defender. True, he still wants to exchange material, neutralize dangerous pieces and contest the initiative. But countersacrifice doesn't always succeed because of the minimal nature of the original sack. All endings aren't automatically won.

The speculative sacrifice of a pawn for kingside attack

is a typical case and a good starting place. An important lesson to learn is that time is not the absolute virtue it was once thought. Nineteen-century theory taught that gambits were sound because a pawn was worth a few extra tempi for development. But today we know that such gambits as the Poisoned Pawn variation of the Sicilian (1. P–K4 P–QB4 2. N–KB3 P–Q3 3. P–Q4 PxP 4. NxP N–KB3 5. N–QB3 P–QR3 6. B–KN5 P–K3 7. P–B4 Q–N3 8. Q–Q2 QxP) are quite playable for Black although he is far behind in development.

More important in the defender's list of priorities are the care and repair of weaknesses and the coordination of pieces. The defender can be very patient in bringing his pieces out. (Page Zhdanov!)

Consider Black's pawn-grabbing in Brinckmann-Nimzovich, Berlin 1927: *1. P–K4 N–QB3 2. P–Q4 P–Q4 3. PxP QxP 4. B–K3 P–K3 5. B–K2!? QxNP! 6. B–B3 Q–N3 7. N–K2.* There are many ideas of defense that suggest themselves, mainly beginning the development of new pieces. After all Black is fighting only with queen and knight so far.

White seems to have excellent compensation in terms of time and space, and it appears he can increase both elements by continuing to attack the Black Q. Then, when he is castled queenside he can try to smash open the center with P–Q5.

However, Black takes time to ease his queenside problems

with 7. . . . *N–N5!* 8. *N–R3 N–Q4.* Temporarily the P–Q5 possibility is shelved, the QN is performing real services rather than mere sentry duty on QB3, and Black has shortened the long white-square diagonal of the enemy KB.

Subsequent analysis showed that the best White could hope for was 9. N–N5! P–QB3 10. N–B4! NxN 11. N–B7ch K–Q2 12. NxR, after which 12. . . . N–N7ch leads to double-edged play in a position of approximate material balance. In the game cited White preferred to conserve his edge in development with *9. N–QB4,* but after 9. . . . *Q–B3! 10. N–N3 Q–Q1* Black had ended the misplacement of his pieces without danger. Then, and only then, was Nimzovich ready to develop, and he did it smoothly after *11. Q–Q2 KN–B3 12. N–K5 P–B3 13. 0–0!? B–Q3.* Black won in 35 moves.

Taking time for the important things is a vital consideration. In a 1960 Russian game (Byvshev-Lyavdansky) White offers an odd gambit: *1. P–K4 P–QB4 2. N–KB3 N–KB3 3. P–K5 N–Q4 4. N–B3 P–K3 5. N–K4 N–QB3 6. P–B4 KN–N5 7. P–QR3 N–R3 8. P–Q4 Q–R4ch! 9. P–QN4!? PxP 10. P–B5,* and after *10. . . . PxPch 11. B–Q2 N(R)–N5 12. B–K2* he has some compensation because of his stranglehold of a few center squares. The temptation for Black is to take the money and run, that is, for him to play . . . Q–Q1, ... N–Q4 followed by . . . B–K2 and castling.

The return to simple development has its virtues but that would leave White's central grip unchallenged. It would also put the Black king in a position to be attacked. Of course, eventually Black will castle kingside but there is no rush to provide White with a target. Instead of that Black sought to loosen the grip: *12. . . . P–QN3!*. (13. N–Q6ch BxN 14. BPxB Q–Q4 with the intent of following with . . . B–N2 and perhaps . . . P–QR4 eases Black's task.) If White had given the knight check he would have relaxed his pawn center's hold and Black could have ignored central play. For this reason he went for broke with a second pawn sacrifice: *13. 0–0 PxP 14. PxP BxP 15. Q–B1 B–K2 16. RxP Q–Q1 17. N(4)–N5.*

Again Black was tempted to continue routinely with 17. . . .

P–KR3 and 18. . . . 0–0, but that only encourages 19. BxRP, the kind of sacrificial chance that White has been playing for. Black correctly took time to put his queenside in order: *17. . . . R–QN1 18. R–Q1 P–QR4 19. R–R4 P–R3 20. N–K4 B–N2 21. B–B3 N–Q4!*. Notice that White is denied easy targets to pound with his heavy pieces. This is what makes Black's queenside action possible.

The third stage begins with White's desperate *22. RxN!? PxR 23. N–Q6ch BxN 24. PxB*. And again in a postsacrifice situation Black is tempted into natural developing moves such as 24. . . . 0–0. But again that would be playing into White's hands after 25. R–KN4 P–B3 26. QxP R–B2 27. B–Q3!.

Black calmly broke up the danger with *24. . . . P–Q5! 25. NxP NxN 26. RxN Q–N4! 27. Q–B1 P–R4!*, the last two moves stopping R–N4. Only then did he consolidate after *28. P–R4 Q–QB4 29. Q–R1* with 29. . . . 00–!. Castling on the 29th move isn't a record. The Soviet Yearbook recalls Yates-Alekhine, San Remo 1930, when the world champion resisted the urge until the 36th move. But this was not necessary in this game as it ended simply: *30. R–Q1 KR–K1 31. B–KB1 R–K3! 32. BxNP Q–B4 33. R–Q3 B–B3 34. R–KN3 R–KN3 35. RxR QxR 36. B–N2 R–N5 37. B–B3 R–N8 38. QxP QxP mate*.

Another fine example comes from the world championship match of 1963 and arose out of *1. P–Q4 P–Q4 2. P–QB4 PxP 3. N–KB3 N–KB3 4. P–K3 P–K3 5. BxP P–B4 6. 0–0 P–QR3 7. P–QR4 N–B3 8. Q–K2 B–K2 9. PxP BxP 10. P–K4! KN–N5* (to stop the dangerous attacking formation begun with 11. P–K5 and QN–Q2–K4) *11. P–K5 N–Q5 12. NxN QxN 13. N–R3!*.

White's last move involves a sacrifice of the KP which is very sharp and dangerous. The knight move serves two functions—protecting the KB and thus threatening 14. P–KR3 NxKP 15. R–Q1 and also threatening the direct 14. N–B2 to force Black's queen out of communication with its knight. The most important feature is that on the immediate capture of the pawn, 13. . . . NxKP 14. B–K3! Q–Q3 15. KR–Q1 Q–K2 16. BxB and 17. QR–B1, White has connected rooks and is ready to exert tremendous pressure on the queenside lines. It wasn't worth the risk, Tigran Petrosian concluded.

Therefore he played *13. . . . BxN 14. RxB NxKP*, which presented White with his biggest problem. As we well know, the most difficult tasks in the middlegame are not those of calculation but of choice. Botvinnik thought for 40 minutes as he rejected one by one the appealing but inexact alternatives: 15. R–Q1 Q–N5! (not 15. . . . QxB 16. QxN 0–0 17. B–R6 P–B3 18. Q–N3) 16. P–B3 Q–B4 or 16. Q–Q2 0–0.

White's selection of *15. P–QN3!* solved the problem of protecting the KB while creating the possibility of 16. B–N2. A new crisis looms for Black. Petrosian decided upon *15. . . . Q–B4!*, another fine defensive move, which anticipates B–N2 and readies himself for . . . NxB and . . . B–Q2, followed by queenside castling. He also had to consider 16. P–QN4!? QxB 17. QxN 0–0 18. R–QB3 and conclude that 18. . . . P–B3! would be solid and sound.

Botvinnik chose the trickier *16. R–R2!* so that on *16. . . . NxB*

17. PxN B–Q2 as played, he could continue *18. B–R3 Q–B4 19. R–Q2!*. The attack is just as hard to play in these positions as the defense, but White's accurate plan anticipates 19. . . . BxP 20. R–Q5 or 19. . . . 0–0–0 20. B–K7! QR–K1 21. B–Q6, with good chances to penetrate Black's defenses with heavy pieces.

Petrosian handled the next few moves very subtly. His king is trapped in the center. But even if he has to return his extra pawn to bring his king to safety, he stands better because of superior pawn structure in the ending. The immediate problem is the threat of R–Q5 and KR–Q1. The resolution was *19. . . . B–B3 20. R–K1 P–KR4! 21. Q–K3! P–B3!* (better than 21. . . . R–R3 or 21. . . . P–R5 because of 22. R–Q5! and Q–B5). White saw that Black was about to escape with . . . K–B2, which connects his rooks. Then Petrosian would have no problems protecting his black squares and would be able to challenge the queen file. Therefore, White played *22. QxKPch*, entering an inferior endgame. Excellent, precise and patient handling of a difficult gambit.

SPECULATIVE SACRIFICES: PIECES

Players don't just sacrifice pawns; they offer heavier wood. A speculative minor piece sack for one, two or three pawns is especially difficult for the defender because his opponent is getting something tangible in return for his offer. On many occasions we've seen a lesser master accept the knight sack of a Tal or an Alekhine, brave off the immediate threats and then discover to his horror that he is losing the ending because of the attacker's passed pawns.

It is nearly impossible in most modern opening variations to prevent a speculative piece sacrifice which grants the attacker a few pawns and the initiative. Too many possibilities exist. But most of them are unsound. The difficulty is that by "unsound" we mean a sack which will backfire *against proper defense*. Against second-best defense, the sacrifice may work brilliantly.

All right, your opponent has sacrificed a piece and you have
satisfied yourself through a bit of calculation that his immediate
threats are not terminal. (You are, of course, remembering to
look for his threats every move.) You should appreciate that
your opponent may have great flexibility in building long-range
threats. Therefore, your first priorities are to determine what
the most likely dangers of the near future are and to protect
your most vulnerable points for a long siege.

Case in point:

Tal-Keres, USSR 1959—*1. P–K4 P–QB3 2. P–Q4 P–Q4 3.
N–QB3 PxP 4. NxP B–B4 5. N–N3 B–N3 6. N–B3 N–Q2 7.
P–KR4 P–KR3 8. B–Q3 BxB 9. QxB KN–B3 10. B–B4 Q–R4ch
11. P–B3 P–K3 12. 0–0 B–K2 13. KR–K1 0–0 14. N–B5 KR–K1
15. NxP?!*

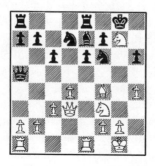

There's nothing to do but accept the sacrifice and await
events: *15. . . . KxN* and now *16. N–K5.* Here is Black's opportunity to appraise the position. Is there an immediate threat?
Yes, 17. Q–N3ch would hurt. Assuming that this can be anticipated, Black sees that he has picked up a knight in return
for a pawn. He may also lose another pawn, the KRP or KBP,
in the next few moves and still be materially superior. But it is
hard to conceive of how Black could give up a second pawn
without also granting White serious tactical chances.

Black no doubt considered *16. . . . NxN* but rejected it because the minuses outweigh the pluses. A dangerous attacking piece, the N, is eliminated, but Black gives up an equally good defensive piece and facilitates the entrance of another attacking piece (the rook or QB after 17. BxN or 17. RxN) to the kingside theater. And since 16. . . . N–B1 17. Q–K3! N–N1 18. Q–N3ch or 17. . . . P–R4 18. B–R6ch K–N1 19. Q–N5ch are unnecessarily unpleasant, Black played *16. . . . R–R1!*.

Although this leads to the disconnection of rooks, it is perfectly in keeping with our principle of economy. This one rook will be temporarily taken out of central play and used to defend both of the major kingside weaklings, the KBP and KRP. Then, with a rook on KR2 he would be ready to bring his QN to KB1 where it covers the K3 and KN3 squares. This arrangement covers all the weak spots in the armament.

The game continued *17. Q–R3* (with the threat of 18. NxKBP) *R–R2! 18. P–B4 N–B1 19. QR–Q1 R–Q1 20. B–Q2 Q–N3 21. B–B3 K–N1*, completing the defensive alignment. The next step was the ousting of the only really obnoxious piece: *22. R–K3 N–K1! 23. R–N3ch N–N2 24. QR–Q3 P–B3! 25. N–N6 NxN 26. RxN*, and following *26. . . . K–B2* there were only technical problems of consolidation to solve. Tal resigned on the 46th move as he ran out of steam.

Beyond the immediate threats lies the long-range danger of the attacker's just bringing more and more developed pieces to the scene of the kingside killing ground. The above game might have turned out differently if White didn't have so much difficulty getting his attack force together. The defense just had to build a secure house for his king and he could do that several moves before being threatened.

In another example, played in the world championship match of 1960, Tal made a similar sacrifice, this time for two pawns:

Tal–Botvinnik—*1. P–K4 P–QB3 2. P–Q4 P–Q4 3. N–QB3 PxP 4. NxP B–B4 5. N–N3 B–N3 6. KN–K2 N–B3 7. P–KR4 P–KR3 8. N–B4 B–R2 9. B–B4 P–K3 10. 0–0 B–Q3 11. NxKP!? PxN 12. BxP*

What was going on through the two players' minds indicates something of the different approaches of instinctive attackers and defenders. The lightning-quick calculator Tal was analyzing complex variations such as 12. . . . . BxN 13. PxB B–N1 (to cover K3) 14. Q–K1! Q–K2 15. B–B8! and determining that he had excellent chances. The sober incumbent champion Botvinnik didn't focus on forcing lines. Instead, he concentrated on variations in which he got his pieces into coordination and his king to a "house." For example, he looked at . . . QN–Q2 and . . . Q–B2 followed by . . . K–B1 and . . . R–K1.

Actually Botvinnik's instincts were correct although his sequence was wrong. Besides 12. . . . . Q–B2 13. R–K1 QN–Q2 as played, White could have solidified the position of his good bishop with 13. N–R5 K–B1 14. P–KB4! and P–B5. But 12. . . . . QN–Q2, the more exact move, would transpose into the game line after *13. R–K1 Q–B2!*. Now it appears that what Botvinnik had chosen to calculate were the possible discovered checks in this position. White doesn't have a strong discovery, surprisingly enough, and Tal settled for *14. B–N8ch K–B1 15. BxB RxB 16. N–B5.*

This new situation shows that Botvinnik has weathered the first wave of attack and now must anticipate the introduction of White's second string of forces, his QR and Q for example. Black hit upon a constructive sacrifice of the third pawn after concluding that his most important goal, besides a protected king "house," is the communication of his pieces. He accomplished this with *16. . . . P–KN3! 17. BxPch K–N1 18. NxB QxN 19. B–N5 R–K2.*

For the cost of the KRP, Black's KR emerges from isolation and Black is in a position to seize the most valuable open line, the K-file. The most effective White piece, his KN, is knocked off KB5. And the Black king reaches safety at KN2. Botvinnik's position was ideally suited for a fighting middlegame (although Tal chose an inferior ending with *20. Q–Q3 K–N2 21. Q–KN3?*). Black's victory came in a long knight-vs.-pawns ending in which Botvinnik always had the winning chances.

A third example shows the importance of countering the opponent's middlegame threats before they occur. It begins with a bishop-for-two-pawns sacrifice played in Lombardy-Keres, Mar del Plata 1957:

> *1. P–Q4 N–KB3 2. P–QB4 P–K3 3. N–QB3 B–N5 4. P–K3 P–QN3 5. N–K2 B–R3 6. P–QR3 B–K2 7. N–B4 P–Q4 8. PxP BxB 9. PxP!? B–R3 10. PxPch KxP*

Black must recapture the pawn because otherwise White's knight and queen have too many opportunities (10. . . . K–B1? 11. N–K6ch). That leaves White with two pawns—and a tough choice of how to continue the initiative. For example, he could win a third pawn by forking two targets with 11. Q–N3ch K–K1 12. N–K6. However, this would enable Black to consolidate more easily after 12. . . . Q–Q2 13. NxPch K–Q1 and . . . K–B1 Black has excellent chances then of wresting the initiative from a less-developed White. A postal game, Czerniakow-Batik 1955–56, went 14. N–K6ch K–B1 15. B–Q2 N–B3! 16. N–B4 N–QR4 17. Q–B2 Q–B3 and later won.

Lombardy chose *11 P–K4!* with the strong plan of using his wedge of central pawns to prepare the way for his pieces. If he can play P–K5 and Q–N3ch, Black is in trouble. White could also simply fortify his center with B–K3 and QR–Q1 or KR–K1 before Black gets a chance to consolidate with . . . R–KB1 and . . . K–N1.

Keres's comment is very perceptive here. He points out that Black must put immediate pressure on the White pawns because otherwise the enemy center would outweigh a relatively small amount of sacrificed material. Therefore, Black played *11. . . . P–B4!*.

The first point is that 12. P–K5 can be met by 12. . . . QxP!, returning material for advantage. The second is that 12. P–Q5 QN–Q2 13. P–Q6 B–KB1 or 13. N–K6 Q–QN1 14. P–B4 R–K1 leads to positions in which White can make only apparent progress. Black is ready to sacrifice back his piece in return for two pawns and a positionally superior middlegame. Black's pieces can very easily become more active than White's in that case.

What followed was *12. B–K3 N–B3 13. Q–N3ch,* which forced *13. . . . P–B5* (otherwise 14. Q–R4 hurts). After *14. Q–Q1* White had made P–K5 a strong threat and had eased the assault on his center begun by 11. . . . P–B4.

But Keres now responded *14. . . . B–Q3!,* after which White could not avoid the countersacrifice of Black's extra piece because of the 15. . . . BxN threat. The game went: *15. P–K5 NxKP 16. PxN BxKP 17. KN–Q5 R–K1 18. NxN QxN,* and Black was already superior. He won a long endgame.

A final example of piece-versus-pawns raises a few questions about dealing with a mass of advancing enemy pawns. The ques-

tions are provoked by a variation of the Alekhine's Defense
and the stem-game of Vasiukov-Spassky, 26th USSR Championship in 1959:

1. P–K4 N–KB3 2. P–K5 N–Q4 3. P–QB4 N–N3 4. P–B5
N–Q4 5. B–B4 P–K3 6. N–QB3 P–Q3!? 7. NxN PxN 8. BxP
P–QB3! 9. BxKBPch! (otherwise Black has no problems after
9. B–N3 PxKP 10. Q–R5 Q–K2) KxB 10. BPxP

White's intentions are obviously to advance his pawns by way
of 0–0 and P–KB4–5 or some such arrangement. Black's object,
of course, is to stop them. But that is not easy, e.g., 10. . . .
B–K3 11. N–R3! followed by N–N5ch or N–B4. Black's task is
to meet White's threat in one of two ways (1) by tactically
diverting White's attention and keeping his hands full until Black
can return the piece effectively or (2) by establishing an iron
blockade. The third method of meeting threats that we considered in Chapter Three, minimizing the effect, doesn't appear
possible.

Black's 10. . . . Q–K1! was a good beginning because it created
a pin on the K-file (threat of . . . BxP) and caused White some
tactical problems. On 11. Q–K2 Black can continue with 11. . . .
B–K3 and 12. . . . B–Q4 or with 11. . . . P–B4 12. N–B3 BxP!
(13. PxB QxQch and . . . R–K1ch is excellent for Black).

White found a finesse in 11. Q–B3ch K–N1 12. Q–K3, which

stops the countersacrifice and forces Black to concentrate on blockade. The game now continued *12. . . . B–K3 13. N–K2 N–Q2*, setting the stage for a critical decision.

Vasiukov decided in favor of *14. 0–0*, a natural move which, however, is met by a fine rejoinder: *14. . . . NxP! 15. QxN B–B5!* *16. QxQ RxQ*, and White fought his way into a drawn ending with *17. P–Q3 BxP(6) 18. R–Q1! BxN 19. P–Q7 R–Q1 20. B–N5! BxR* *21. RxB B–K2! 22. BxB K–B2 23. BxR RxB*.

A more difficult issue is what happens if White takes time to stop Black's threat with 14. P–Q4 or 14. P–B4. The former move is not adequate, we discover, because of 14. P–Q4 B–B5, and it is difficult to avoid a strong 15. . . . BxQP!. But 14. P–B4!? looks strong.

Again the choice is reduced to the two options of blockade and tactical counter. The tactical idea is 14. . . . Q–N3 15. 0–0 R–K1 or 15. . . . B–Q4. There are some good points to 15. . . . B–Q4, such as 16. N–N3 P–KR4 17. P–B5 Q–K1 18. P–Q4 P–R5 19. N–K2 BxQP! 20. PxB QxPch 21. BxQ R-K1 22. K–B2 R–R4, with excellent play as suggested by Soviet Grandmaster Kholmov. But it is not so advantageous for Black after 18. P–K6! BxQP 19. PxN QxP 20. P–Q3! R–K1 21. N–K4.

On the line 14. . . . Q–N3 15. 0–0 R–K1 there are great complications following 16. N–N3 BxQP 17. P–B5 (17. PxB B–B5!) BxBP 18. NxB B–B4 19. P–Q4 or 16. N–N3 B–Q4 17. P–B5 Q–N5 18. P–K6 N–B3 19. P–K7 BxKP 20. PxB K–B2, and the defender is justified in looking for a simpler way of surviving into the ending.

The answer to his question is the blockade: 14. . . . P–KN3! 15. 0–0 B–N2 16. P–Q4 N–N3 17. N–B3 N–Q4! 18. NxN BxN 19. B–Q2 Q–K3 20. P–QR4 P–KR4 and 21. . . . K–R2 as played in a later Russian game.

Before we turn to other issues under the heading of sacrifice and the gain of material, we should recall another Tartakoverism: "It is wisest to sacrifice your opponent's pieces."

CHAPTER SIX:

Further Questions About Material

As usual, the connotation of certain words and phrases dealing with the gain and loss of material is shaded in favor of the attacker. "Sacrifice" suggests risk, daring and excitement. But "Pawn-grabbing" suggests foolhardiness, greed and waste of time. Subconsciously we all root for the sacrificer and disdain the player who, with just as much courage, lunges out to capture enemy material and then carefully fends off the threats.

Even Nimzovich, the champion of Heroic Defense says early on in *My System*, "Never play to win a Pawn while your development is yet unfinished!" True, he left open one loophole, "A center Pawn should always be taken if this can be done without too great danger." Today we know that even by capturing the opponent's QNP with our queen—a practice proscribed in virtually every primer—the defender may live happily ever after (or at least into the endgame).

In his day Steinitz was quite content to argue his judgments about acceptable risk-taking over the board. He lost a number of games with his own patented negative-gambits such as 1. P–K4 P–K4 2. N–KB3 N–QB3 3. P–Q4 PxP 4. NxP Q–R5! (5. N–N5 QxKPch or 5. . . . B–N5ch first and a subsequent . . . K–Q1 to cover QB2). But the strength of his ideas is now widely agreed upon by modern analysts.

There is no clear rule-of-thumb to guide a player who is undecided on whether to go pawn-hunting. It is another matter of "judgment," that ill-defined gray area of chess knowledge that seems to be acquired only through experience. We can suggest, however, that it is better to take a pawn when you can get an inferior game by refusal or when you can beat off the immediate threats of the other side very easily. It is even wise to provoke a sacrifice when the alternative to provocation is humble submission to attack.

That was the case in Mora-Taimanov, Lyons 1955, which began:

1. P–K4 P–K4 2. N–KB3 N–QB3 3. B–N5 P–QR3 4. B–R4 P–QN4 5. B–N3 N–R4 6. NxP NxB 7. RPxN Q–K2 8. P–Q4 P–Q3 9. N–KB3 QxPch 10. B–K3 B–N2 11. Q–K2 B–K2 12. N–B3 Q–N5 13. R–KN1 N–B3 14. 0–0–0 0–0? (14. . . . P–N5! 15. N–R2 N–Q4) 15. P–Q5! KR–K1 16. R–Q4 Q–B1 17. Q–Q3! R–N1 18. N–K4 P–QR4 19. B–N5 NxN 20. RxN B–B1 21. R–KR4

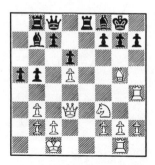

Two decisions have to be made by Black. First, how bad is 21. . . . P–N3? The answer is, pretty bad since Black will have to take extreme measures to stop 22. P–KN4 and R–N3–R3 or 22. B–B6 and N–N5. The second decision concerns the consequences of 21. . . . P–R3 22. BxP. Taimanov determined that he could live with the sacrifice and that it would be better to be attacked and have an extra piece than be attacked and have nothing.

The moves *21. . . . P–R3* and *22. BxP PxB* were played but then White erred with 23. *N–N5?*, an attractive move but one that allows Black to run to safety with his material edge. Play continued 23. . . . *B–N2 24. RxP Q–Q2! 25. Q–R7ch* (25. R–R8ch BxR 26. Q–R7ch K–B1 27. QxBch K–K2 28. Q–R4 K–Q1!! wins because the double check is not decisive) *K–B1 26. N–K6ch PxN 27. R–B6ch BxR* (now 27. . . . K–K2 28. QxBch K–Q1 is a different story after 29. R–B7 R–K2 30. Q–N8ch) *28. QxQ BxP 29. QxBP KR–Q1 30. K–N1 P–R5!*, and Black had a winning queenside mating attack on top of his material superiority.

What would have happened on the stronger 23. P–KN4!, one might ask? The threat of P–N5 could be met by 23. . . . . BxP! 24. QxB Q–K3 25. Q–Q2 Q–K7, forcing queens off the board. Taimanov's decision was obviously the correct one.

The virtue of provocation is also apparent when the defender can realize a positional improvement—Rubinstein-Levenfisch, Karlsbad 1911:

1. P–Q4 P–K3 2. P–K4 P–Q4 3. N–QB3 N–KB3 4. B–KN5 B–K2 5. P–K5 KN–Q2 6. BxB QxB 7. Q–Q2 0–0 8. P–B4 P–QB4 9. N–B3 P–B3 10. KPxP QxP?! 11. P–KN3 N–B3 12. 0–0–0 P–QR3 13. B–N2 N–N3 14. KR–K1 N–B5 15. Q–B2 P–QN4

It is not simple for White to proceed in the middlegame because of Black's queenside demonstration. White would like to pile up his heavy pieces against the weak KP and assault it with B–KR3 and N–KN5 at some time in the future. But to do that he would have to ease the tension on his Q4 square. The obvious idea is 16. PxP but that walks into 16. . . . NxP (not 16. . . . P–N5 17. N–QR4) 17. KxN P–N5, regaining the piece after having opened up the White king position.

But Rubinstein had better judgment and he played *16. PxP!* provoking *16. . . . NxP 17. KxN P–N5 18. N–Q4!,* and after *18. . . . PxNch* he played *19. K–R1!.* The result of the last few moves is that White's problem on Q4 is over and his king position is quite secure. Without that Black pawn on QB3, a pawn that can be captured in any ending, Black would be better off because then he has a pin against the king along the long diagonal. As it is, Black has virtually no attack. His position crumbled after *19. . . . NxN 20. QxN R–N1 21. R–K3 P–N4 22. RxBP! PxP 23. PxP B–Q2 24. P–B6 QxQ 25. RxQ B–K1 26. B–R3 R–B3 27. P–B7 R–QB1 28. RxP! RxQBP 29. BxPch Resigns.* Provocation plus countersacrifice plus judgment equals positional advantage.

And once again, it is better to accept a pawn sacrifice when its refusal would mean a relatively more dangerous position than would arrive through acceptance. A case in point is a Smyslov-Botvinnik game from their 1954 championship match:

1. P–K4 P–QB4 2. N–QB3 N–QB3 3. P–KN3 P–KN3 4. B–N2 B–N2 5. P–Q3 P–N3 6. KN–K2 P–Q3 7. 0–0 B–N2 8. P–B4 P–B4! 9. P–KN4?!

Black's last move grabs an additional share of the center and blocks P–KB5. To force that breakthrough White has just offered a pawn. On 9. . . . PxNP he will continue 10. P–B5, followed by moving knights to Q5 and (hopefully) K6. There is no simple method of warding off these threats. Therefore, a critical choice has to be made.

Black's decision to accept the pawn may have been based on a thorough analysis of the tactical chances. But, considering Botvinnik's style, we could conclude that he played 9. . . . PxNP because on other moves White obtains too strong an attack, free: 9. . . . N–R3 10. P–N5 N–B2 11. PxP PxP 12. N–N3, followed by queen or knight to R5, or 9. . . . Q–Q2 10. NPxP PxP 11. N–N3, after which White must penetrate on some kingside squares.

After 9. . . . *PxNP 10. P–B5 Q–Q2 11. N–B4* (11. N–Q5 might have been more exact, although on 11. . . . N–Q5 Black is quite solid) Black found a strong method of countering White's plans for N–K6 and N–Q5. He played *11. . . . PxP 12. PxP B–Q5ch! 13. K–R1 BxN! 14. PxB N–K4.* The point of the 11th and 12th moves is that now the long diagonal of Black's QB leads to the White K. The point of the 13th move is to stop QN–Q5. The loss of the two bishops is relatively minor because neither of White's bishops functions particularly well in the resulting pawn formation.

White had nothing better than *15. Q–K2 N–KB3 16. BxB,* entering a terrible endgame (which he lost after *16. . . . QxBch 17. Q–N2 QxQch 18. KxQ P–B5!*) because neither 15. P–B4 BxBch 16. KxB Q–N2ch nor 15. Q–K2 N–B3 16. N–K6 B–B6 or 16. P–Q4 N–B6 was of any weight. Black won speedily.

THE JOY OF PAWN-GRABBING

It is surprising how often even the very best players are reluctant to take a tempo or two to capture a weak pawn. The excuse is usually, "I can always do that in the endgame," or "I didn't want to take my pieces away from my kingside," or some such.

In the great New York 1927 tournament book, Alexander Alekhine was dumbfounded when trying to explain this game:

Marshall-Vidmar: *1. P–K4 P–K4 2. N–KB3 N–QB3 3. N–B3 N–B3 4. B–N5 B–N5 5. 0–0 0–0 6. P–Q3 BxN 7. PxB P–Q3 8. B–N5 Q–K2 9. KBxN? PxB 10. R–N1 P–KR3 11. BxN QxB 12. Q–K2 Q–K3! 13. N–R4!? Q–B3? 14. N–B3 Q–K3 15. N–R4 Q–B3? 16. N–B3 Q–K3 Draw.*

Why in heaven's name, Alekhine asked, can't the QRP be taken by Black on move 13 or 15 (and, if the game had continued, surely on move 17, 19, 21, etc.)? He suggests *14. P–QB4* to block the retreat of Black's queen, but then *14. . . . Q–R4 15. P–B4 PxP 16. RxP Q–KN4* (*16. . . . P–N4 17. N–B5*) *17. QR–KB1 P–QR4!* is hardly enough compensation. Marshall had no answer and neither did Vidmar.

The decision of whether or not to grab an enemy pawn is one of the most common in chess. Sometimes we forget how often it occurs because we believe that in certain familiar positions such-and-such-a-pawn is usually poisoned and thus blot its capture out of our thoughts. Sometimes we reject a pawn capture because we automatically assume that because the opponent weakens our pawns—or bottles up a knight, or gains the two bishops, or plants a rook on the seventh rank, etc.—he *must* have compensation. That isn't always true. And furthermore, the inhibition against sweeping pawns off the board is not that the opponent has adequate compensation but that he has *more* than adequate compensation.

Bent Larsen has often been on both sides of the pawn-grabbing question and we cite his game with Smyslov (White) from the 1959 Moscow tournament:

1. P–K4 P–QB4 2. N–KB3 N–QB3 3. P–Q4 PxP 4. NxP P–K3 5. N–QB3 B–N5?! 6. N–N5 P–QR3? (6. . . . N–B3!) 7. N–Q6ch K–K2 8. B–KB4! N–B3 9. B–B4 Q–R4 10. 0–0 N–K4 11. NxBch? QRxN 12. B–QN3

Should Black grab a pawn with *12. . . . BxN 13. PxB QxBP?*
What are the evils that arise as a result? Well, White obtains two
good bishops in a position in which they can play a major role.
Black's king is in the center and when it is castled "by hand,"
it will leave the defense of Black's weakest pawn, the QP.

On the other hand, Black's heavy pieces occupy squares which
will control several important lines for the foreseeable future.
White will not be able to bring his queen into action easily,
for example, while Black's queen is on QB6.

Black took the pawn and then consolidated into a normal
middlegame position quickly: *14. R–K1 P–Q3 15. Q–K2 KR–Q1
16. QR–Q1 K–B1.* Note that 16. P–QR4 (to stop . . . P–QN4)
could be met by 16. . . . N–B3 and 17. . . . N–Q5. Black's problems
are not over, despite the new security of his king. White could
choose between doubling rooks against the QP—probably the
best idea—or the kingside attack involving P–KB4.

Smyslov chose the latter plan: *17. K–R1 P–QN4 18. B–N5
N–N3 19. B–Q2 Q–B2 20. P–B4 K–N1 21. R–KB1.* Black now
prepared for another of our defensive friends from Chapter
Two, the seizure of a foothold in the center. He played *21. . . .
Q–B3*, in order to meet 22. QR–K1 with 22. . . . P–Q4!.

White played *22. B–R5*, but on *22. . . . R–K1 23. R–Q4* Black
had another advance in the center: *23. . . . P–K4! 24. PxP PxP
25. R–N4 N–B5* followed by . . . N–K3–Q5 or –B4. Black had
a winning game (although he misplayed later and only drew).

Notice that White could have played more solidly to obtain compensation—doubling rooks on the Q-file—but Black's decision to take the pawn was correct in any event.

What makes the decision to go pawn-hunting so difficult is that there are usually other methods of securing good play but ones which involve less risk—and, naturally, less reward. To repeat an earlier comment, one of the hardest skills to acquire is the ability to make good choices among reasonable alternatives.

Here is a case from Bled 1961 between Udovcic and Bisguier:

1. P–QB4 N–KB3 2. P–KN3 P–K3 3. B–N2 P–Q4 4. N–KB3 B–K2 5. 0–0 0–0 6. P–N3 P–B4 7. PxP NxP 8. B–N2 N–QB3 9. N–R3 P–QN3 10. N–B4 B–N2 11. P–Q4 R–B1 12. P–K4 N–B3 13. P–K5 N–Q4 14. PxP BxP 15. KN–Q2!?

White's idea is N–K4, followed by occupying Q6 with a knight. Black would like to confuse the White pieces with 15. . . . P–QN4, but that permits 16. N–K4!. However, Black can play a solid defensive line with 15. . . . B–K2 16. N–K4 R–B2, so that on 17. N(K)–Q6 he can play 17. . . . B–R3, intending . . . P–QN4, and on 17. N(B)–Q6 he can play 17. . . . B–R3, intending . . . P–KB4!. Yet another idea is 15. . . . N(3)–K2 followed by 16. . . . N–B4, to cover his Q3 hole.

But there is another idea, *15. . . . B–R3 16. N–K4 N–R4!?*. This will force White into conceding a queenside pawn because he cannot get out of the pin on his QN. White can't avert the sack with 17. NxB because of 17. . . . BxN! 18. PxB NxP. But is this a good sacrifice to provoke? Here it must be part calculation and part judgment that is called into question. Bisguier went ahead and took the pawn.

In the game, White chose *17. R–B1 B–K2 18. Q–N4*, with the tactical idea of N–B6ch in hand. White also prepared to put a rook on Q1 and get out of the pin on his knight. At this point, Black could back off from grabbing a pawn but 18. . . . K–R1 19. N(K)–Q6 and 18. . . . NxN 19. PxN N–N5 20. KR–Q1 are not palatable.

Black played *18. . . . NxN! 19. PxN RxP 20. RxR BxR*, and now *21. N–B6ch K–R1* leaves Black remarkably secure. This position had to be foreseen and carefully evaluated before taking the pawn, but Black decided he would be quite safe. On 22. QxB PxN White can't try the obvious 23. R–Q1 because of 23. . . . N–K6! 24. RxQ NxQ and neither 23. PxP BxP 24. B–QR3 R–KN1 nor 23. BxN! QxB (23. . . . PxB 24. PxP! BxP 25. BxBch and 26. QxP is also playable) 24. QxQ PxQ 25. PxP B–B4 looks like an advantage for White. But the last possibility, at least, gives him a playable game.

White went too far with his expectations: *22. Q–R4? B–Q6! 23. R–Q1 B–N3* and was quickly lost: *24. Q–N5 (24. BxN PxB 25. RxP QxR) PxN 25. PxP B–B4 26. P–KR4 R–N1! 27. BxN B–B7! 28. Q–R6 RxPch 29. K–R2 R–N3 30. B–K4 B–Q3ch 31. B–K5 BxR*, at which point his flag mercifully fell.

When grabbing pawns the defender must remember that he is a . . . defender. That is, he should realize he has a material advantage and does not necessarily need counterplay. He can be content wth exchanges and liquidations. Too often the pawn-grabber acts as if he wants to equalize piece play and obtain just as much space as the attacker while still keeping his extra material. It rarely works out.

Take the situation when Black accepts the gambit pawn of the Alekhine-Chatard attack in the French Defense: *1. P–K4*

P–K3 2. P–Q4 P–Q4 3. N–QB3 N–KB3 4. B–KN5 B–K2 5. P–K5 KN–Q2 6. P–KR4!? BxB 7. PxB QxP!? 8. N–R3 Q–K2.

The gambit is almost always rejected these days although Black has excellent resources. On 9. Q–N4, for example, Black can hold the position with 9. . . . P–KB4! 10. Q–R5ch P–N3 11. Q–R6 N–B1 12. N–B4 P–QB3 (to stop sacrifices on Q4), and White must still prove the worth of his gambit.

The more natural move is 9. N–B4 after which 9. . . . P–QR3 is usually played to stop 10. N–N5. The novice pawn-grabber would play 9. . . . P–QB4? and be in trouble after 10. N–N5. Or he might try 9. . . . P–QR3 10. Q–N4 K–B1 11. Q–B3! K–N1 12. B–Q3 P–QB4? (losing to 13. BxPch! RxB 14. RxR KxR 15. 0–0–0!, with a violent attack on the KR-file), similarly thinking that Black should *always* play the attack on the base of the White pawn chain.

But when Black has an extra pawn he can play more conservatively. Even 9. . . . P–KN3!? comes into consideration, e.g., 10. B–Q3 N–B1 11. Q–Q2 Q–N4!, tying up a few pieces, or 10. Q–N4 N–QB3 11. 0–0–0 N–N3, followed by . . . B–Q2 and . . . 0–0–0. Static pawn weaknesses are worth a pawn.

Even in the main lines of the analysts, 9. N–B4 P–QR3 10. Q–N4, Black has a solid game with 10. . . . P–KN3 11. 0–0–0 N–N3 12. B–Q3 QN–Q2 13. R–R6 (13. BxNP BPxB 14. NxNP R–KN1) N–B1 14. QR–R1 B–Q2 or 11. Q–N3 N–N3, but not after 11. Q–N3 P–QB4? 12. QNxP! with a winning attack).

Black has a secure middlegame in these lines as long as he stops the sacrificial ideas on his Q4 and KN3. But the pawn-grabber does not need immediate counterplay (. . . P–QB4) in addition to material.

HOW MUCH IS ENOUGH?

When the sacrificer's initiative begins to run out of steam he can do either of two things—batten down the hatches and try to save the endgame or continue the attack with additional sacrificial fuel. In the latter case, it doesn't matter how many pawns you are behind if all endgames are lost anyway.

That poses a new puzzle for the defense. Now that the game is going your way you want to make sure that you have enough material to win with. But if there is another pawn available to make completely certain . . . ? You don't want the attack to be revived but then you don't want a mere draw after what you've gone through. A similar puzzle involves countersacrifice. How much material do you need to have the winning chances in the ending, and how much must you return to avoid mate?

A dramatic example of this occurred in a turn-of-the-century game between those American rivals, Pillsbury and Marshall:

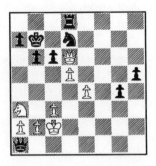

After an up-and-down middlegame Black (Pillsbury) is a rook ahead. He could have consolidated better but here he is on the verge of a decisive simplification. The main thorn in his queenside is the threat of PxPch, e.g., 31. . . . PxP 32. QxPch or 32. N–N5.

Pillsbury, unfortunately, tried to hold onto the bulk of his material and played *31. . . . R–KB1??*. After *32. PxPch K–R1 33. PxN* it was his turn to attack and he did with *33. . . . R–B7ch 34. K–N3 QxNPch 35. K–R4*. But suddenly *Black resigned* because on *35. . . . P–N4ch 36. K–R5 QxPch 37. K–R6*, he has run out of checks and is about to be mated himself.

In his notes, Marshall quotes the analysis of a Viennese amateur: 31. . . . N–B4!! 32. QxR (or 32. QxPch K–N1 33. N–N5 R–QB1) Q–B8!! 33. PxPch KxP, and now Black will win despite material equality because of his advanced kingside pawns. For example, 34. Q–Q5ch K–B2 35. Q–K5ch K–N2 evades the perpetual check, or 34. N–N1 P–N6 35. N–Q2 (35. Q–Q5ch K–B2 36. Q–K5ch K–N2 37. QxNP loses to 37. . . . Q–K7ch 38. N–Q2 QxNch!) 35. . . . P–N7 36. Q–B8ch K–N4 ditto.

The irony of Black's losing when he preserves a big material edge but winning in an equal-material ending is not lost on the grandmasters. They know that you don't need more than a certain amount to win a position and that anything more is superfluous.

In the following position, from Unzicker-Bronstein, Göteborg 1955, Black has his choice between simplification or taking more material:

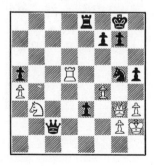

Black could play 38. . . . QxN 39. RxN Q–N7, which is good enough to win the king-and-pawn endings after either 40. RxQRP Q–KB7! 41. R–K5 RxR 42. PxR P–R5! or 40 R–K5 RxR 41. PxR Q–KB7! 42. P–R4 P–N3 43. K–R3 K–B1. Perhaps because of shortness of time Bronstein did not choose this direct but somewhat unclear simplifying line.

Instead, he made the appealing pawn promotion: *38. . . . P–K7 39. RxN P–K8(Q).* White had one last throw, *40. RxPch K–R1 41. Q–N5,* with threats of 42. Q–R6 mate or 42. RxP and 43. Q–N7 mate. If Black hadn't foreseen this, it would have been very disturbing because there is no simple method of beating off White's desperate bid. But Bronstein hadn't forgotten how much material he needed to win, and he played *41. . . . QxPch! 42. QxQ* (42. KxQ R–K7ch mates) *R–K7* and *White Resigned* because the Black K escapes rook checks by moving to KR3.

We've already said that the decision to start taking pawns and other material is a complicated one. Equally complicated is deciding when to stop. Witness Gipslis-Korchnoi, Semifinals 25th USSR Championship 1958:

1. P–K4 P–QB4 2. N–KB3 P–Q3 3. P–Q4 PxP 4. NxP N–KB3 5. N–QB3 P–QR3 6. B–KN5 P–K3 7. P–B4 P–R3 8. B–R4 Q–N3 9. Q–Q2 QxP 10. N–N3 Q–R6 11. B–Q3 B–K2 12. 0–0 NxKP! (so far this is the 7th game of the 1972 Spassky-Fischer match) *13. BxN! BxB 14. P–B5*

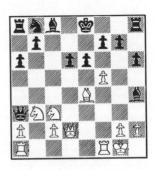

White's recapture on K4 with a bishop instead of a knight has its points, e.g., 14. . . . P–K4 15. N–Q5 B–Q1 16. P–B6, or 14. . . . 0–0 15. P–B6 BxP 16. RxB! or 14. . . . P–Q4 15. PxP!? PxB 16. Q–B4 B–B3 17. N–Q5. Korchnoi finds a satisfactory response in *14. . . . Q–N5!*, tying White to his QN and protecting Black's QN2 so that he can move his own QB.

White proceeded with *15. PxP BxP 16. N–Q4,* but was further confused by *16. . . . B–N4!*, which stops 17. Q–B2 QxQN 18. NxB by way of 18. . . . B–K6. Gipslis forged on with *17. Q–Q3 B–QB5 18. Q–R3.* Now what does Black do?

Before taking the Exchange at KB1 he should consider the serious consequences of 19. Q–B8ch. If that isn't pleasant for him, he should play the simple 18. . . . 0–0!, which brings his king to safety and threatens to play 19. . . . BxR without danger. On 18. . . . 0–0 Black would have an easy game after 19. QR–N1 Q–B4 or 19. Q–B5 P–KN3. The most serious line is 19. R–B5, threatening RxB, but then 19. . . . Q–N3! (threatening . . . QxNch and . . . B–K3) is strong, e.g., 20. RxB QxNch 21. K–R1 R–K1! 22. R–Q1 Q–B3 (or 22. . . . RxB).

This would have been the sound policy. Korchnoi apparently overlooked *20. N–K6!* after he played *18. . . . BxR? 19. Q–B8ch B–Q1.* The knight is immune because of the variation 20. . . . PxN 21. QxPch B–K2 22. Q–B8ch B–Q1 23. B–N6ch. Although in the actual game Black consolidated skillfully with *20. . . . Q–N3ch 21. KxB N–B3! 22. NxPch K–B1 23. QxR KxN 24. R–QN1 Q–Q5,* White could have made things very complex with 21. K–R1! which preserves the KB-file. (In this line, note that 21. K–R1 N–B3 22. NxPch K–B1 23. N–K6ch PxN 24. RxBch K–N2 25. QxR? B–B3! loses but 25. Q–Q7ch! and 26. QxKP wins.)

CONSOLIDATION AND VIGILANCE

Once the initial sacrificial crisis is over, the defender's task changes. He is no longer concerned primarily with beating off the attack but rather with consolidating his material advantage and coordinating his pieces. His greatest danger is overconfidence

—letting up after being under considerable pressure for several moves.

Young players are especially prone to blunders after weathering an attack well. Twenty-two-year-old Alexander Alekhine proved himself to be one of the strongest players in the world at the great St. Petersburg tournament of 1914, but that same year in the same city he lost this fiasco to another rising star:

Alekhine-Bogolyubov, Russian Championship 1914: 1. P–K4 P–K4 2. N–KB3 N–QB3 3. B–N5 B–B4 4. P–B3 KN–K2 5. P–Q4 PxP 6. PxP B–N5ch 7. B–Q2 BxBch 8. QxB P–QR3 9. B–R4 P–Q4 10. PxP QxP 11. N–B3 Q–K3ch 12. K–B1! Q–B5ch 13. K–N1 0–0 14. P–Q5 R–Q1? (14. . . . N–R2) 15. Q–K1! B–N5 16. B–N3 Q–B5 17. PxN BxN 18. QxN BxBP, and now White should win easily with his extra piece. The simplest consolidating idea is N–K2–N3. But White played 19. P–KR4? R–Q7 20. R–KB1?? and lost to 20. . . . R–K1! 21. Q–N5 RxBP! 22. BxPch K–R1! 23. R–Q1 QxB 24. R–Q2 P–R3 25. RxR R–K8ch 26. K–R2 QxR 27. Q–N4 BxP White Resigns.

A mature grandmaster can be psychologically defeated as well, as in the curious Tal-Geller game from the 25th USSR Championship. After a spectacular Exchange sacrifice this position resulted:

White's 25. BxN was met by 25. . . . PxB??, which lost to 26. R–K7 since 26. . . . QxR is met by a queen check on KN4. What happened to Geller? He explained:

"After my opponent's adventurous, to me, twelfth move I considered myself obliged to punish him. . . . Now I remained the Exchange ahead, the direct threats to my king had been repulsed and I considered victory to be near. A simple analysis of the natural 25. . . . QxB showed that I couldn't hope to win after that. But I must have a win. . . . My opponent's 'incorrect' play simply demanded punishment and since 25. . . . QxB didn't win then I made the other without a second's thought."

When consolidating, the defender must first establish to his own satisfaction that his position is well protected against threats. Then he thinks about maximizing the activity of his pieces. His most important ally is the threat of exchanging material into a winning ending.

A good example of this was the Botvinnik-Stein game played in the Soviet team championship of 1964. Stein played a speculative sacrifice of his queen for rook and bishop:

1. P–QB4 P–KN3 2. N–QB3 B–N2 3. P–Q4 N–KB3 4. P–K4 0–0 5. B–K3 P–Q3 6. P–B3 P–N3 7. B–Q3 B–N2 8. KN–K2 P–B4 9. 0–0 N–B3 10. B–QB2?! P–K4! 11. PxKP PxP 12. B–N5 P–KR3 13. B–KR4 N–Q5 14. N–Q5 NxN?! 15. BxQ N–K6 16. Q–Q3 QRxB (16. . . . QNxB 17. B–R4) 17. QxN(3) NxB 18. Q–B3 NxR 19. RxN B–R3

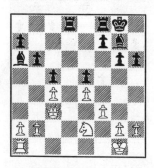

White's *20. Q–B2!* was an important step in activating his pieces, chiefly his knight, which can now get to Q5 via QB3.

White noted that 20. . . . P–QN4 21. N–B3 PxP 22. Q–R4 made things easy. The game proceeded: *20. . . . P–R4 21. Q–R4 R–Q7 22. N–B3 B–B1*, and now *23. R–Q1!* gave Black the choice of trading rooks or surrendering the Q-file.

After 23. . . . *RxP 24. N–Q5* Black had sufficient compensation for his queen in a material sense. But his pieces simply were no match for White's. White, in fact, threatened to win a rook with 25. Q–R3 R–QB7 26. Q–N3 R–K7 27. K–B1. Black made a brave attempt with *24. . . . B–K3!*, hoping for 25. Q–R3 BxN 26. QxR BxBP.

But White gave no second chance: *25. QxP! BxN 26. KPxB P–QN4 27. P–Q6! PxP 28. P–Q7 P–B6 29. QxP! P–B7 30. R–QB1 R–Q1 31. RxP B–B1 32. Q–B8 R(7)–N1 33. QxQR! Resigns.*

Simplification must help the defender and that is why the consolidation process can run so smoothly. By constantly offering exchanges the defender drives the attacking pieces further and further back. A case in point:

Tal-Bhend, Zurich 1959—*1. P–Q4 P–QB4 2. P–Q5 P–Q3 3. P–K4 P–KN3 4. N–KB3 B–N2 5. B–K2 N–QR3 6. 0–0 N–B2 7. N–B3 P–B4!? 8. B–Q3 PxP 9. NxP N–KR3 10. B–KB4 0–0 11. Q–Q2 N–B2 12. P–B4 P–QN4 13. QR–K1 R–N1 14. P–QN3 P–K3 15. KN–N5 NxN 16. BxN Q–Q2 17. N–B3 P–N5 18. PxP NxP 19. N–Q5 B–N2 20. B–K4 NxB 21. QxN K–R1*

Tal played 22. *BxP?!* with the idea of 22. . . . PxB 23. N–K7 and strong threats of NxPch and Q–R4ch. On Black's 22. . . .

BxN he played *23. R–K7.* However, Bhend retreated his queen to Q1 and Tal discovered that 24. Q–R5 can be met by 24. . . . B–N1!.

White put on the best face and played *24. KR–K1.* From here on Black concentrated on avoiding traps set by his opponent and seizing the initiative by threat of exchange. He played *24. . . . B–B2!*, utilizing the pin of White's rook. Notice that 24. . . . B–N1 would leave White considerable play after 25. Q–R5 because of his threat of 26. R–K8 RxR 27. RxR Q–B2 28. QxP mate.

There followed: *25. B–B2 R–N2! 26. P–KR4 RxR 27. RxR P–KR3 28. Q–B5 B–N1 29. Q–K4 P–Q4! 30. PxP QxP.* As long as Black keeps one queenside pawn he should be able to win the endings that occur after an exchange of queens. Tal was steadily forced backward: *31. Q–N6 Q–Q5! 32. Q–N3 R–B2 33. R–K4 Q–N7 34. B–Q3 B–Q5 35. R–K2 Q–B8ch 36. K–R2 Q–KB5 37. R–K8 QxQch 38. PxQ K–N2 39. B–B4 R–B1 40. R–K7ch K–B3 41. RxP BxB 42. PxB K–B4 43. R–K7 R–QR1 44. R–K2 R–R6 45. K–R3 P–R4* and *White Resigned.*

ILLUSTRATIVE GAMES
CANDIDATES TOURNAMENT 1953

BRONSTEIN   EUWE

1. P–Q4 N–KB3 2. P–QB4 P–K3 3. N–QB3 B–N5 4. P–K3 P–B4 5. B–Q3 P–Q4 6. N–B3 0–0 7. 0–0 N–B3 8. P–QR3 BxN 9. PxB QPxP 10. BxBP Q–B2 11. B–Q3 P–K4 12. Q–B2

Before continuing into this heavily analyzed opening we pause to quote from David Bronstein's introduction to the game in his classic tournament book:

Keeping the opposing king in the center where it can be assaulted by a queen and rooks is nearly always worth a pawn; sometimes even a piece. These attacks are of two kinds—(1) the king remains on the eighth rank, hemmed in by its own men, (2) the king walks out to the sixth, sometimes even to the fifth rank and tries to find shelter in the wings.

In this game we find an example of the second type of attack. A defender's main weapon in these cases is cold-bloodedness, and my opponent used it all the way. At one point I was compelled to break off my calculations in order to determine just exactly who was attacking whom!

The opening position is a familiar one. White seeks P–K4 and the kingside expansion of his pawns and minor pieces. Black pressures White's center and seeks to contain his bishops.

12. . . .	R–K1
13. P–K4	KPxP!?

An easier road to equal play lay in 13. . . . P–B5, which results in a theoretically even ending—14. BxP PxP 15. PxP N–QR4 16. B–Q3 QxQ 17. BxQ NxP and 18. . . . B–B4. Euwe's choice is much sharper because White's center comes under fire in the middlegame rather than in the ending.

14. PxP	B–N5
15. QxP	. . .

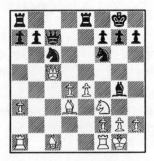

White refuses an interesting challenge: 15. P–K5 would force the variation 15. . . . BxN 16. PxN NxP 17. BxPch K–R1 18. PxPch KxP 19. B–N2, and now 19. . . . QR–Q1 or 19. . . . Q–B5. Despite the aerated king position, Black has good pieces'

play in view of his threats of . . . R–K7 or . . . R–KR1. On
19. . . . Q–B5, for example, White would be in hot water on
20. PxB R–K4! 21. BxN PxB, with . . . R–N4ch or . . . R–R1
in mind. White could try the endgames with 20. Q–B5 QxQ
21. BxQ B–B3 or 20. QxP KxB 21. QxN QxQ 22. BxQ, but Black
would have excellent drawing chances in either case.

This may be a better plan for White in retrospect. White
chooses an equally complicated line which appears superior
at first glance. (Twenty years later it was pointed out that
15. . . . BxN! 16. PxB Q–Q2, threatening the QP and 17. . . .
NxKP with perpetual check, was strongest here.)

15. . . .	KNxP
16. BxN	RxB
17. N–N5!	. . .

An excellent attacking idea which begs Black to remove the
QP and permit White to use his bishop on the long diagonal.
For example, 17. . . . RxP 18. B–N2 R–Q2 19. Q–B2 P–KN3
20. N–K4 is so strong that Black would do best to countersacrifice with 18. . . . Q–B5. The speed with which the attack
can change hands, incidentally, is revealed in 17. P–Q5 (to win
a pinned knight) BxN 18. PxB R–KR5 19. P–B4 Q–Q2!, breaking the pin and threatening 20. . . . Q–N5ch.

17. . . .	R–K2!
18. Q–B2	P–KN3
19. N–K4	B–B4!

This explains why Black played the weakening 18. . . . P–KN3
in preference to 18. . . . P–B4. Black understood that he was
provoking a dangerous sacrifice. White has no other way of
meeting the threats to his QP and N.

20. N–B6ch!	K–N2
21. Q–Q2!	KxN

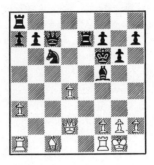

"I was quite satisfied at this point," wrote Bronstein. "The Black king cannot get back to KN2 and will have to run the gauntlet of rooks, queen, bishop and perhaps even pawns. My opponent, however, showed not the least sign of despair—a fine example for young players who tend to become nervous when mate is threatened and by that alone make their defensive task more difficult."

With his next move White creates three very powerful threats, the obvious fork P–Q6, the natural check B–N2 and the subtle cutoff of retreat Q–R6.

22. P–Q5	R–Q1!!

A tremendous answer. A casual glance will convince that 22. . . . Q–Q3 23. Q–R6! QxQP 24. B–N5ch and 25. KR–K1ch is deadly. But the move chosen threatens to meet 23. Q–R6 with 23. . . . RxP. It also stops P–Q6 and provides a safe way of returning the extra piece.

23. B–N2ch	N–K4
24. P–B4	Q–B4ch
25. K–R1	. . .

Another point of 22. . . . R–Q1 comes to light in 25. B–Q4 RxP! 26. BxQ RxQ 27. BxRch KxB 28. PxN B–K5 or 26. PxNch K–K3 27. BxQ RxQ 28. BxR KxB, and Black should draw despite the loss of the Exchange.

25. ...	RxP
26. PxNch	K–K3

Not 26. . . . K–N2 27. Q–N5, threatening RxB or P–K6ch. Here Bronstein notes that despite regaining his piece, "White still has many strategic obstacles to overcome. The Black king is surrounded by its own pieces which will display an alarming tendency to whip up a counterattack at the first opportunity. The Black king also has many more flight squares available to him than if he were castled. Finally White's first rank is vulnerable with his king on KR1."

27. Q–N5	K–Q2
28. QR–B1?	...

Oddly enough this is White's last chance to gain a major edge. With 28. P–QR4 and 29. B–R3 he should be able to penetrate on the dark squares or win the Exchange in a situation more favorable than that in the note to move 25.

28. ...	Q–N3
29. B–B3	R–K1
30. B–N4	R(K)xP

Black has a second pawn to console himself with, and he need not worry about 31. RxB because of 31. . . . PxR! 32. Q–N8 K–K3!, with a draw at least. In many of the variations to occur in the next few moves White rejects ideas because they offer him only a perpetual check. But it is likely that he has no more than a draw no matter what he does now.

31. Q–R4	P–QR4
32. B–K1	P–R4
33. B–B2	Q–R3
34. B–N3	R–K5

Although it has been in the middle of the board on the second or third rank for several moves, Black's king is secure. With his heavy pieces in front, Black is not afraid to move his most valuable piece around, e.g., 35. Q–N5 K–K3!. Both players were on the verge of forfeiting on time here but White nevertheless sprang his double-edged last try.

35. RxB!?!   RxQ

It may also be safe to capture the rook but instinctively it is better to remove the queen. With the queen off the board Black can bring his king back to safety behind his kingside pawns without danger of penetration by White's heaviest piece. The alternative, 35. . . . PxR 36. R–B7ch K–K1 37. R–B8ch is only a draw unless White is ready for 37. . . . K–Q2 38. Q–Q8ch K–K3 39. Q–K8ch K–B3 40. Q–R8ch and another half dozen checks. Isn't it much simpler to take the queen?

36. RxRch   K–K3
37. QR–Q1   . . .

Just in time Bronstein noticed that 37. R–K5ch?? K–B3 38. R–B1ch allows mate in one move! The rest is fairly simple.

37. . . .   Q–B5!
38. R–Q6ch   K–K2
39. R–Q7ch   K–B3

40. BxRch	QxB
41. R–B1ch	K–N4

Draw

Since 42. R–Q5ch! and 43. RxQRP removes Black's winning chance.

HASTINGS 1961–62

J. LITTLEWOOD   BOTVINNIK

1. P–K4 P–QB4 2. N–KB3 P–Q3 3. P–Q4 PxP 4. NxP N–KB3 5. N–QB3 P–KN3 6. B–K3 B–N2 7. P–B3 P–QR3!? 8. B–QB4 P–QN4 9. B–N3 B–N2 10. Q–Q2 QN–Q2

White has chosen the most popular and recently the most effective attacking formation against Black's Dragon Variation. The novelty, 7. . . . . P–QR3, begins a queenside initiative by Black before he has castled and placed his king as a stationary target on the kingside. White could have anticipated this with 8. Q–Q2 in order to meet 8. . . . . P–QN4 with 9. P–QR4!, a move which creates weaknesses throughout Black's queenside whether he plays 9. . . . . PxP or 9. . . . . P–N5. White could always castle kingside later. But Black could also temporize, e.g., 8. . . . . QN–Q2 and 9. . . . . Q–B2 before . . . P–QN4.

11. 0–0–0?   **. . .**

To understand why this is a mistake one must examine 11. B–R6! which forces the issue on the kingside. Black can abandon kingside castling with 11. . . . BxB 12. QxB N–B4, but then White's development is very simple whereas Black's is difficult: 13. 0–0–0 NxBch 14. BPxN! Q–N3 15. K–N1 0–0–0 16. P–QN4! and 17. N–N3 as in a later Botvinnik game. The alternative is 11. . . . 0–0, the move Black has been trying to delay. White could then proceed with his attack: 12. P–KR4 N–B4 13. P–R5 NxB 14. RPxN P–N5 (else 15. PxP RPxP 16. BxB mates) 15. N–Q5! BxN (15. . . . NxN removes a vital kingside defender) 16. PxB, followed by 17. PxP or 17. N–B6 or even 17. BxB. Black can never really get away with . . . NxKRP because of P–KN4 and death along the KR-file.

11. . . .	N–B4

Black can eliminate a dangerous attacker on any subsequent move with . . . NxB(ch). One of the reasons White's formation is so popular is that the B on QN3 is an excellent defensive piece as well. Even if it is exchanged for a Black N, the White king position remains relatively secure.

12. K–N1	NxB
13. BPxN!?	. . .

Seven moves later, this move can be harshly criticized. The reason for this unusual recapture—unusual because the tried and true principle states a player should make pawn captures toward the center (13. RPxN)—is both defensive and offensive. The defensive idea is that after a later . . . P–QN5 White's QB2 will not be as vulnerable. Also, Black will not be able to open the complete QR-file with . . . P–QR4–5xP. The offensive idea is based on the use of the QB-file later on with R–QB1 and on the exploitation of weak black squares with P–QN4 and N–N3.

Although valid in many other similar positions, this move is inferior here for tactical reasons that are nearly impossible to foresee from this position.

13. . . .   0–0

Now Black has done as much preliminary spadework on the queenside as he can without the use of heavy pieces such as his KR. Castling is safe. Notice that if White takes precautions on the queenside with 14. P–QN4 he allows . . . R–QB1–B5!. Perhaps best is 14. R–QB1 and 15. KR–Q1, although this is an admission that the traditional mating attack with P–KR4–5 must be passed over.

14. B–R6   BxB!
15. QxB   P–N5!

Black is walking on thin ice and he must act quickly. Only under certain conditions will the capture on KR3 work for him because if White is left alone for a few moves he will mate after P–KR4–5. The White Q cannot be driven off Black's KR3 by pieces. On other devices White will either obtain a decisive attack (15. . . . R–B1? 16. P–K5! or 15. . . . Q–N3 16. P–KR4 K–R1 17. P–R5 R–KN1 18. PxP RxP 19. Q–R2 followed by N–B5 or P–KN4) or a big positional edge (15. . . . P–K4 16. N–B2! and N–K3–Q5).

16. P–K5?   . . .

Despite its apparent strength, this is the losing move. If White moves his QN he is conceding the loss of the initiative, however: (a) 16. N–Q5 can be met by either 16. . . . BxN 17.

PxB Q–Q2 followed by . . . R–QB1–B4 or . . . P–K4 or by
16. . . . NxN 17. PxN BxP 18. N–B5! PxN 19. RxB P–B3! (not
19. . . . P–K3 20. RxQP! QxR 21. Q–N5ch, with perpetual
check) 20. RxBP Q–K1 and . . . Q–B2 or . . . Q–N3. Black is
better in almost every endgame because he has passed pawns
in the center but White cannot create a passed pawn easily on
the queenside. (b) 16. QN–K2 can be met by 16. . . . P–K4
17. N–B2 P–R4, with a faster attack than White's, or 16. . . .
P–K3 17. P–KR4 Q–K2 18. P–R5 P–R4 19. PxP BPxP.

| 16. . . . | N–Q2! |

A fine resource which forces White into a desperate sacrificial attack. The point of 16. . . . N–Q2 is to meet 17. PxP with
17. . . . P–K4!, (although 17. . . . PxN 18. N–B5 PxN 19. Q–N5ch
K–R1 20. PxKP is not dangerous because of 20. . . P–B7ch!
followed by a queen check and . . . R–KN1).

White probably counted on 16. . . . PxN 17. PxN KPxP, which
favors White's better pawn structure after 18. PxP. Black's use
of *Zwischenzugs* in this game is both entertaining and instructive.

| 17. P–KR4 | PxN |
| 18. P–R5 | QPxP! |

Yes, keep taking because 18. . . . P–B7ch 19. NxP P–N4 20.
QxNPch K–R1, which stops the mate, gives White good practical
chances after 21. PxP. White cannot stop for 19. NPxP here
because 19. . . . PxN 20. PxNP N–B3 or 20. RxP Q–R4 kills his
attack.

| 19. RPxP | . . . |

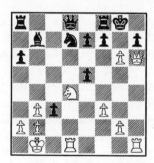

19. . . .   **N–B3!**

Only here did White discover that the move he had banked on (20. N–B5) fails to 20. . . . P–B7ch! and . . . Q–B1ch followed by the capture of his knight.

Without the additional energy from this knight, White's attack is dead because the Black knight covers the king position perfectly. The rest was mop-up:

20. QNPxP PxN 21. PxRPch K–R1 22. RxP Q–R4 23. Q–K3 N–Q4 24. Q–Q2 NxPch 25. K–R1 QR–Q1 26. R–QB1 QxPch (Simplest. Black needs only one extra piece.) *27. QxQ NxQ 28. RxR RxR 29. Resigns*

17TH USSR CHAMPIONSHIP 1949

NEZHMETDINOV   CHISTYAKOV

1. P–K4 P–K3 2. P–Q4 P–Q4 3. N–QB3 N–KB3 4. B–KN5 PxP 5. NxP B–K2 6. N–N3!? P–QN3 7. B–N5ch P–B3 8. B–K2 B–N2 9. N–B3 QN–Q2 10. O–O P–KR3 11. BxN PxB?!

This game highlights a clearance sacrifice of a pawn by which White seeks to bombard the Black king, hidden from view behind a wall of Black pawns. While the pawns offer an apparent barrier this does not completely stop the tactical tricks of the attacker.

Black has deliberately provoked a double-edged middlegame with his 11th move. He did not recapture on his KB3 with a

piece because of the pressure that would have followed 11.
. . . NxB 12. N–K5 and 13. B–B3 or 11. . . . BxB 12. N–R5. Instead of the relative peace he could have obtained with 10.
. . . 0–0 or 10. . . . Q–B2 and 11. . . . 0–0–0, Black wants a
middlegame in which he has the two bishops and attacking
chances along the KN-file.

12. P–Q5?!　　　　　　　　　. . .

White takes up the challenge and responds with a speculative
pawn offer based on the use of the Q4 square for his knight.
Although that hardly seems enough, we can look ahead a few
moves to forecast an attacking formation with a knight on
Q4, a bishop on KR5, rooks on Q1 and K1 and a queen somewhere. White will then be threatening sacrifices on K6 and
KB7 as well as the line-opening P–QB4. To effect that same kind
of arrangement without the pawn sacrifice would be impossible.
(Where else but Q4 can the White KN go to with any effect?)
In retrospect, we can say it was better to play 12. R–K1 or
12. N–R5. But sitting at the board it is an attractive sack.

12. . . .　　　　　　　　　　　BPxP

Black has little choice. He can't refuse the offer without
making even greater concessions (12. . . . P–K4 13. PxP BxP
14. N–B5 or 12. . . . Q–B2 13. PxKP PxP 14. N–Q4), and he

can't take with the KP because then White will mine the K-file with N–B5 and R–K1.

13. N–Q4   B–B4!

A wise decision—eliminating the strongest White attacking piece. It should be clear that Black will not be able to castle queenside in time to avoid White's threats on KB7 and K6 (15. . . . Q–B2 16. B–R5 N–B4 17. P–QN4 or 15. . . . N–B4 16. B–R5 Q–Q2 17. P–KB4), nor is it desirable. Black's king is much safer in the center although it will have to be moved to KB1 in some cases.

By giving up his black-squared bishop Black is not making much of a concession because White has already exchanged off *his* black-squared bishop and cannot exploit the dark squares quickly. Black decides in favor of a defensive formation with his K on KB1 to cover KN2. His other pieces can snipe at White from obvious squares—the QR from QB1, for example. Black also decides against advancing his central pawns unless there is a compelling reason to do so. There is no excuse for loosening a quite solid pawn structure.

14. B–R5   BxN
15. QxB   K–B1!

It would seem that Black's center pawns are protection enough for his valuables, but look at 15. . . . Q–K2? 16. N–B5! PxN 17. KR–K1 N–K4 18. P–KB4 Q–B4 19. QR–Q1!, followed by regaining the piece with tremendous pressure in the center.

16. KR–K1   R–B1
17. Q–N4ch   . . .

White's problem is that there are no targets. If he pauses to protect his QBP Black can begin his counterthreats with 17. . . . Q–B2 or 17. . . . R–B5. White's check contains a few traps: 17. . . . R–B4 puts a piece on a clumsy square and makes P–QB4 easier after 18. QR–Q1—and 17. . . . Q–K2 walks into

18. QxQch! KxQ 19. N–B5ch K–B1 20. N–Q6, e.g., 20. . . . R–B2
21. NxP R–N1 22. N–Q8 (Chistyakov).

17. . . .	N–B4
18. QR–Q1	Q–B2
19. Q–KR4	. . .

Now White has his target. There was no longer any pressing
point to P–QB4 because that would only open up a file to
Black's heavy pieces and a diagonal to his bishop. It will be
effective after 19. . . . Q–Q1 20. P–QB4!. By the way, how
does Black protect his KB3? On 19. . . . Q–K2 White has 20.
N–B5 and on 19. . . . K–N2 White can play 20. Q–N4ch K–R2
21. Q–KR4 for a repetition of moves. That leaves only 19. . . .
P–B4, which invites the Q to KB3, and 19. . . . N–Q2, which cuts
communication along the second rank and encourages 20. BxP
KxB 21. Q–R5ch and N–B5 or RxKP.

| 19. . . . | P–B4! |

Black has calculated this line: 20. Q–B6 R–R2 21. B–N6 N–Q2!
22. Q–R4 PxB 23. RxKP Q–Q1! 24. Q–N4ch K–B2 25. QR–K1
N–B4, a mixture of confusing the attacker's pieces, offering to
trade and consolidating.

| 20. P–QB4! | . . . |

The thought involved is 21. PxP BxP 22. NxP. The purpose, as distinct from the immediate threat, is to use the Q-file in connection with Q–B6.

20. . . .   **PxP!**

But Black has prepared a neat countersacrifice: 21. Q–B6 R–R2 22. NxP PxN 23. BxP QxB! 24. R–Q8ch RxR 25. QxRch K–N2 26. R–K7 K–N3, with three pieces for the queen, an easy win.

21. QxP   **R–KN1**

Black has the counterattack in hand now and he forces a series of simplifications with threats. The first threat is 22. . . . P–B5.

22. P–B4   **Q–K2!**

Uncovering the threat of 23. . . . N–K5 and also planning to put the queen on KR5. Now 23. NxP walks into 23. . . . RxPch 24. K–B1 Q–B3.

23. Q–Q4	N–K5
24. B–B3	NxN
25. BxB	QxB
26. PxN	. . .

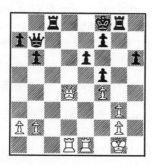

White has begun to think of defense himself. But he can still lay traps. For example, 26. . . . RxP walks into a cute one:

27. Q–R8ch K–K2 (27. . . . R–N1 28. QxPch K–K2 29. RxPch! or 28. . . . R–N2 29. Q–R8ch or even 28. . . K–K1 29. RxPch! PxR 30. QxPch K–B1 31. QxPch K–K1 32. R–K1ch K–Q1 33. Q–B6ch K–B2 34. Q–K5ch! and mates) 28. RxPch!!, mating or winning the queen. Vigilance!

26. . . .	R–B7!
27. Q–Q6ch	Q–K2
28. Q–N8ch	K–N2
29. Q–K5ch	Q–B3
30. R–Q7	QxQ
31. PxQ	RxP
32. R–QB1	K–N3!

Black stays awake to the end. He prepares to meet 33. R(1)–B7 with 33. . . . K–R4, after which his king is safe from perpetual check threats: 34. K–R2 P–B5! 35. PxP R(7)xPch 36. K–R1 K–R5 37. R–Q1 RxP 38. RxBP K–R6 39. R–Q3ch R–N6 (Chistyakov). The rest was simple because White could stop either the loss of more pawns or the penetration of enemy rooks, but not both:

33. RxRP R–Q1! 34. K–R2 R(1)–Q7 35. R–KN1 R–K7 36. R–R4 P–N4 37. R–R7 RxKP 38. P–R4 P–N5 39. P–R5 R–R7 40. P–R6 R(4)–K7 41. R–N7 RxP 42. RxNP P–R4 43. Resigns

1959 CANDIDATES TOURNAMENT

FISCHER   SMYSLOV

1. P–K4 P–QB4 2. N–KB3 P–K3 3. P–Q4 PxP 4. NxP N–KB3 5. N–QB3 P–Q3 6. B–QB4 B–K2 7. 0–0 P–QR3 8. B–N3 P–QN4 9. P–B4 0–0 10. P–B5?

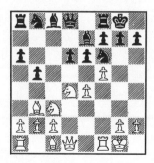

With his tenth move White has begun a campaign of speculation, a campaign that requires Black to be vigilant at all times despite the occasionally overwhelming nature of his position. At several points it appears that his advantage is absolute—and then White comes back with ideas to complicate the issue.

For the record, White's 10. P–B5 is a good idea strategically if only the first player had enough time. In the same tournament by transposition Fischer obtained a lost position after 7. B–N3 P–QR3 8. P–B4 0–0 9. Q–B3 Q–B2 10. 0–0?! P–QN4 11. P–B5? P–N5 12. N–R4 P–K4 13. N–K2 B–N2 14. N–N3 QN–Q2 15. B–K3 B–B3! 16. B–B2 Q–N2 17. KR–K1 P–Q4! against Tal. Blacks counterplay simply comes too quickly.

10. . . .   **P–N5!**

Confusing the opposition and provoking the sacrifice 11. PxP?! PxN 12. PxPch K–R1 13. Q–B3, which is easily repulsed via 13. . . . N–B3! 14. NxN Q–N3ch 15. K–R1 QxN 16. B–N5 PxP 17. QR–K1 B–N5! 18. Q–B4 B–R4, as in Jansa-Polugaevsky, Kapfenberg 1970, which was speedily won by Black.

11. QN–K2   **P–K4**
12. N–KB3   **B–N2**

There was no reason for 11. . . . NxP (12. B–Q5 Q–N3ch 13. K–R1 N–B7ch 14. RxN, winning a piece) when Black could gain time with a developing move. The KP is not running away. But 11. . . . NxP 12. B–Q5 B–N2! is OK.

13. N–N3	NxP!

Now this is safe and correct although Black can also obtain an easy middlegame with 13. . . . QN–Q2 followed by . . . N–B4 or . . . P–QR4. But a pawn is a pawn is a pawn. . . .

14. NxN	BxN
15. Q–K1	BxN

Again there is a temptation to proceed into an equal-material middlegame with 15. . . . B–QB3 16. QxNP P–Q4, but the extra pawn is worth a little trouble—especially since Black gains time with his next few moves.

16. RxB	N–B3
17. Q–K4	N–Q5
18. R–R3!	. . .

The first of many little traps: 18. . . . NxB?? loses to 19. P–B6 (theatening mate at KR7) P–N3 20. Q–R4 P–KR4 21. PxB. White wins back the initiative for the next few moves because of this.

18. . . .	B–B3
19. B–Q5	R–B1
20. P–B3	PxP
21. PxP	N–N4

The knight's only square, but good enough because it begins the attack on the weak QBP. The secondary idea in Black's mind is the removal of White's blockading bishop from Q4, which would allow . . . P–Q4 and . . . N–Q3–K5 or . . . P–Q5. The third threat, as usual, is the exchange of pieces leading to a won ending.

22. B–Q2	R–B4!

Simply because he is a pawn ahead does not mean Black has an easy time of it. His move provides fuel for both the primary and secondary threats as well as containing a trick of his own: 23. . . . Q–N3 24. B–K3 NxP!. Black's rook move prepares for . . .

N–B2 and . . . P–Q4–5, which would win before White could muster strength for new threats.

23. K–R1		Q–Q2
24. B–N3!		P–Q4
25. Q–B3		N–Q3!

Caution is in demand here, as White threatens 26. Q–R5 P–R3 27. BxRP, a threat which would work well after 25. . . . P–Q5?. Black's knight maneuver provides a counterthreat against the KBP and the addition of an overbearing centralized knight on K5. 26. BxP loses to 26. . . . P–K5.

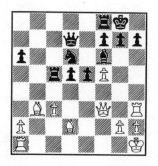

26. R–KB1		N–K5
27. Q–R5		P–R3
28. BxP		PxB

No chance to refuse this sack because of the threat of 29 BxNP. Black had calculated a safe course for his king after 29. QxRP: 29. . . . R–N1 30. B–B2 B–N2! 31. Q–R7ch K–B1 32. BxN PxB 33. P–B6 BxP 34. RxB R–N8ch. But not 29. . . . N–N4? 30. R–N3 Q–K2 31. P–KR4.

29. B–B2!?　　　　　. . .

Not adequate to save the game but frightening enough to upset an experienced defender who had previously satisfied himself that he could win if he avoided mate after 29. QxRP.

Fischer's choice gains a significant tempo in some variations, e.g., 29. . . . R–N1 30. BxN PxB 31. QxRP B–N2 32. R–N3 P–B3 33. QxP, with some cheapo chances (33. . . . R–B3 34. RxBch or 33. . . . R–KB1 34. Q–N5 R–QB3 35. P–KR4). Psychologically it's a good try.

29. . . .	B–N4
30. P–B6	R–N1
31. BxN	PxB
32. R–N3	. . .

And how does Black handle the twin threats of P–KR4 and QxP? This was Black's last major test.

32. . . .	Q–B4!

Of course. The good defender always discerns weaknesses in the opposing camp (in this case the eighth rank) as well as in his own. The text move allows him to transpose into an ending as surely won as if he were a rook ahead.

33. K–N1	Q–N3!
34. Q–K2	R–B3!
35. P–KR4	RxP
36. RxR	QxR
37. Q–R5	. . .

It's a permanent piece sacrifice after 37. QxKP Q–B5! 38. QxQ PxQ 39. R–N4 P–KB4. The nicest point in Black's concluding series is that 37. PxB is met by 37. . . . Q–B5! 38. Q–N4 P–KR4, not 37. . . . PxP 38. Q–R5. Black won straightforwardly now:

37. . . . Q–B5 38. K–R2 K–N2 39. PxB PxP 40. QxNPch QxQ 41. RxQch K–B3 42. R–R5 R–N8 43. K–N3 R–KB8! 44. R–R4 K–B4 45. R–R5ch K–K3 46. R–R6ch P–B3 47. R–R4 P–K6 48. R–K4 P–B4! Resigns

STUDY EXAMPLES
(Answers on Page 261)

1. White is a rook behind but he has 1. N–B6ch and 1. B–B6 on tap. What do you do as Black?

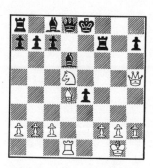

2. White plays 1. RxB and 2. B–N5. What then for Black?

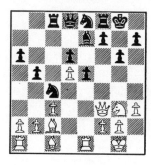

3. White plays 1. N–B5. How does Black respond?

4. Black is temporarily a piece ahead but what does he do about it?

5. White's last move was 1. P–B5!?. What do you do for Black?

CHAPTER SEVEN:

Avoiding Loss

What do you mean "avoiding loss"? Hasn't everything we've examined so far been concerned with that? Yes, but we've concentrated on the period of a game when the defender is faced with major decisions which, if handled well, will lead to a pleasant middlegame. But if the First Crisis is handled badly then the defender has to worry. Now let's consider the later crises.

The essence of good defense is making it hard for the opponent to win. This sounds obvious but it's not so. Hundreds of thousands of games have been lost when the defender liquidates a bad middlegame position and forces the players into an ending which is hopelessly lost for him. Or when the defender, rather than stonewalling his way through to the ending, not giving up an inch, decides to make a desperate bid for complications—which destroy his defense perimeter in a few moves.

The good defender has to be defeated several times during a game. An opening blunder, the careless loss of a pawn, the failure of his initiative, the ruining of his pawn structure—these are all things he can accept and still put up a good fight.

Consider this notorious book trap in the Queen's Indian Defense: *1. P–Q4 N–KB3 2. P–QB4 P–K3 3. N–KB3 P–QN3 4. B–N5 P–KR3 5. B–R4 B–N2 6. P–K3 B–N5ch 7. QN–Q2??*, and now *7. . . . P–KN4 8. B–N3 P–N5* wins a piece because of the threat of *. . . N–K5* once White's KN moves. This position has occurred twice in international tournaments. On both occasions White was a strong grandmaster. Some players would resign immediately to save face. But neither grandmaster did so —and neither lost:

Bogolyubov-Tarrasch, Göteborg 1920—9. P–QR3 PxN 10. PxB PxP 11. BxNP BxB 12. R–KN1 B–N2 13. B–R4 P–Q3 14. P–K4 QN–Q2 15. Q–B3 Q–K2 16. R–N4 P–K4 17. P–Q5 0–0–0 18. K–K2 QR–N1 19. QR–KN1 RxR 20. RxR P–KR4 21. R–N3 K–N1 22. Q–B5 B–B1 23. B–N5 P–R5 24. R–KB3 Q–B1 25. BxN NxB 26. QxN B–N5 27. P–R3 Q–R3?? 28. PxB Resigns

Uhlmann-Kinmark, Halle 1963—9. N–K5 N–K5 10. QxP BxNch 11. K–K2 B–N5? 12. B–R4 B–K2 13. Q–N7 R–B1 14. N–N6! PxN 15. QxPch R–B2 16. Q–N8ch R–B1 17. Q–N6ch Draw

Remember that *it takes several mistakes to lose a game.* A bad position is not the same as a lost game. Only further mistakes by you can make that transition from bad to lost.

For successful defense a player has to know two things: (1) that he is in trouble, and (2) why he's in trouble. Only when the defender knows that he has to defend can he put up a tough resitance. And only when he realizes which aspects of the position are his weaknesses and which are his strengths will he know what to preserve and what to change.

The position above arose in Speyer-Schlechter, St. Petersburg 1909, after *1. P–K4 P–K4 2. N–KB3 N–QB3 3. B–N5 P–QR3 4. B–R4 N–B3 5. 0–0 B–K2 6. R–K1 P–QN4 7. B–N3 P–Q3 8. P–B3 B–N5 9. P–Q3 0–0 10. P–QR4 P–N5 11. QN–Q2 R–QN1 12. B–B4 Q–B1 13. N–B1? N–QR4 14. B–R2 PxP 15. PxP B–K3! 16. N–K3? N–N6 17. BxN BxB 18. Q–Q2 B–K3 19. B–R3 Q–Q2.*

Sloppy opening play has left White with a weak queenside. Before he is overrun with Black pieces White should think about counterplay in the center with 20. N–B2 and 21. P–Q4 or about queenside protection with P–B4, Q–R5 and KR–N1.

However White didn't realize the dangers in the position and he hesitated: *20. P–R3 KR–K1 21. P–B4 P–B4!*, and now *22. P–N4?*. If Speyer understood the situation he could have tried to cover all the queenside weaknesses with Q–B2, N–Q2 and KR–N1. Another possibility, pointed out by Lasker, was 22. N–Q5 followed by KPxN and preparations for P–KB4 after the knight is captured on Q5. But White's 22. P–N4 naively starts a pawn storm at a point when time is of the essence. As we suggested in the section on counterplay, a pawn storm may be thorough but it is slow.

Schlechter continued *22. . . . R–N6*, and only now did White go on the defensive: *23. Q–B2 KR–N1 24. N–Q2 R(6)–N2 25. KR–N1.* But now Black had a new target, the kingside, and he skillfully exploited it: *25. . . . P–KR4 26. P–B3 N–R2! 27. RxR RxR 28. R–N1 B–N4 29. N(3)–B1 N–B1! 30. RxR QxR 31. B–B1*

B–Q2. In face of . . . Q–N5 or . . . N–K3–Q5, White lost a
pawn after *32. N–N1 BxP*, and soon the game.

Failure to recognize the dangers in the position and a vacil-
lating manner were the culprits in that game. An equally common
error is misjudging the positive and negative aspects of a position:

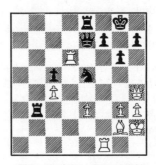

Here is a late middlegame from the 1953 Candidates Tournament. White's pawns are very bad. But his pieces are active and
he can put up a difficult defense with 36. R(6)–KB6! RxP 37.
B–Q5!. White's loss of a pawn is not decisive as long as he has
threats against Black's kingside.

But White (Najdorf) played *36. QxQ??,* "an incredible con-
ceptual error" as he himself said later. In the ending Black's
kingside has no threats against it and Black (Geller) won
speedily: *36. . . . RxQ 37. B–Q5 RxP 38. R–Q8ch K–N2 39. R–QB8
N–Q6 40. R–QR8 R–K7ch 41. K–N1 R–Q7 42. R(8)–R1 N–N5
White Resigns.*

WHAT KIND OF WEAKNESS?

The nature of the weakness that makes your game bad determines what kind of defense is appropriate. If, for example,
you have static weaknesses—that is, vulnerable points that
cannot be easily repaired—you have to determine how they
can be attacked. If the answer is "easily," then you must strike

back fast. If the answer is "with difficulty," you can rely on waiting tactics. Similarly, if your problem is a loss of material you have to decide how easily the opponent can consolidate his advantage. If a series of exchanges leading to a lost endgame is foreseeable, you must seek counterchances. But if exchanges are difficult to achieve or if you can establish an impregnable fortress in the ending, then waiting tactics are appropriate.

This instructive example was played in the 1974 US Championship between Ken Rogoff (White) and Bernard Zuckerman:

> *1. P–QB4 N–KB3 2. N–KB3 P–KN3 3. P–KN3 B–N2 4. B–N2 0–0 5. 0–0 P–B4 6. P–Q4 PxP 7. NxP N–B3 8. N–QB3 NxN 9. QxN P–Q3 10. Q–Q3 P–QR3 11. B–Q2 B–B4 12. P–K4 B–K3 13. P–N3 R–N1?! 14. QR–B1 N–Q2 15. Q–K2 N–B4 16. N–Q5 P–QR4 17. KR–Q1 P–N3*

White has won the battle of the opening by making . . . P–QN4 and . . . P–KB4 difficult for Black. Beginning with his last two moves Black turns from seeking counterplay to prevention of White's progress (stopping P–QN4 and P–B5). Although White has a clear advantage it is still a long way from victory. His first middlegame sortie was *18. P–KR4*, to weaken Black's kingside with P–R5xP. This doesn't change the basic nature of the position but gives White some later prospects of kingside exploitation.

There followed *18. . . . P–KR4* and *19. B–N5!*. White's bishop cannot be driven away with . . . P–KR3 anymore. Black made the first of several crucial mistakes at this point. He can defend his KP with 19. . . . R–K1 and throw the middlegame issue back to White. How would White make progress? He cannot bring additional pressure on the weak points at K7 or QN6. He could try a tactical idea with 20. P–K5 BxP 21. NxPch RxN 22. QxB PxQ 23. RxQch RxR 24. BxR, but after all this brilliance, Black stands well with 24. . . . R–Q7.

What else is there? Well, White can try to advance on the queenside with Q–B2, P–R3 and P–QN4. That looks like the most promising idea. But Black has excellent chances of forestalling this, e.g., 20. Q–B2 Q–Q2 21. P–R3 P–R5 22. PxP (22. P–N4 N–N6 and . . . N–Q5) BxN 23. KPxB QxP. This last point is significant. Black can readily afford . . . BxN *when White has made weaknesses of his own.* It appears that White cannot make progress without making weaknesses. Therefore waiting tactics with 19. . . . R–K1! are dictated.

However, Black played *19. . . . BxN?* to ease the pressure on his KP. After *20. KPxB R–K1 21. B–R3* White had made considerable progress since the diagram without any risk. Now, instead of a queenside advance, White can plan for P–KN4 which will expose the Black king to danger. The only defending piece near the king is Black's bishop.

Black appreciated this and handled the next few moves well: *21. . . . B–B3! 22. B–K3 K–N2!.* White didn't want to exchange off a pair of bishops (especially when 22. BxB PxB would give Black a good open file). Black's last two moves, moreover, have killed prospects of P–KN4 for the time being because, for example, 23. P–KN4 PxP 24. QxP R–KR1 would show White's kingside to be weaker than Black's.

White again has a problem of making his considerable advantage count. Black has covered his weaknesses well. If White returns his thoughts to playing for P–QN4 he creates the counterplay Black has been seeking. Black will occupy the QR-file and pressure White's queenside pawns then. Rogoff put off a decision and quietly began to maneuver: *23. R–B2 Q–B2 24. K–R2.*

Here again Black made a crucial error. No winning plan for White is evident and White's last two moves clearly do not indicate what it would be. Black should temporize and await developments. But Black played *24. . . . P–K3?* to obtain play on the K-file. The drawback, of course, is that it simplified White's task immensely by giving him the target he has been seeking.

After *25. PxP NxP 26. R(2)–Q2 QR–Q1 27. B–N2 N–B4 28. R–Q5 R–K4 29. Q–B3 RxR 30. QxR* White had tremendous pressure on the QP and Black's kingside and queenside. Further provocation by Black increased this advantage: *30. . . . B–K4?! 31. B–N5! P–B3 32. B–K3 P–B4 33. B–N5!* and Black made his last error with *33. . . . R–KB1,* instead of *33. . . . R–K1 34. P–B4 B–B6 35. QxQP QxQ 36. RxQ R–K7,* with some chances. After *33. . . . R–KB1* White's endgame was easily won with *34. P–B4 B–B3 35. QxQP.* White won in 44 moves.

Black's weaknesses in this instance were static but not easily exploitable. A different situation is illustrated by Lilienthal-Smyslov, USSR Absolute Championship 1941:

1. P–Q4 N–KB3 2. P–QB4 P–K3 3. N–QB3 B–N5 4. Q–B2 P–Q3 5. P–KN3 P–B4?! 6. PxP PxP 7. B–N2 N–B3? 8. BxNch!

PxB 9. *N–B3 0–0* 10. *0–0 R–K1* 11. *B–N5! BxN* 12. *QxB N–K5* 13. *Q–K3 NxB* 14. *NxN P–K4* 15. *N–K4?*

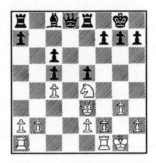

White's opening play has cleverly created a sickly pawn formation in his opponent's camp and he is ready to grab the first QBP. It was wiser to play 15. KR–Q1 first, however. Black has exploitable, static weaknesses and waiting tactics are hopeless. Therefore, Black took action with *15. . . . Q–Q5!* 16. *P–N3 B–N5!*.

This is better than 16. . . . QxQ because White's doubled pawns are easily protected whereas Black's aren't. Now 17. KR–K1 can be met by 17. . . . QR–Q1 18. NxP BxP!, e.g., 19. RxB QxRch or 19. QxB QxN. This tactical trick allowed Black to stave off the first middlegame crisis: *17. N–B3 P–K5!* 18. *QR–Q1 Q–K4.*

White missed an effective move in 19. N–R4 and chose *19. R–Q2.* This allowed Black to offer a brilliant pawn sacrifice which was best refused: *19. . . . QR–Q1!* 20. *RxR?! RxR* 21. *NxP P–B4* 22. *N–B3 QxQ* 23. *PxQ R–Q7.* Black held the ensuing ending by continuing the policy of activating his pieces even at a cost: *24. R–Q1! R–B7!* 25. *R–Q3 BxP* 26. *R–Q8ch K–B2* 27. *NxB RxN* 28. *R–Q7ch K–K3!* 29. *RxRP* (29. RxNP RxQRP 30. RxKRP R–N7 31. R–QN7 P–R4 is drawn, says Botvinnik) *P–N4* 30. *RxP RxQRP* 31. *R–R6ch K–K4* 32. *RxP K–K5* 33. *RxP P–B5!* 34. *KPxP K–B6* (the point is that because of . . .

P–B5 Black's king cannot be driven from this square) *35. P–R3 R–R8ch Draw.* White cannot escape perpetual check.

To repeat, the nature of your weakness determines the kind of defense necessary—sometimes active, sometimes passive. This goes for material as well as positional advantage:

Von Freymann-Vidmar, St. Petersburg 1909: *1. P–Q4 P–Q4 2. P–QB4 P–K3 3. N–QB3 P–QB4 4. P–K3 N–KB3 5. N–B3 N–B3 6. P–QR3 B–Q3 7. PxBP BxP 8. P–QN4 B–Q3 9. B–N2 0–0 10. B–Q3 P–QR4 11. P–N5 N–K4 12. NxN BxN 13. Q–K2 P–QN3? 14. 0–0 B–N2 15. KR–Q1 Q–K2 16. N–R4 BxB 17. QxB N–Q2 18. PxP PxP 19. B–B5 QR–Q1 20. BxN RxB 21. NxP*

Black's queenside weakness has cost him a pawn. It is easy to imagine White's making that pawn count because it is an outside passed pawn which can be protected without problems. Therefore, Black cannot rely on his chances to blockade the pawn and stop White's progress. Black must complicate.

Vidmar proceeded to do this with *21. . . . R–Q3 22. N–R4 R–KR3*, with a threat of 23. . . . Q–R5 24. P–R3 QxN. White parried this with *23. R–Q4*, but after *23. . . . Q–B2! 24. P–R3 R–B1!* Black had succeeded in making the win difficult because of his active pieces and control of the only open file. The transformation of Black's game is remarkable.

In the continuation White had problems in consolidating his edge: *25. QR–Q1 R–KN3 26. R(4)–Q3* (allowing the strong

26. . . . . P–Q5!, which Black misses) *P–R3 27. R–Q4* (not 27.
R–B3 RxPch! 28. KxR P–Q5ch) *K–R2 28. R(1)–Q3 Q–K4 29.
Q–Q2 R–B5! 30. N–B3 Q–KN4.* The complications proved to be
so great that White blundered with *31. P–B4 Q–N6 32. NxP??
R–B8ch* and mates. However, Black's position was strong enough
to make lengthy defense possible.

The opposite side of the coin is suggested by the game Bis-
guier-Portisch, Bled 1961:

*1. P–Q4 P–K3 2. P–QB4 N–KB3 3. N–QB3 B–N5 4. N–B3
P–B4 5. P–K3 N–B3 6. B–Q3 BxNch 7. PxP P–Q3 8. P–K4 P–K4
9. P–Q5 N–K2 10. 0–0 P–KR3 11. N–K1 P–KN4?! 12. P–B3
N–R4 13. P–N3! N–N2 14. N–N2 B–R6 15. R–N1 Q–Q2 16.
R–B2 BxN 17. RxB N–N3 18. Q–N3 R–QN1 19. Q–N5 K–K2
20. KR–N2 Q–B1 21. Q–R4! P–R3 22. R–N6*

After a spirited middlegame of maneuver White is about to
cash in on the queenside with 23. Q–N3 and 24. RxNPch. Note
that Black couldn't have preserved the integrity of his queenside with 20. . . . . Q–B2 because of 21. QxP!. Black cannot cover
his QN2 with additional protection in the next two moves.
Therefore, he must lose a pawn.

Faced with this inevitability Portisch must answer the same
question as Vidmar in the previous example. But the situation
is quite different. Black cannot complicate the game sufficiently
to distract White from the consolidation of his extra pawn.

But he can make the use of that pawn difficult. And he did with: 22. . . . N–B1! 23. Q–N3 N–Q2 24. RxNP RxR 25. QxR QxQ 26. RxQ R–QN1!!.

The genius of this defense lies in the difficulty White would have in winning an ending with two bishops and an extra pawn against two knights. The extra White pawn is on White's QB3 and it would be virtually impossible to make it count after 27. RxR. Therefore White played 27. R–R7! R–N3 28. P–KR4. On 28. . . . P–B3, the natural move, Black would have difficulty after 29. B–B2! threatening 30. B–R4. Black's second rank has been weakened by . . . P–B3 and he could no longer play . . . N–K1–B3 as a defense.

With this in mind, Black played 28. . . . N–K1! 29. PxP PxP 30. BxPch P–B3 31. B–R4 K–Q1, planning . . . N–B2 and . . . K–B1–N1, winning the White rook! White played 32. R–R8ch N–N1 33. B–B2, but after 33. . . . K–B1 34. R–R7 N–Q2 he took a repetition-of-moves draw with 35. R–R8ch N–N1. On 35. B–R4 N–B2 36. BxNch KxB 37. BxP Black should win after 37. . . . K–B1 38. P–N4 (38. P–B4!) K–N1 39. RxN KxR 40. P–N5 K–Q2 41. P–N6 K–K1. An amazing illustration of defensive obstacles placed in the way of inevitable victory.

STONEWALLING

The dichotomy of passive vs. active defense is one of the least understood problems of chess technique. Instead of determining the proper strategy, most defenders do what suits their mood rather than what the position dictates. And because it is much more agreeable to force the issue and seek complications, the stonewall strategy is the most neglected of skills.

Stonewalling has a bad reputation because it is essentially negative and passive. The emphasis is on holding the line, not conceding anything. But the defender has the psychological edge of having established the ground rules for play. He can always spot a slight error in the aggressor's moves and return to complications. And the onus is on the aggressor to make something of the position. Quite often it means giving the aggressor just enough rope to hang himself:

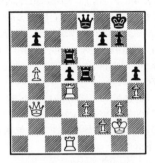

The diagram is taken from Larsen-Keres, San Antonio 1972. Black has a major liability on Q4 which has been attacked by the maximum number of White pieces. Keres makes an interesting decision. Rather than cling to the defense of the QP he sacrifices it in order to enter an ending with only kingside pawns. We've mentioned earlier that such endings are much more easily drawn than ones with pawns on both flanks—even endings with equal numbers of pawns.

Keres played 27. . . . *R–QN3 28. RxP RxNP 29. RxR(K)! RxR* (29. . . . QxR 30. R–Q8ch and 31. QxP) *30. QxP R–QB4.* Black is eager to trade off one of the remaining heavy pieces (31. . . . Q–B3ch) because that would virtually certify a draw. White, for his part, must try to avoid exchanges, avoid perpetual check and yet make his pawn count. Play continued: *31. R–Q6 P–N3 32. R–Q7 Q–K3 33. R–Q8ch K–N2 34. Q–N4 Q–B5 35. Q–N2ch Q–B6 36. Q–N7* (36. Q–N8 Q–K4!) *R–B4 37. Q–K7 Q–N7 38. Q–B8ch K–R2 39. Q–N8ch K–R3 40. R–Q2 Q–KN2! 41. Q–R8 K–R2.*

So far, no progress. Black's pieces have remained active enough to protect his king and threaten perpetual check. Now White made a minor error after which a draw should have been a foregone conclusion: *42. P–K4? Q–B6!,* which forced rooks off the board.

We might draw the curtain here except White played on: *43. PxR QxR 44. Q–N7 K–N1 45. P–B6 Q–Q1! 46. Q–B6 K–R2 47. Q–QB3 Q–Q4ch 48. P–B3 Q–R7ch 49. K–R3 Q–N8 50. K–N2 Q–R7ch 51. K–B1 Q–R3ch 52. K–K1 Q–K3ch 53. K–B2 Q–R7ch 54. K–N1 Q–N8ch 55. K–N2 Q–R7ch 56. K–R3 Q–N8.* Now *57. K–N2 Q–R7ch* is drawn by repetition of the same position three times. What makes this example intriguing is that White made one last try to win . . . and lost: *57. P–N4 Q–R8ch 58. K–N3 Q–N8ch 59. K–B4? Q–R7ch 60. K–N5?? Q–N6! 61. Q–K3 PxP 62. Q–B4 QxP 63. QxP Q–K6ch*, followed by winning the BP after *64. Q–B4 Q–K7! 65. Q–N3 Q–N4ch 66. K–B4 Q–B4ch.* White resigned on the 91st move.

Patient defenders have won a good many games through careful, solid play against an opponent who takes too many risks to win. The onus is on the player with the advantage. Even a pathetically lost game can be held if things are made difficult enough for him.

This position occurred in a world championship game (Tchigorin-Steinitz, 1889) and the fact that Black didn't lose swiftly is surprising. That he didn't lose in the long run is shocking. That he nearly won is astounding: *1. P–K4 P–K4 2. N–KB3 N–QB3 3. B–B4 B–B4 4. P–QN4 BxNP 5. P–B3 B–R4 6. 0–0 Q–B3? 7. P–Q4 KN–K2 8. P–Q5! N–Q1 9. Q–R4 B–N3 10. B–KN5 Q–Q3?! 11. N–R3 P–QB3 12. QR–Q1 Q–N1 13. BxN KxB 14. P–Q6ch K–B1 15. Q–N4 P–B3 16. B–N3.*

Black played well in this extremely unpleasant position: *16. . . . P–N3* (not 16. . . . N–B2 17. N–R4 B–Q1 18. Q–B4 N–R3 19. N–B5) *17. N–B4 K–N2!* (17. . . . N–B2 18. QNxP! PxN 19. Q–B4 N–R3 20. NxP is too strong) *18. P–QR4 N–B2 19. NxB PxN 20. BxN KxB 21. NxPch K–N2!* (not 21. . . . PxN 22. P–B4). But White had regained his pawn and had to win another after 22. N–B4.

Steinitz continued to play tenaciously with *22. . . . P–QN4 23. PxP* (23. N–N6 R–R3 gets rid of Black's awful QB) *Q–R2! 24. P–N6 Q–R5 25. Q–B5 R–K1*. At least Black has gotten his queen out of self-imprisonment and brought his king to relative safety. The "only" other problem besides his material minus is the bind White has placed on the center and queenside. Black may never be able to move his QB.

There followed more maneuvering until Black had protected his kingside: *26. P–B3 Q–B7 27. N–K3 Q–N6 28. R–N1 Q–B2 29. N–B4 R–R5 30. R–N4 R–R3*. Black miraculously keeps his hopeless position from collapsing. Notice that he has taken the sting out of P–K5 and made penetration along the QR-file difficult for White. But White finally stumbled upon the right idea: *31. Q–Q4 K–N1 32. N–K3 R–R6 33. R–R4! R–N6 34. KR–R1! K–N2 35. R–R8 R–N4!*.

Black has one idea to complicate White's inevitable victory after doubling rooks on the eighth rank. Steinitz will play . . . P–QB4 and . . . RxNP. Even this is not enough because on *36. R–N8! P–B4! 37. Q–Q5 RxNP*, White should have won with 38. QxQch! KxQ 39. KR–R8 R–B3 40. N–Q5 and N–K7 or N–B7. But White made two slips: *38. KR–R8? Q–B1 39. N–B4 R–B3 40. P–B4? P–QN4!*, and Black suddenly stood better.

Black later erred and only drew, but *41. RxP B–R3 42. RxR QxR 43. RxP RxR 44. QxR QxP* should have given Black's better pieces and kingside pawns good winning chances.

How did Black survive? It was a mixture of careful anticipation of threats (16. . . . P–N3 and 17. . . . K–N2), the activation of his pieces (22. . . . P–QN4 and 23. . . . Q–R2) and the continual irritation of White's winning plans (. . . Q–R5–B7–N6–KB2,

. . . R–QN4 and . . . P–B4, and finally . . . P–QN4). By posing new problems for White whenever possible, Black frustrated his opponent nearly into a loss. And, of course, some help from White was necessary.

OBJECTIVITY AND PRACTICALITY

Creating problems for the opponent is the key to making victory difficult. Often this can be done by following the general principles of good chess. But every experienced player knows that frequently the objectively best move in a position would be one that simplifies matters in a fashion that aids the other side. The best move in practical terms is something that may be antipositional and which, if correctly handled, would lose faster than the theoretically "correct" plan. But the pragmatic move creates new decisions for the opponent to resolve and therein lies the source of error.

In this position young Mikhail Botvinnik has been out-played by Vladimir Alatortzev (White) in a 1933 tournament game which began: *1. P–Q4 N–KB3 2. P–QB4 P–K3 3. N–QB3 B–N5 4. N–B3 P–QN3 5. P–K3 B–N2 6. B–Q3 0–0 7. 0–0 P–Q4 8. PxP PxP 9. P–QR3 B–Q3 10. P–QN4 QN–Q2 11. N–QN5 B–K2 12. N–K5 P–QR3 13. QN–B3 P–B4 14. NPxP PxP 15. R–N1 Q–B2?? 16. NxN NxN 17. Q–N3! QR–N1 18. NxP BxN 19. QxB RxR 20. BxR.*

The correct plan according to general principles is 20. . . . PxP 21. PxP N–B3 and 22. . . . R–Q1, as Ragosin pointed out. But he noted that Botvinnik's 20. . . . *P–B5!?* was the best practical chance. White had to worry about a passed enemy pawn and had to consider the win of a second pawn with 21. BxPch.

It's true that with 21. Q–K4! N–B3 22. Q–B2, followed by the advance of White's central pawns, Black would be in a very bad way. His survival chances would be worse than if had played 20. . . . PxP. Nevertheless, 21. Q–K4 and 22. Q–B2 is a very difficult plan to find.

Alatortzev actually played *21. BxPch? KxB 22. Q–K4ch K–N1 23. QxB,* but after *23. . . . P–B6!* he had problems despite two extra pawns. If he brings his bishop to QR3 with 24. P–QR4 P–B7 25. B–R3, Black has an easy time with 25. . . . R–N1 26. R–B1 Q–B3 27. P–R3 QxP. And, as played, Black had powerful play after *24. P–K4 P–B7 25. P–Q5? R–N1 26. P–N3 Q–B1.*

The upshot of this was that Black eventually won a hard game after *27. Q–N5 Q–B5 28. P–B3 R–N6 29. Q–Q2 R–Q6 30. Q–K2 N–K4 31. K–N2 R–Q8 32. QxQ NxQ 33. P–Q6 K–B1 34. P–QR4 K–K1 35. K–B2 N–Q7! 36. R–K1 NxBP!.*

THE DEMAND FOR COUNTERPLAY

One bad piece, the saying goes, makes for a bad game. In bad positions the priority is placed on fighting for piece activity even at the cost of material:

In this game from the Ninth Soviet Championship Black's foremost problem is not his weak queenside pawns or the prospect of being mated; it is the lack of coordinated piece play, highlighted by his QB on QR1. Black solved this problem with 28. . . . *P–B4!* 29. *PxP N–K5!*, and he liquidated the position skillfully: 30. *R–K3 NxQBP* 31. *P–KR4 B–Q4!* 32. *BxB PxB* 33. *RxP NxNP* 34. *R–K4 Q–N2* 35. *Q–Q3 KR–B1* 36. *R–K1* (36. R–Q7 N–B4!) *N–B4* 37. *Q–Q1 N–K3* 38. *R–Q7 R–B2* 39. *R–Q6 QR–QB1* 40. *N–N5 R–B8* 41. *QxR RxQ* 42. *RxR N–B5!* 43. *R(1)–QB6 Q–N8ch* 44. *K–R2 Q–KB8* 45. *K–N3! N–K7ch* 46. *K–B3 N–N8ch!* and draws by perpetual check.

A more recent example was Auerbach-Karpov, USSR Championship 1970: 1. *P–QB4 P–QB4* 2. *N–KB3 N–KB3* 3. *N–B3 P–Q4* 4. *PxP NxP* 5. *P–K3 P–K3* 6. *P–Q4 N–QB3* 7. *B–Q3 B–K2* 8. *0–0 0–0* 9. *P–QR3 N–B3* 10. *PxP BxP* 11. *P–QN4 B–Q3* 12. *N–K4!* *NxN* 13. *BxN Q–K2* 14. *B–N2 P–B4?* 15. *BxN PxB* 16. *B–K5! BxB* 17. *NxB*, and now Black is one move away from being paralyzed by 18. R–QB1. But he played 17. . . . *P–B4!* 18. *R–B1 PxP* 19. *N–B6 Q–B3* 20. *PxP B–R3* 21. *R–K1 B–N4!* 22. *Q–Q6! BxN* 23. *RxB QR–K1* 24. *P–N3 Q–K2* 25. *R–Q1 R–B2* 26. *Q–B5 QxQ* 27. *PxQ R–N2* 28. *R–R6 R–QB1* 29. *P–B6 R(2)–QB2* 30. *R–Q7 RxR!* 31. *PxR R–Q1* 32. *RxRP K–B2*, and Black just drew on the 52nd move.

A third example with the same freeing move but in a different setting occurred in Capablanca-Botvinnik, Moscow 1936:

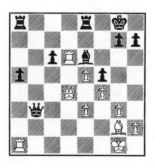

Black's problems center on his weak pawns and bad bishop. But he managed to draw without improving either one of these situations. Black played 35. . . . *P–B4!*, with the idea of occupying the QB-file once the pawn was captured. The pawn was lost anyway and White should have played 36. Q–Q2 with the threat of 37. RxB! RxR 38. B–Q5 Q–N3 39. Q–R2, as Capablanca said.

But at the board the former world champion played *36. QxP?* *KR–QB1* 37. *Q–N6?* (better 37. Q–Q4), and Black obtained excellent drawing chances with *37. . . QR–N1 38. QxQ BxQ*, because 39. RxP leads to 39. . . R–B8ch 40. K–B2 R–B7ch 41. K–B1? B–B5ch or to perpetual check. White played *39. B–B6!*, but Black's *39. . . . P–R5!* offered another pawn for a draw (40. BxP BxB 41. RxB R–B8ch 42. K–N2 R–N7ch 43. K–R3 R–KR8). Capa played *40. P–N4 PxP 41. K–B2 K–B1 42. K–N3* but agreed to a draw when the game was adjourned because of the simplifying 42. . . . R–N3 43. B–K4 RxR 44. PxR R–Q1.

In each of these cases Black's problems only appeared to be centered on his weak QBP. The real weakness was the absence of counterplay. When the QB-file was opened after the liquidation of the bad pawn, Black's game blossomed.

Besides the questions of attitude and strategy we've examined so far there are specific tactical ideas that can benefit the defender in his bid to avoid loss—the perpetual check, the desperado, bishops of opposite color, and the defense perimeter.

PERPETUAL CHECK

At the Olympiad in Skopje in 1972 young Ljubomir Ljubojevic of Yugoslavia took great delight in showing off the following position and challenging his grandmaster elders to find the one move for White that forced a draw:

Some of the finest masters of the day were baffled by the problem and doubted that the draw could be apparent after only one move. Inevitably the observers threw up there hands and asked for the solution which Ljubojevic revealed to be 1. N–R6!!.

This devilish move protects the remaining squares on the KN-file that previously were unprotected. The point is that now White threatens a perpetual check with his rook up and down the KN-file. Black can only avoid perpetual check by transposing into a hopelessly drawn rook-and-pawn ending.

Perpetual check is the last refuge a desperate defender. It is not, as many examples would indicate, just something that happens when an attacker fails to mate and can only repeat the position. The defender, if he's awake, can find a multitude of opportunities for perpetual in his games:

This is a 1947 game between Soviet masters Simagin and Aronin. White is two pawns down but he plays the beautiful and apparently crushing 22. *RxP!!?* which threatens 23. B–N6 mate as well as 23. QxQ. The position appears hopeless for Black but he saves half a point with 22. . . . *P–K5!!*, which blocks the diagonal of the mating bishop and opens a diagonal of his own. White must play 23. *QxQ* and accept the draw after 23. . . . *BxPch 24. K–R1 B–N6ch 25. K–N1 B–R7ch.*

Another fine example was Lasker–Alekhine, St. Petersburg 1914: *1. P–K4 P–Q4 2. PxP N–KB3 3. P–Q4 NxP 4. N–KB3 B–N5 5. P–B4 N–N3 6. N–B3 P–K4! 7. P–B5 PxP 8. N–K4 N(3)–Q2 9. QxP Q–K2 10. B–QN5! N–B3* (10. . . . P–QB3 or 10. . . . P–B4 is met by 11. 0–0! and R–K1) *11. BxN PxB 12. 0–0 BxN 13. PxB 0–0–0 14. Q–R4 N–K4 15. K–N2 Q–K3! 16. QxRP Q–B4 17. Q–R8ch K–Q2 18. R–Q1ch?* (18. Q–R3) *K–K3! 19. QxR QxPch 20. K–N1 B–K2! 21. Q–Q4 Q–N5ch 22. K–R1 Q–B6ch 23. K–N1 Q–N5ch* and draws.

DESPERADO

The desperado is a tactical resource in which you use your doomed piece to eat as much material as possible before it dies.

A simple illustration of this is the Scotch Opening variation beginning with *1. P–K4 P–K4 2. N–KB3 N–QB3 3. P–Q4 PxP 4. NxP N–B3 5. N–QB3 NxP.* The best method of answering this is 6. QNxN Q–K2 7. P–B3 P–Q4 8. B–QN5 followed by 0–0 and R–K1. But our interest centers on what happens after 6. *KNxN.*

Then after 6. . . . *NxN!* both sides must continue to make captures with their galloping knights. If White stops for 7. PxN he remains a pawn behind after 7. . . . NPxN. Therefore, 7. *NxQ NxQ 8. NxBP NxBP 9. NxR NxR* is a likely continuation, with Black remaining a pawn ahead temporarily.

A spectacular example of desperado that comes to mind is Hearst–Evans, US Intercollegiate 1950:

1. P–QB4 N–KB3 2. N–QB3 P–KN3 3. P–Q4 P–Q3 4. P–K4 QN–Q2 5. P–KN3 B–N2 6. B–N2 P–K4 7. KN–K2 0–0 8. 0–0 P–B3 9. P–KR3 PxP 10. NxP N–N3 11. P–N3 P–Q4 12. KPxP PxP 13. B–R3 R–K1 14. P–B5 N–K5 15. Q–Q3? N–Q2 16. N–R4 N–K4 17. Q–B2 B–Q2! 18. QR–Q1 Q–B1 19. K–R2 BxN and now 20. BxN

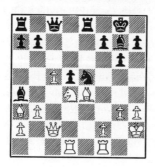

White's *Zwischenzug* capture is made to avoid 20. PxB N–B5, which gives Black's knight a dominating position. But Black's 20. . . . N–B5!! appeared to settle the issue by threatening 21. . . . RxB and 21. . . . NxB. Two pieces are *en prise* and one must be lost.

But White rose to the occasion with 21. N–N5!!, which protects one of the bishops and allows him to meet 21. . . . BxN with 22. PxN BxP 23. B–Q3, with chances of survival. The other difficult line would be 21. . . . RxB 22. PxB P–QR3 23. RxP! PxN 24. QxR NxB 25. KR–Q1, with complications enough to keep White alive. (Unfortunately Black still had a winning game with 21. . . . BxN! 22. PxN BxP 23. B–Q3 P–QN4! 24. Q–N1 Q–R3, when White missed better chances with 24. BxB QPxB 25. R–Q6.)

A more recent example of desperado play was Tal-Keres, Candidates Tournament 1962: 1. P–K4 P–K4 2. N–KB3 N–QB3 3. B–N5 P–QR3 4. B–R4 N–B3 5. 0–0 B–K2 6. R–K1 P–QN4

7. *B–N3 0–0* 8. *P–B3 P–Q3* 9. *P–KR3 N–QR4* 10. *B–B2 P–B4* 11.
P–Q4 N–Q2 12. *QN–Q2 BPxP* 13. *PxP N–QB3* 14. *P–R3 PxP*
15. *N–N3 N(2)–K4* 16. *KNxP B–B3* 17. *B–Q2?* *NxN* 18. *NxN*
N–Q6! 19. *N–B6?* *NxBP!* 20. *Q–B3?* *NxPch!* 21. *K–R2* (21. *QxN*
Q–N3ch) *B–K4ch!* 22. *NxB PxN* 23. *KR–Q1 N–B5!*, and Black
won.

BISHOPS OF OPPOSITE COLOR

The drawing finesse of obtaining bishops of opposite color
seems like a dirty trick. After all, if one player has won a pawn
—or even two pawns—after much hard work it doesn't seem
fair that his opponent should be able to draw the game simply
because their bishops do not share control of the same squares.
But chess can be unfair.

Take this sharp game from the 24th USSR Championship
between Stolyar and Tal:

1. *P–K4 P–QB4* 2. *N–KB3 P–K3* 3. *P–Q4 PxP* 4. *NxP P–QR3*
5. *P–QB4 N–KB3* 6. *N–QB3 B–N5* 7. *B–Q2 0–0?!* 8. *P–K5!*
N–K1 9. *N–B2 B–K2* 10. *B–Q3 QN–B3* 11. *Q–K2 Q–B2* 12.
P–B4 P–B3 13. *PxP NxP* 14. *0–0 P–QN3* 15. *N–K4! P–QN4!*
16. *PxP PxP* 17. *K–R1 B–N2* 18. *P–QR3 N–QR4* 19. *N–Q4*
Q–N3 20. *N–KB3 N–B5!* 21. *NxNch BxN* 22. *B–N4 KR–Q1*
23. *N–K5*

Black's problems on the kingside remain critical in view of the threats of Q–R5 and NxN. Tal played *23. . . . N–K6* to force *24. R–KN1*, after which *24. . . . N–B4! 25. Q–R5 Q–Q5!* broke the brunt of the attack at the cost of a pawn. The game continued *26. BxN PxB 27. QxP Q–K5! 28. QxQ BxQ 29. B–Q6* (otherwise *29. . . . P–Q3) QR–B1 30. KR–K1 B–N2 31. QR–B1 BxN*, and a draw was soon agreed.

And from the same tournament: Tal-Spassky—*1. P–K4 P–K4 2. N–KB3 N–QB3 3. B–N5 P–B4 4. N–B3 N–B3 5. PxP N–Q5 6. NxP B–B4 7. 0–0 0–0 8. N–B3! P–B3 9. NxN BxN 10. B–Q3* (*10. B–R4! P–Q4 11. N–K2* allows White to consolidate much more easily) *P–Q4 11. N–K2 B–K4 12. N–N3*, and now *12. . . . N–K5!* simplifies into a drawish position after *13. BxN* (*13. NxN PxN 14. BxP Q–R5!*) *PxB 14. P–Q3 PxP 15. QxP QxQ 16. PxQ BxN! 17. RPxB BxP.*

White was still a pawn ahead but this is only a theoretical advantage in endings of this kind. Tal played on: *18. P–Q4 QR–Q1 19. B–K3 R–Q4 20. KR–B1 R–QN4 21. P–N3 R–Q1 22. R–B4 R(1)–Q4 23. QR–QB1 K–B2 24. R–R4 P–QR3 25. R–B5 B–Q6 26. R–R3 R(N)xR 27. PxR B–N4 28. P–QN4 R–Q8ch 29. K–R2 B–B5 30. B–B4 R–KB8 31. B–K3*, and a draw was agreed. White's extra kingside pawn does not afford a sincere winning idea.

THE DEFENSE PERIMETER

This is a special strategic case in which the defender can put together an impregnable line of protection around his pieces. No breakthrough is possible that can upset the mutual assistance of the defender's forces.

An exceptional case of the defense perimeter came up in a youth tournament in Belgium in 1970:

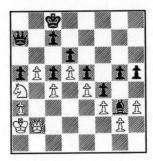

White's last move, 45. Q–N2, prepares for 46. P–N6. That break would lead to an exchange of queens and the inevitable battle between a strong White knight and a Black bishop sharply restricted by its own pawns. To avert this, Black played 45. . . . Q–N3!!.

This ingenious blocking idea should not save Black because White can maneuver his knight back to QN3 and his king to QR4 after which Black's QRP is dead. But why spend several moves to win a pawn when you can take a queen immediately? White played *46. NxQch? PxN* and then discovered there was no method of penetrating the Black position because of the locked pawn chains.

White tried *47. P–KR4* before . . . P–R5 was played but after *47. . . . PxP 48. Q–Q2 P–R6! 49. PxP P–R5* the draw was certain.

This many seem an extreme situation but the idea is not uncommon. In the 1971 Candidates Match between Hübner and Petrosian the young German master drifted into a difficult position with the White pieces after *1. P–K4 P–QB4 2. N–KB3 P–K3 3. P–Q4 PxP 4. NxP N–KB3 5. N–QB3 P–Q3 6. B–QB4 B–K2 7. B–K3 0–0 8. P–B4? P–Q4! 9. B–Q3 PxP 10. QNxP N–Q4 11. Q–B3 NxB 12. QxN Q–N3 13. 0–0–0 R–Q1 14. P–B3 N–B3 15. N–KN5 BxN 16. PxB NxN 17. PxN P–K4?!* (*17. . . . B–Q2!*) *18. QxP B–K3 19. K–N1 R–Q4 20. Q–K4 P–N3.*

White determined that he was on the verge of obtaining a lost game because he could not prevent the loss of his QP by normal means. He hit upon a queen sacrifice which established a completely invulnerable setup: *21. B–B4!! B–B4 22. BxR BxQch 23. BxB R–Q1 24. P–R4 RxP 25. RxR QxR 26. BxP K–B1 27. B–B3 Q–B7 28. K–R1! Draw!* White can draw simply by moving his bishop along its diagonal. When Black plays . . . P–QR4–5 he will stop it with P–R3. And when Black exchanges off kingside pawns with . . . P–B3 and later . . . P–N4, White plays PxP. There was no method of penetration.

A third illustration comes from the 1953 Candidates Tournament:

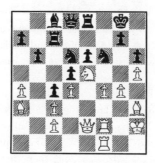

Boleslavsky (White) has a crushing position, and now the exact *36. BxN* (eliminating an irritating defender) *QxB 37. P–N5* and *R–N2* should have won. He preferred *36. B–KN2? N(Q)–K5 37. R–B3 N–Q2 38. N–N6 N(2)–B3 39. N–K5 N–Q2 40. K–N1? NxN 41. BPxN*, and in this critical position Black played *41. . . . N–N4!!*.

When White played *42. R–B8ch* Black answered *42. . . . RxR* and offered a draw which was accepted(!) because *43. RxRch QxR 44. BxQ KxB* establishes an ironclad defense perimeter. Black might even have winning chances.

ILLUSTRATIVE GAMES
20TH USSR CHAMPIONSHIP

BOLESLAVSKY   KERES

*1. P–K4 P–K4 2. N–KB3 N–QB3 3. B–N5 P–QR3 4. B–R4
N–B3 5. 0–0 B–K2 6. R–K1 P–Q3 7. BxNch PxB 8. P–Q4 N–Q2
9. QN–Q2 0–0 10. N–B4 PxP? 11. KNxP N–N1 12. Q–B3 B–B3
13. B–K3 B–Q2 14. QR–Q1 R–K1 15. N–B5 BxN 16. PxB*

A dubious opening variation mixed with a premature surrender
of the center (10. . . . P–B3!) gives Black a very pessimistic
middlegame. How will he ever develop his queenside pieces?

16. . . .   P–Q4?!

This is a courageous though not entirely sound method of
getting into the game. Black might do better with 16. . . . P–QR4
followed by . . . Q–Q2 and . . . N–R3–N5. The move chosen asks
for a liquidation of the center with N–R5 and P–B4.

17. N–R5   BxP!

Since he must lose a pawn on the queenside anyway Black
keeps material in balance. He is *not* threatening . . . B–B6 because
White could answer the bishop move with B–KN5!, attacking
the Black Q and first rank. Black's reasoning in taking the pawn
is sound. If he can't develop smoothly, why not force White to do

something? The onus is on White now to prove he has compensation for a pawn.

| 18. P–B4! | Q–B1 |

Now the threat of . . . B–B6 is on. White should move his bishop to one of the appealing squares, B5, B4 or Q2. Best is 19. B–B4! so that if Black plays the same continuation as in the game White has 22. BxP! N–Q2 23. QxP, with a likely win.

19. B–Q2?!	PxP
20. RxRch	QxR
21. NxP(4)	B–B3
22. B–R5	Q–B1

Black's position is bad but not lost. He is prepared to defend his weaknesses and develop with . . . R–R2–N2 if necessary. For his part, White should try 23. Q–K4 followed P–B4 with with the dual idea of N–K5 and P–KN4–5.

| 23. Q–Q3 | P–R3! |

Always a good idea as long as there is no immediate threat. The prospect of getting mated on the first rank has been hanging in the air for several moves. White's last move indicates he doesn't have a forceful plan and this encourages Black to put his house in order before developing his last pieces. Remember— "take time for the important things."

| 24. N–K3 | P–B4! |

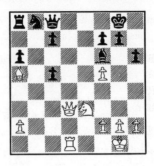

The threat was simply 25. N–N4 B–K2 26. P–B6, busting up
the kingside at a time when Black's pieces cannot join the king's
defense. On 25. . . . B–N4 in that line, White could play P–KN3
to support P–KR4. But Keres sacrifices a pawn to get his pieces
out. He is willing to accept the kingside pawn structure after
25. N–Q5 N–B3! 26. NxBch PxN 27. B–B3 N–Q5!.

25. Q–Q5	P–B3
26. QxP(5)	N–Q2
27. Q–Q6	R–R2
28. R–QB1	N–K4!

Another fine move to activate Black's pieces. On 29. P–B4
he intends 29. . . . R–Q2 30. Q–B5 N–Q6 31. QxP QxQ 32. RxQ
B–Q5 and . . . R–K2. Black knows that as long as he keeps the
number of pawns on the *queenside* even he has good drawing
chances. A kingside majority for White should not win.

29. N–Q5	N–N5

Now the ending with 30. QxP QxP 31. Q–B8ch QxQ 32.
RxQch K–R2 should be defensible after 33. P–KR3 R–Q2!.

30. P–KR3	R–Q2!
31. Q–B5!	Q–N2!

Of course not 31. . . . RxN 32. QxR. The real trick in the
position is 32. N–N6 B–Q5! 33. QxP BxPch and . . . BxN. You

can only find these chances if you look for them. Who would think that Black has tactical chances in this position?

32. NxBch	NxN
33. QxP	R–Q8ch!
34. K–R2	Q–N1ch
35. Q–B7?	...

The queen ending with 35. B–B7 RxR 36. QxR Q–B1 37. P–N4! N–Q4 38. B–B4 offers White his last winning hope.

35. ...	QxQ
36. RxQ	R–Q4
37. B–N6	R–N4!

Exact to the end. Black may lose after 35. . . . RxP 36. R–R7 because White's QRP runs fast.

38. R–B8ch	K–R2
39. R–B6	N–Q4

Again there were losing chances with 39. . . . RxP 40. B–Q8! RxP 41. RxP.

40. B–Q4	N–N5!
41. R–B7	Draw

SAN REMO 1930

NIMZOVICH   TARTAKOVER

1. P–Q4 P–Q4 2. P–QB4 N–QB3 3. N–QB3 P–K4? 4. BPxP NxP 5. P–K3 N–B4 6. P–K4 N–Q3 7. P–B4 PxP? 8. BxP

Black's eccentric opening play has put him in a very bad way. White threatens P–K5 followed by B–N5ch and P–K6 with a quick mating attack. To forestall this with further concessions such as 8. . . . P–KB3 wouldn't prevent White from obtaining a dominating position after 9. N–B3 and P–K5.

    8. . . .   **P–QR3!**

A surprisingly good move in such a depressing position. Black anticipates 9. P–K5 N–N4 10. NxN PxN 11. BxPch P–B3! with a counterthreat of 12. . . . Q–R4ch. White can accept the pawn sacrifice more calmly with 10. BxNch PxB 11. NxP but then 11. . . . B–N5ch 12. B–Q2 Q–R5ch or 12. N–B3 R–R4! eases Black's pain considerably.

        9. B–Q3   **N–K2**
       10. B–N3   **N–N3**
       11. Q–R5!   **Q–Q2!**

Not 11. . . . P–KB3 12. P–K5! and Black covers the QN4 square again while threatening to remove most of his middlegame problems with 12. . . . Q–N5.

       12. P–KR3   **N–N4**
       13. N–B3   **B–B4**
       14. N–K5!   **Q–K2!**

Another finely calculated move which averts the kingside problems that follow 14. . . . NxN 15. BxN 0–0 16. R–KB1 or 16. B–B6!?. Black's efforts to obtain counterplay are quite remarkable.

15. QNxN	PxN
16. NxN	...

16. BxPch K–Q1! gives Black potent counterchances, e.g.,
17. NxN QxPch or 17. K–Q1 B–Q3 18. NxN BPxN 19. BxB PxB
20. Q–K2 R–B1, as pointed out by Alekhine.

16. ...	BPxN
17. Q–K5!	...

Now 17. BxPch P–B3! 18. PxP 0–0 can be dangerous for White
for the temporary gain of two pawns. The following exchanges
couldn't be avoided and they maintain White's superiority.

17. ...	P–B3
18. R–KB1	R–B1
19. P–R3	RxRch
20. KxR	B–Q2
21. R–B1	B–N3
22. R–Q1	QxQ
23. BxQ	PxP
24. PxP	K–B2

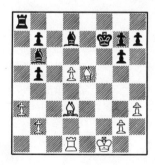

Black has weak pawns on both flanks while White has an excellent passed pawn in the center. Black's endgame begins with
the exchange of black-squared bishops so that he can blockade
the QP with his K on Q3.

25. B–Q6	**K–N1**
26. B–N4	**R–QB1**
27. R–K1	**B–QB4!**

White must allow the exchange because of the threat of
28. . . . R–B1ch. Black has no difficulty in blockading White's
winning chance, the QP, after 28. R–B1 BxB 29. RxRch BxR and
. . . K–B1–K2–Q3.

28. BxB	RxB
29. B–K4	K–B1
30. K–B2	P–N5!

Now Black can take over the QN-file after 31. PxP R–B5 and
. . . R–N5.

Black had to fight off one more determined try: *31. K–K3
PxP 32. K–Q4! R–R4 33. PxP RxRP 34. K–B5 R–R3 35. B–B3
R–KB3* (so that he can play . . . P–N3ch) *36. R–QN1 P–QN4
37. B–K2 R–B7 38. R–KB1* (38. B–B3 BxP) *RxR 39. BxR K–K2
40. BxP B–B1 41. B–Q3 B–Q2 42. B–B2 B–B1 43. K–B6 K–Q1
44. B–Q3 B–Q2ch 45. K–Q6 B–B1*, and White agreed to a draw
after 20 more moves. Black's control of the QP's queening
square stops all winning attempts.

ANSWERS TO STUDY EXAMPLES

CHAPTER TWO

1. Black plays 1. . . . P–N4!!, returning a sacrificial pawn to keep the dangerous line closed. In a 1957 world championship game Botvinnik stood much better after 2. BxNP Q–Q3 3. R–R4 N–B3! 4. BxN QxB 5. RxPch K–R1 6. K–N1 R–KN1 because he had the attack and his own king was covered by a White pawn on KR5.

2. White kept the queenside solid with a sacrifice. 1. PxP Q–R3 2. R–N5! B–B3 3. N–Q2! BxR 4. RPxB Q–R6 5. N–N1 Q–R4 6. P–QR4 P–K3 7. N–B3 N–K2 8. N–K4 P–B4 9. Q–B3 in Auerbach-Korchnoi, 31st USSR Championship 1963, which ended in a draw.

3. Black repaired his weakness on KN3 before White had time to play P–QN4, N–B2–Q3 and P–K5ch. The game went: 1. . . . B–QB3 2. Q–B3 B–K1! 3. P–QN4 B–N3! 4. N–B2 Q–Q5 5. N–R3 P–K4 6. N–B2 R–N7 7. K–R2 Q–B5 8. R–Q1 R–N6 9. N–Q3 QxKP *White Resigns* (Uhlmann-Karpov, Leningrad 1973).

4. The threat of 1. BxP PxB 2. RxP can always be handled by 2. . . . B–KB3. But it's a good idea to eliminate the White QB now: 1. . . . B–KN4! 2. BxB QxB 3. R–R5 Q–N3 as in Makaganov-Panov, Leningrad 1936, which went 4. N–N3 N–B3 5. N–B5 BxN 6. KPxB? Q–K1! 7. RxP?! (else . . . P–K5!) PxR 8. RxP P–K5 9. Q–K3 Q–K4ch 10. K–B1 R–R8

11. R–N6ch K–R1 12. P–N5 KR–R1! 13. R–R6ch N–R2 14. P–N6 RxNch *White Resigns.*

5. In Taimanov-Panno, Majorca 1970, Black actually stood better after 1. . . . R–B1! 2. N–R5 N–K1! (3. BxNP Q–N4) 3. R–K3 P–B3 4. B–Q4 although a draw was agreed here.

6. White's bishop is his best piece, and once it is exchanged off, White's black-square weaknesses are evident. Spielmann-Yates, San Remo 1930, went 1. . . . Q–N3 2. R–Q2 B–B1! 3. R(2)–K2 B–Q3! 4. Q–B1 P–N4! 5. BxB QxB 6. R–B1 R–B1 7. R(2)–KB2 B–K1 8. N–B3 R–N2 9. Q–Q2 P–KR4! with a winning game.

7. Black's counterplay began with a clever redeployment: 1. . . . K–N1! 2. N–B4 Q–B1! 3. QN–K2 QN–Q1 so that he can play . . . P–QB4. Olafsson-Petrosian, Bled 1961, continued 4. Q–QN3? P–B3 5. B–Q3 P–B4 6. PxP BxBP 7. N–R3 NxKP! 8. B–KB4 QN–B2 9. B–QN5 K–R1 and Black won quickly.

8. Obviously foolhardy is 1. . . . NxB 2. NxN Q–N1 after which White has a choice of strong followups. And 1. . . . N–QN5 2. B–B4 RxRch 3. RxR R–Q1 4. RxR QxR is bad because of 5. P–K4! with a big endgame initiative for White. But 1. . . . N–Q5! 2. NxN NxB 3. N–B5 NxN 4. BxN P–B3 (Botvinnik-Keres, USSR Absolute Championship 1941) led to equality.

9. 1. B–Q6? was played but 1. P-K4! followed by 2. N–R2 and N–N4 would have crippled Black's phalanx and given White good chances.

CHAPTER THREE

1. Black plays 1. . . . RxRch 2. RxR N–K7ch! 3. RxN and . . . B–K3! after which White must pause to watch his first rank. In Grechkin-Geller, Sverdlosk 1951, White fell apart with 4. P–KN3 R–Q8ch 5. K–N2 Q–B5 6. RxB QxR 7. Q–B2 Q–Q4ch 8. K–R3 P–N3!.

2. Black's only kingside target is KR2 and he threatens it by way of . . . B–B1 and . . . R–KR4. None of White's other

pieces can watch KR2; so in Petrosian-Gligoric, Zagreb 1965, White played 1. Q–N1!! and after 1. . . . B–N5 2. R–R5 B–K7 3. N–N3 B–QN5 4. R–R4 R–N1 5. N–K5 R(1)–N4 6. RxP B–Q3 7. R–B8ch K–N2 8. R(R)–R8 RxN(4) 9. PxR BxP 10. R–B5 and won.

3. 1. . . . Q–K8ch! does it: 2. RxQ N–B7ch 3. K–N1 NxRch and 4. . . . PxQ.

4. The threat is P–B6. Black could stop that with 1. . . . P–KB3 but then White turns his attention to attacking the base with P–KN4–5. In Kan-Ryumin, Leningrad 1934, Black played the sharp 1. . . . B–B3! which also exchanged off a dangerous piece. The doubled pawns were a minor inconvenience since White could not easily attack them. After 2. BxB PxB 3. Q–R5 K–R1 4. R–B4 R–KN1 5. R–R4 R–N2 6. N–Q4 Q–K2 (notice that on 1. . . . P–KB3 White could now plant a knight on K6) 7. N–K2 N–Q2 8. N–B4 K–N1 and Black held on.

5. White threatens to double rooks on the KR-file in the next five moves and then play P–KB4. Black played 1. . . . K–N1! 2. K–N2 K–B2 3. R–KR1 K–K2 4. R–R5 K–Q1 5. QR–KR1 K–B1 6. N–Q1 QR–KB2 7. N–K3 R–N3 8. N–B5 K–B2 (Gufeld-Taimanov, Moscow 1969) and Black was quite safe on the queenside where no pawn-breaks were possible.

CHAPTER SIX

1. Simplify with 1. . . . B–KN5! 2. QxB BxPch! 3. KxB QxN and Black wins (Perfilyev-Botvinnik, USSR 1925) with his extra Exchange: 4. B–B6 (4. Q–N8ch K–K2 5. QxR Q–R4ch) Q–B3 5. B–R4 K–B1 6. Q–N5 P–KR3 7. Q–K5 K–N1 8. R–Q5 R–K1, etc.

2. It's not serious after 1. RxB PxR 2. B–N5 Q–N5!, e.g., 3. BxP P–B4 4. N–B2 Q–N3 5. R–KB1 B–K5 6. N–K3 QR–K1 (Tal- Korchnoi, Candidates Tournament 1962).

3. Yates-Rubinstein, Hastings 1922, went 1. N–B5 B–N4! 2. Q–N4 BxB 3. QRxB N–N2 4. NxN KxN and White has only transposed into a bad bishop vs. good knight ending. Black

won soon after 5. R–N1 P–B4 6. Q–K2 Q–N4 7. P–QR4 P–K5. Notice that 1. . . . PxN? 2. QxP N–B3 3. B–R6! K–R1 4. B–N5! loses for Black.

4. Black preserved his extra piece with 1. . . . K–B2! 2. BxN BxN 3. PxB B–R4 4. R–Q7 N–N3! 5. RxP KR–QB1! 6. RxP BxN 7. B–R3ch K–B3 and soon won (Pollock-Tchigorin, Hastings 1895).

5. There's no crisis if Black calmly plays 1. . . . B–N1!!, e.g., 2. P–B6 QxBP or 2. PxNP N(2)xP 3. PxPch QxP 4. N–N5 Q–B3 5. R–B1? N–N5! 6. Q–B3 QxNch winning as in Spielmann-Keres, Nordwijk 1938.